W9-ASR-501

Tiberius Sempronius Gracchus

Tiberius Sempronius Gracchus

TRADITION AND APOSTASY

Alvin H. Bernstein

CORNELL UNIVERSITY PRESS

ITHACA AND LONDON

Cornell University Press gratefully acknowledges a grant from the Andrew W. Mellon Foundation that aided in bringing this book to publication.

First published 1978 by Cornell University Press.
Published in the United Kingdom by Cornell University Press Ltd., 2-4 Brook Street, London W1Y 1AA.

Library of Congress Cataloging in Publication Data
(For library cataloging purposes only)

Bernstein, Alvin H
    Tiberius Sempronius Gracchus.

    Bibliography: p.
    Includes index.
    1. Gracchus, Tiberius Sempronius. 2. Rome—History—Servile Wars, 135–71 B. C. 3. Land tenure (Roman Law)
DG254.5.B47   937'.05   77-12663
ISBN 0-8014-1078-9

Printed in the United States of America by Vail-Ballou Press, Inc.

3-1-79

For Charles, sine qua, non.

Contents

Abbreviations and Short Titles

Astin, *SA*   A. E. Astin, *Scipio Aemilianus* (Oxford, 1967).

Badian, *FC*   E. Badian, *Foreign Clientelae, 264–70 B.C.* (Oxford, 1958).

Badian, *TGBRR*   E. Badian, "Tiberius Gracchus and the Beginning of the Roman Revolution," *Aufstieg und Niedergang der Römischen Welt,* ed. by H. Temporini (New York, 1972).

Broughton, *MRR*   T. R. S. Broughton, *The Magistrates of the Roman Republic,* 2 vols. (New York, 1951–1952).

Brunt, *IM*   P. A. Brunt, *Italian Manpower 225 B.C.–A.D. 14* (Oxford, 1971).

CAH   S. A. Cook, F. E. Adcock, and M. P. Charlesworth, eds., *Cambridge Ancient History,* Vols. VIII–IX (Cambridge, 1930 and 1932).

CIL   *Corpus Inscriptionum Latinarum.*

Crawford, *RRC*   M. H. Crawford, *Roman Republican Coinage,* Vol. II (Cambridge, 1974).

Degrassi, *ILLRP* A. Degrassi, *Inscriptiones Latinae Liberae Rei Publicae* (Florence, 1965).

Dessau, *ILS*   H. Dessau, *Inscriptiones Latinae Selectae,* 3 vols. (Berlin, 1892).

Fraccaro, *Studi* P. Fraccaro, *Studi sull'età dei Gracchi,* Vol. I (Città di Castello, 1914).

Frank, *ESAR*   T. Frank, ed., *An Economic Survey of Ancient Rome,* Vol. I (Baltimore, 1933).

Gelzer, *Kl. Schr.* M. Gelzer, *Kleine Schriften,* Vols. I–III (Wiesbaden, 1962).

Gruen, *RPCC*   E. S. Gruen, *Roman Politics and the Criminal Courts, 149–78 B.C.* (Cambridge, Mass., 1968).

Jacoby, *FGrH*	F. Jacoby, *Die Fragmente der griechischen Historiker* (Berlin, 1923–1930; Leiden, 1940——).
Malcovati, *ORF*	H. Malcovati, *Oratorum Romanorum Fragmenta Liberae Rei Publicae* (3d ed., Turin, 1966).
Meyer, *Caes. Monarchie*	E. Meyer, *Caesars Monarchie und das Principat des Pompeius* (Stuttgart, 1922).
Mommsen, *Gesam. Schrift.*	T. Mommsen, *Gesammelte Schriften,* Vols. I–VIII (Berlin, 1904–1913).
Mommsen, *Röm. Gesch.*	T. Mommsen, *Römische Geschichte,* Vols. I–V (Berlin, 1903–1904).
Mommsen, *Röm. Staats.*	T. Mommsen, *Römisches Staatsrecht,* Vols. I–III (3d ed., Leipzig, 1887–1888).
Ogilvie, *COL*	R. M. Ogilvie, *A Commentary on Livy. Books 1–5* (Oxford, 1965).
Peter, *HRR*	H. Peter, *Historicorum Romanorum Reliquiae,* Vols. I–II (Leipzig, 1906–1914).
RE	A. Pauly, G. Wissowa, et al., *Real-Encyclopädie der Classischen Altertumswissenschaft* (Stuttgart, 1894——).
Riccobono, *FIRA*	S. Riccobono, *Fontes Iuris Romani Anteiustiniani* (Florence, 1941).
Scullard, *RP*	H. H. Scullard, *Roman Politics 220–150 B.C.* (2d ed., Oxford, 1973).
Taylor, *RVA*	L. R. Taylor, *Roman Voting Assemblies from the Hannibalic War to the Dictatorship of Caesar* (Ann Arbor, 1966).
Taylor, *VDRR*	L. R. Taylor, *The Voting Districts of the Roman Republic* (Rome, 1960).
Toynbee, *HL*	A. J. Toynbee, *Hannibal's Legacy: The Hannibalic War's Effects on Roman Life,* Vols. I–II (London, 1965).
Walbank, *COP*	F. W. Walbank, *A Historical Commentary on Polybius,* Vols. I–II (Oxford, 1957–1967).

Preface

At the center of the calamitous events of 133 B.C. stands the figure of Tiberius Sempronius Gracchus, the controversial tribune whose assassination signaled a major turning point in Roman history. Most commentators, ancient and modern, agree that his death was the first instance of the civic violence that thereafter became a recurrent feature of the last century of the Republic. They agree about little else, however: issues central to understanding what happened in 133 and the future course of the Roman revolution remain subjects of scholarly dispute. The important question of why the tribune proposed a law to reclaim public land illegally held by the wealthy and distribute it to the poor persists not only because it holds psychological interest, but because of disagreements on more tangible questions. To explain why Tiberius behaved as he did we must know precisely what he did. Yet specialists still dispute, for example, who among the populace were meant to benefit from the law he proposed. Were they mainly urban residents or were they rather the rural landless who were to be resettled on the public lands? Were the recipients to be exclusively Roman citizens, or Italian allies as well? How would resettlement affect beneficiaries' draft status and thus the total manpower available for military service?

Tiberius' actions cannot be interpreted in isolation from his contemporaries' perceptions of them; yet here, too, scholarly disagreements are more than a matter of emphasis. What was the ruling oligarchy's attitude to Tiberius, the proposed law, and the methods used to secure its passage? What legal issues were raised by Tiberius' removal of his tribunician colleague, Octavius, from office? What was the Senate's opinion of the proceedings? What were the duties of a tribune of the People? These questions in turn reflect even more basic disagreement among scholars over the way the Republic's constitutional and political machinery worked, over Rome's relations with her allies, over the state of the peninsula's economy, and over the reliability of the sources.

The source material that exists for 133 B.C. is too fragmented to permit definitive solutions to most of the problems posed above. Anyone attempting to reconstruct the events of that year has to work with incomplete evidence. Examining the sources is like contemplating a difficult jigsaw puzzle created by a perverse demiurge who has withheld a great number of the parts. The closest the scholar can come to assembling a whole picture is to fit together what pieces remain wherever they interconnect, so as to suggest the nature of what is missing. He may thus draw from his limited sources some idea of the overall scheme, that is, of the interplay of circumstance and event that constituted the ancient reality. The procedure is fraught with dangers, and a careful, plausible coherence is often the most that can be expected.

To be sure, a number of scholars have tried this kind of reconstruction. No new version could fully transform our general understanding of the period without sacrificing judiciousness for originality. That understanding, nevertheless, is far from complete, and many specific cruxes, with important implications in a broader context, require further exploration, despite the notable scholarly advances of the past half-century. Since Hugh Last published his section on the Gracchi in the ninth volume of the *Cambridge Ancient History* (1932), there has been a steady flow of work on their period. The continuing debate has engendered valuable studies of the free and servile populations of the Italian peninsula; the Republic's formal constitutional structures and how they worked in practice; the unwritten rules that regulated the behavior of the governing oligarchs; the relationship of Roman civil and criminal law to the political system; the deep changes wrought in the economic and social patterns of life, and their ramifications; and the prejudices, personal interests, and reliability of the sources. Collectively, this diverse, rather unwieldy body of new information and theory demands a reinterpretation of the so-called Gracchan revolution. The individual contributions need to be weighed for their effect on the total picture of the period because they assume their full value only when placed in proper relation to one another and to data already at the scholar's disposal. Where they conflict, as where their mutual implications are unclear—and such difficulties occur constantly—reconstruction must take the form of original synthesis: synthesis, because the raw material is not really new, and original, because the inadequacies of the sources necessitate the exercise not only of rigorous historical judgment but also of historical imagination, without which the myriad details cannot take shape so as to suggest a reasonable, harmonious whole.

Tiberius Gracchus himself, for all the scholarship concerned with him, has remained a cardboard figure. His picture rarely takes on any life beyond that of a modern stereotype, whether he is seen as radical revolutionary or well-meaning conservative. This book avoids putting him in modern dress. It traces his development within the social context of his age, in an attempt to integrate the man with his time and thereby to arrive at a coherent account of his actions. It views Tiberius' family history, his upbringing, his early career, and the political actions of his maturity as the sources report them, in light of the ethos of second-century Roman society. This perspective reveals an ambitious young politician driven to a premature death by the conflict between what he was and what was expected of him, as well as by the discrepancy between the opportunities that fate allowed him and the destiny to which he felt he had been born.

Though this approach attaches importance to the psychological disposition of Tiberius Gracchus, the book is hardly psychohistory. Nor was it inspired by the discovery of new literary, epigraphical, or numismatic evidence, or by a new historiographical technique. It aims unashamedly to provide in the end that old-fashioned phenomenon, "une histoire d'événement." To do this it re-examines the ancient evidence in light of modern research. Obviously, an enormous debt is owed to the scholarly works that have preceded it, particularly some of the more recent literature in the field. It is designed to face those questions, large and small, that could affect our understanding of its main figure and the events in which he played a part. Given the nature of the sources, providing answers often involves a measure of speculation. Where this happens, the book tries to proceed with the appropriate degree of tentativeness. Its goal, however, is definite: to construct a full, reasonable, and suggestive narrative of the life of Tiberius Gracchus from the disparate and disputed materials available. Finally, while the work is written for the professional in that it seeks to advance the scholar's understanding of the events of 133, it does its best to be intelligible to interested readers who are not specialists.

In the course of writing this book I have accumulated important debts. The time necessary for its completion was bought with generous grants from my home university, Cornell, from its Society for the Humanities, and from the National Endowment for the Humanities. Several good friends, Ralph Johnson, Donald Kagan, Richard Polenberg, Meyer Reinhold, Robert Tannenbaum, and L. Pearce Williams, read the entire typescript and made many valuable suggestions for its improvement. For their help and encouragement, and especially for their friendship, I am deeply grateful. Thanks to Cornell University Press's anonymous readers, I was able to correct a number of embarrassing errors that might otherwise have appeared in print. I should also like to thank Roberta Ludgate, who first deciphered my untidy scrawl, Pat Guilford, who turned that much-amended early draft into the final typescript, and Maureen Meaney, who nobly took on the task of preparing the index.

Harvard University Press has been kind enough to allow me to use throughout the translations of the Loeb Classical Library. They will enable readers who do not know Greek and Latin to locate a quoted passage easily and to see it in its broader context.

My greatest debt, however, is to my wife, who alone knows the cost of the book's composition. With the patience of Griselda she sometimes delicately, sometimes ruthlessly, reshaped and amended my primitive prose and helped bring the book to its present form. If there is lucidity or elegance in the pages that follow, she is responsible.

ALVIN H. BERNSTEIN

Ithaca, New York

Tiberius Sempronius Gracchus

1   Res Familiares

quam ob rem peto a vobis, ut me sic audiatis, neque ut
omnino expertem Graecarum rerum neque ut eas nostris in
hoc praesertim genere anteponentem, sed ut unum e togatis
patris diligentia non inliberaliter institutum studioque discendi
a pueritia incensum, usu tamen et domesticis praeceptis multo
magis eruditum quam litteris.

—Cicero, *De Re Publica* i.36

In the centuries between his tribunate and the present, Tiberius
Gracchus has taken on as many forms as Proteus. His intentions
and motives have been seen in different lights from age to age and
commentator to commentator. He appears variously as one who
sought to alleviate human suffering; to set up a tyranny; to increase his *clientela* and thereby his political power; to drain from
the capital the disruptive surplus of the urban citizenry; to ensure
that Rome would have enough manpower to maintain her legions
and foreign dominions. He was inspired by liberalizing philoso-
phies from abroad; personal animosities and public rivalries; political ambition fired by a highborn mother early widowed; a conservative's longing to return the citizenry to a pastoral Golden Age.
These are only some of the explanations, ancient and modern, of
Tiberius' departure from previous mores, as well as of his uncommon tenacity. Their very number and range suggest greater complexity than the advocates of any one of them would be happy to
allow, as well as the difficulty involved in deciding why a man
does what he does. His actions provide clues to the man, but important, too, are the forces that worked on him, not merely during
his political career, but during his formative years. A study of the
actions of a historical figure, if confined to his maturity, can lose
valuable insights that could have eased the task of understanding.
This is particularly true in the case of a young Roman, scion of
a noble house, whose childhood was regarded as a preparation for

his adult public life. He received in these years a unique education in his family's history and traditions, its accomplishments and lore.

The education of a Roman aristocrat was controlled by his family with an exclusiveness difficult for the contemporary mind to grasp, particularly because the Roman nobility, at least at the beginning of the second century, had no official system of education.[1] The child grew up in a fiercely authoritarian family unit that secluded him from potentially corrupting outside influences. The baby was kept first at his mother's breast and later at her knee. The practice of employing wet nurses, common among the Greeks, was avoided as an unworthy abrogation of maternal responsibility. An elderly female relative would undertake the serious business of the Roman toddler's play until the child showed some capacity for real understanding, whereupon the father began his son's education. Under his direct supervision technical skills, both intellectual and physical, were taught as necessary, but the emphasis was strongly on building character through emulation of paternal and ancestral examples, with abstract speculation and theoretical learning relegated to second place.[2] The declaration that Cicero assigns to the cultured Scipio Aemilianus illustrates the order of values: "I must ask you not to think me entirely ignorant of Greek literature nor disposed, especially in political questions, to prefer them to our own. See me rather as a true Roman, liberally educated thanks to my father's diligence, and eager for knowledge from boyhood, yet trained much more by experience and by the precepts I learned at home, than by any I received from the study of books."[3]

Through his middle teens the aristocratic adolescent remained under his father's tutelage. From him he learned to read, write, and hunt, to fight in Roman armor, and by him was introduced to the law and to the workings of the Senate. If his father or another senior member of the family belonged to that august body, the

1. Cic. *Rep.* iv.3.
2. Tac. *Dial.* 28.4, 24.1; Pliny *Epist.* viii.14.4–5; Plut. *Cato mai.* 20.
3. Cic. *Rep.* i.36.

young man would listen at the Senate house door.[4] Even when, during the second century, practical and progressive Romans with a knowledge of and contacts in the Hellenistic world began to employ Greeks to tutor their sons in philosophy and rhetoric in the final stages of their education, the tutors probably were not given a free hand. Plutarch says that even the redoubtable Hellenophile Aemilius Paullus, who made liberal use of Greek tutors, allowed nothing but the pressure of public business to keep him from being present when his sons were in outsiders' hands.[5] However accurate the story, it clearly reflects an ideal.

Above all, however, Roman education concentrated on indoctrination into the traditions of the family, their virtues and deeds, real, embellished, and imaginary. We can get a fair idea of the nature of this central aspect of Roman training, and the powerful impression it must have made on a young man at the threshold of a public career, from an account of the funeral ceremonies of politically distinguished Roman families. When a Roman noble died, his body was carried, usually propped in an upright position, into the forum and to the rostra. The relative who most resembled him, or an actor brought in for the purpose, would put on a mask that reproduced, in uncanny detail, the dead man's features. He walked in front of the bier, followed by others wearing masks of the rest of the family's distinguished dead, each man clad in the robes appropriate to the highest office the ancestor had held during his lifetime, and where appropriate, preceded by the official insignia, the fasces, of those offices. The whole procession therefore consisted of the numerous living images of the family's praetors, consuls, censors, imperators, and triumphators, reaching back through the generations of the family's eminence. Then they sat on ivory chairs, facing the funeral orator, the deceased's adult son, if he had one, some other relative if he had not, who eulogized the achievements and virtues, not only of the man about to be buried, but of all those whose images were

4. Pliny *Epist.* viii.14.4–5; Plut. *Cato mai.* 20; Gell. i.23. Gwynn, *Roman Education from Cicero to Quintilian,* chap. 1.
5. Plut. *Aem. Paull.* 6.

present at the funeral, beginning with the most ancient. After the body's interment the masks, including the newest, were enclosed in a wooden shrine and placed in the most conspicuous position in the house's atrium, there to look down upon their living descendants.[6] Thus domestic galleries of ancestral portraits were built up, brought out for the funeral procession of each member of the family, and also throughout the year on occasions when the dead were commemorated by funerary meals eaten at the tombs by friends and relatives, portions of food being left over for the dead.[7] Polybius closes his account of all this by noting that there could hardly be a more ennobling spectacle for a young Roman aspiring to virtue and fame; he thinks that such constant reiteration of the great deeds of noble men encouraged the Roman young to renew the uncommon feats of bravery of which their tradition was full.[8]

So the family molded their son's moral outlook and passed on to him their ambitions for his future conduct and character. Indeed, great Roman houses came to be identified with certain traits of character: the Claudii were considered proud, the Iunii inflexible, the Aelii Tuberones and the Quinctii austere, and so forth. An extreme example serves to highlight the tendency. Tradition ascribes a specific heroic action to three generations of men bearing the name P. Decius Mus. Father, son, and grandson were all said to have secured victory for Rome in a vital battle by offering themselves as sacrifices to the gods, taking the enemy with them. Decius, the son, preparing to follow his father's example, exclaims, "Why should I hesitate to follow the family destiny? It has fallen to our house to provide the sacrificial victim when our country is in danger." His son, in turn, on the eve of the battle of Asculum, was expected to carry on the tradition. The consternation this prospect aroused in Pyrrhus' camp reportedly induced the

6. The description is from Polyb. vi.53–54. See MacMullen, *Enemies of the Roman Order,* pp. 7–8; Coarelli, *Monuments of Civilization: Rome,* "Sepulcher of the Scipios," pp. 33–36.

7. J. M. C. Toynbee, *Death and Burial in the Roman World,* pp. 46–64, esp. pp. 51, 61–64.

8. Polyb. vi.54.3–6.

general to announce that he had prepared ways of dealing with the eventuality and to send a message to the Roman consuls that this third Decius would attempt his *devotio* in vain.[9]

Whatever the historicity of these events, they illustrate some of the forces at work on minds whose values, quite different from our own, stemmed from an upbringing equally foreign. What Gilbert Murray called the "inherited conglomerate" was not for Tiberius Gracchus what it is for any modern commentator. The modern commentator, of course, cannot divest himself of his own inherited conglomerate as he approaches a historical figure, but he can and should attempt to identify what his subject's is likely to have been. This attempt constitutes an essential step in bridging the perceptional gap that might otherwise limit or distort a modern view of Tiberius Gracchus' intentions and motives. This study needs to begin, therefore, not with his birth in 163, but with an examination of the context in which he would have seen himself—the family history his preceptors would have used to make him aware of his duties in life. It seeks his primary inspiration not across the Adriatic or south to Magna Graecia in foreign philosophical influences, but at home, in the family tradition on which he was raised.

That tradition went back at least to 238, when a Tiberius Sempronius Gracchus attained the consulship, thereby ennobling all his descendants. In that year, between the first two Punic wars, he led an expedition against Sardinia, an island then in Carthaginian hands. The enterprise succeeded without a battle, for

9. For the grandfather, see Livy, viii.9; for the father, Livy, x.28.12–14; for the son, Zonar., viii.5. The episodes are cited by Marrou, *Histoire de l'éducation dans l'antiquité*, pp. 347–349. See Cic. *Rab. Post.* i.2 for sons emulating fathers; Cic. *Off.* i.116, for one's duty to copy one's ancestors. See also Peter, *HRR,* I, 2d ed., p. 174 (Coelius Antipater). According to the same Coelius, Gaius Gracchus told many persons that his brother Tiberius came to him in a dream when he was hesitating over whether to be a candidate for the quaestorship and said: "However much you may try to defer your fate, nevertheless you must die the same death that I did." This happened before Gaius was tribune of the People, and Coelius writes that he heard it from Gaius who had repeated it to many others.

Carthage was too preoccupied at home to resist, and Rome thereby gained her second overseas possession.[10] This Tiberius was the great-grandfather of the tribune for 133.[11]

His son, the tribune's great-uncle, of the same name, has a better-documented and more memorable public career. During the Republic's darkest days immediately after the Roman disaster at Cannae near the east coast, the newly appointed dictator named Gracchus as his second in command, his *magister equitum*.[12] They managed to raise four legions, but these seem to have been a ragtag outfit, including youngsters who still wore the purple-bordered dress of boyhood and, because of the shortage of free manpower, slaves and criminals.[13] The shaky state of Rome's fortunes now induced many of the subject allies in south-central Italy, Capua among them, to rebel. At the same time, Hannibal took the loyal city of Casilinum, just north of Capua, despite Gracchus' persistent and ingenious efforts to resupply it, efforts that apparently helped him attain the consulship for 215.[14] His colleague was killed fighting in Gaul while still consul designate, but Gracchus urged that for the time being the Gauls be ignored and the Romans concentrate exclusively on the Carthaginians. He then set out to organize the available manpower, and at his wish the least efficient of the soldiers recruited earlier for the dictator's army were sent off to less vital service in Sicily. Despite this loss, Gracchus' own army is said to have consisted of twenty-five thousand allies and the slaves who had volunteered for service after Cannae.

10. Polyb. i.88.8–12; Livy *Per.* xx; Zonar. viii.18.

11. Pace Meyer, "Untersuchungen zur Geschichte der Gracchan," pp. 385–386. See Festus 430L and the discussion by Walbank, *COP,* I, 149–150. This Gracchus had been plebeian aedile for 246, and he and his colleague, C. Fundanius Fundulus, fined Claudia, the sister of the consul for 249, 25,000 *asses* for arrogant speech, and built from the various fines of their aedileship a temple to *Libertas* on the Aventine (Livy xxiv.16.9; Livy *Per.* xix). For the sources on this Gracchus' career, see Münzer, s.v. Sempronius (50), *RE,* 1400–1401.

12. Livy xxii.57.9; Zonar. ix.2. For the sources on this Gracchus' career, see Münzer, s.v. Sempronius (51), *RE,* 1401–1403.

13. For the slaves, Livy xxii.57.9–12; Val. Max. vii.6.1; Oros. iv.16.7–8. For the criminals, Livy xxiii.14.3–4; Oros. iv.16.9.

14. Livy xxiii.19.3–12. Scullard, *RP,* p. 57.

King Philip V of Macedonia, who had been keeping a close watch on the course of hostilities in the Italian peninsula, judged that the struggle's outcome was now certain enough for him to throw in his lot with the Carthaginians. He sent ambassadors to Hannibal to conclude an alliance, promising aid in the struggle against the Romans in return for Punic support of his ventures in Greece. On their way home the Macedonian ambassadors were intercepted and turned over to Gracchus, who sent them to the Senate in Rome. Tiberius then joined Q. Fabius Maximus near Capua, followed Hannibal east into Apulia, and wintered at Luceria, where his troops skirmished with the Carthaginians as opportunities arose.[15]

In 214, when Gracchus was still at Luceria as proconsul with his army of slave volunteers, a force of Carthaginian infantry and cavalry under Hanno came to Beneventum, between Luceria and Capua. Tiberius moved to meet them there. In his preparations for the following day's battle, Tiberius promised freedom to any slave who delivered up a Carthaginian head. Though hampered in the battle by the grim literalness with which the slaves accepted his word—Livy explains that they became entirely preoccupied with butchering those who had already fallen, neglecting to assail those who still stood—the Roman forces prevailed, and the rout was reported as being all but complete. The slaves were thereafter freed. Despite a later setback, when Hanno defeated a number of cohorts commanded by a Roman prefect of the allies, a grateful Roman electorate rewarded Tiberius with a second consulship, that for 213.

During this consulship, Tiberius managed only minor successes at Lucania, but they sufficed to make his the only command in Italy that was prorogued: regrettably, for he was slain in an ambush while bringing his troops to Capua.[16] Of his loss one modern scholar has written that it "deprived . . . Rome of an outstanding general." [17] This man must have left a further legacy beyond bequeathing more glory to his family. His campaign of 214 must have taught two lessons: first, the importance of having a large

15. Livy xxiii.32–xxiv.3. 16. Livy xxiv.10–xxv.17.
17. Scullard, *RP,* p. 62.

and adequately trained pool of men available for service, and second, the difficulties involved in using slaves as soldiers. As we shall see later, both points were advanced by Tiberius Gracchus in 133 in his defense of the land reform program.

The nephew of this man, the son of his elder brother Publius, was yet another Tiberius Sempronius Gracchus, consul for 177 and 163, and censor for 169.[18] He became the most distinguished of the family and was the father of the ill-fated tribunes, Tiberius and Gaius. In 190 the Scipios entrusted this Tiberius, whom Livy calls "Far and away the sharpest of the young men of that time," with the vital task of securing from Philip of Macedon safe passage to the Hellespont for their armies.[19] Five years later, in 185, he may again have been a member of an important embassy, this one sent to Thessalian Tempe to hear complaints against Philip lodged by the Thessalians, Perrhaebians, and Atha-

18. P. Sempronius Gracchus is probably to be identified with the tribune for 189. See Münzer, s.v. Sempronius (49), *RE*, 1400, *RE*, 1403–1409. For the sources on the career of Tiberius Sempronius Gracchus, consul for 177, see Münzer, s.v. Sempronius (53). Richard ("Qualis Pater, Talis Filius," pp. 43–55) has rejected Livy's account of how the elder Gracchus persuaded the tribune M. Aburius to withdraw his veto and allow M. Fulvius Nobilior's triumph in 187 (Livy xxxix.5.1–5), claiming it is a propagandistic invention. While Livy may have been influenced in his description of the details of Gracchus' action by a later source with an ax to grind (though not necessarily, as Richard would have it, an anti-Gracchan one), the author's enthusiasm for discrediting Livy has led him to overstate his case. Even if we grant that Livy's account of the story was colored by a later version designed to exaggerate the father's patriotism and calm virtue in order to highlight the sons' disruptive misdeeds, it hardly follows that the report, in its essentials, is not reliable. For present purposes Richard's more general assertion (p. 45) that all else Livy tells us about Gracchus *père* is similarly tainted is not even argued for, much less proved. We may wish to take Livy with a large grain of salt, but excessive skepticism can keep us from the truth no less than credulity.

19. Livy xxxvii.7.11–14: "Ti. Sempronius Gracchus, longe tum acerrimus iuvenum." Tiberius was probably in his late twenties at this time, pace Carcopino, *Autour des Gracques,* p. 70, who thinks he has proved he was born in 208. It seems highly unlikely that an eighteen-year-old would be entrusted with so important a mission, and all Carcopino has really demonstrated is that Tiberius cannot have been born after 208. See *RE, 53,* for a more realistic calculation.

manians.[20] On its way back the embassy protested recent Achaean treatment of Sparta to the Achaean League's magistrates, but they rejected the ambassadors' request that the assembly be convened on the grounds that the Senate had not officially authorized it.[21]

Tiberius' career now reaches a critical turning point as it becomes entangled with the so-called trials of the Scipios—two brothers, both great generals, heads of one of the most powerful families in Rome at the time.[22] During his tribunate, either in 187 or in 184, proceedings were instituted against L. Scipio Asiaticus or P. Scipio Africanus or both concerning accountability for funds derived from their campaigns against Antiochus, ruler of the Seleucid Empire.[23] Before the matter could be concluded, Tiberius

20. Livy xxxix.23.5–27.3, cf. 33.1; Polyb. xxii.6, cf. xxiii.2.7; Paus. vii.8.6. Livy twice mentions Tiberius as one of the three ambassadors (24.13, 33.1) though Polybius (xxii.6) mentions Tiberius Claudius Nero instead. See Geer, "The Scipios and the Father of the Gracchi," p. 385, n. 10.

21. Polyb. xxii.10, cf. xxiii.4.7; Diod. xxix.17; Paus. vii.8.6, 9.1. See Errington, *Philopoemen,* pp. 166–167, for discussion of the incident.

22. The ancient sources provide an unsatisfactory account of the episode, appearing to conflate the date, charges, events, and outcome of the "trials" of P. Cornelius Scipio Africanus and L. Asiaticus. Livy, who gives most detail, nonetheless finds his source, Valerius Antias, inadequate. My concern is, of course, only with the role of Tiberius Gracchus and with how his involvement affected his political fortunes. See Livy xxxviii.50.4–60.10. For other references to these events in the sources, see Polyb. xxiii.14; Val. Max. iii.7.1, v.3.2; Plut. *Cato mai.* 15.1–2; Plut. *Apophth. Scip.* 10; App. *Syr.* 40; Gell. iv.18, vi.19; Dio frags. 63 and 65; Auct. *Vir. Ill.* 49.17; Zonar. ix.20. The great body of scholarly literature that has attempted to unravel the tangle leaves consensus still a long way off. See Mommsen, *Römische Forschungen,* II, 417–510; Münzer, *RE,* s.v. Cornelius 337; Fraccaro, "*I processi degli Scipioni,*" pp. 217–414; De Sanctis, *Storia dei Romani* IV.i, 591–598; Frank, "Italy," p. 371; Haywood, *Studies on Scipio Africanus,* chap. 5; Fraccaro, "Ancora sui processi degli Scipioni," pp. 3–26. For a full bibliography see Scullard, *RP,* p. 290, n. 1, and his own discussion, pp. 290–303. See also Bandelli, "I processi degli Scipioni," pp. 304–342.

23. Livy xxxviii.50.5–12 places the prosecutions of both Publius and Lucius in 187, and Appian (*Syr.* 40) seems to put the accusations against Publius in 187 as well. But in the non-Antiate version the prosecutor of Scipio Africanus is given as M. Naevius, who can definitely be dated to 184 (Broughton, *MRR,* I, 376. See Livy xxxix.52.3–5, cf. xxxviii.56.2 and 5–6). Gellius (iv.18.3–6) also mentions Naevius' attack on Publius.

Gracchus exercised his veto on behalf of a Scipio. The sources are unanimous on this alone, leaving confusion over which man benefited and indeed over whether there may have been two vetoes.[24] The latter possibility is inherently unlikely, as is the need for a veto on behalf of Africanus. At any rate, the story goes that before vetoing, Tiberius had been an enemy of either or both, and that when he intervened he swore an oath that his action did not indicate burial of the old *inimicitia* or the forging of any bond of friendship, but was undertaken solely out of regard for the dignity of the Roman state.[25]

This profession of pure idealism notwithstanding, Tiberius' motive in aiding the Scipios needs closer examination. While the sources agree that *inimicitia* existed, they are not very specific about its cause. One ancient writer produces what he asserts is a speech by Tiberius against Scipio Africanus, while another simply generalizes that "previously they had disagreed on a number of political issues." [26] Nor could hostility have developed long before the trials and veto (or vetoes), whether they occurred in 187 or 184, since Tiberius had in the past been closely connected with the Scipios. He had served under Lucius in Greece and Asia and, as we have seen, had been employed as the Scipios' envoy to Philip in

24. For the prosecution of Publius, see Polyb. xxiii.14; Cic. *De Orat.* ii.249; Livy xxxviii.50.5–12; Diod. xxix.21; Val. Max. iii.7.1; Plut. *Cato mai.* 15.1–2; App. *Syr.* 40; Gell. iv.18; Dio frags. 63 and 65. For the prosecution of Lucius, see Cic. *Prov. Cons.* 8.18; Livy xxxviii.55–56, 60; Val. Max. iv.i.9, iv.2.3; Pliny *NH* praef. 10; Plut. *Cato mai.* 15.1–2; Gell. vi.19; Dio frags. 63 and 65; Auct. *Vir. Ill.* 57.1. For Tiberius vetoing the proceedings against Publius, see Livy xxxviii.52.9; Dio frag. 65. For his vetoing the proceedings against Lucius, see Livy xxxviii.56.10; Gell. vi.19; Dio frag. 65. For the charges against them see Polyb. xxiii.14.7; Livy xxxviii.54.1–12; Gell. iv.18; cf. Dio frag. 63.

25. See Cic. *Prov. Cons.* 8.18; Livy xxxviii.52, 53; Gell. vi.19; Dio frag. 65; Auct. *Vir. Ill.* 57.1. This tradition of prior hostility is rejected by Fracarro, *"I processi degli Scipioni,"* pp. 260–264, and by Carcopino, *Autour des Gracques,* pp. 47–60, but defended by Geer, "Scipios and Father of the Gracchi," pp. 381–388. Livy xxxviii.52.11 for Publius, xxxviii.57.4; Gell. vi.19.7 for Lucius.

26. Livy xxxviii.56.11–13. Gell. vi.19.6: "ob plerasque in republica dissensiones."

190. This is hardly the sort of task allotted gratuitously to an *inimicus,* though neither is it so specialized a mission as to require the talents possessed only by this political opponent.[27] Finally, the state of relations between Tiberius Gracchus and Cato, archenemy of the Scipios, sheds no helpful light; the sources allege, what surely must be true, that Cato was the man behind the prosecution of the Scipios, yet hint at both political alliance and political ill will between Tiberius and Cato at this period.[28]

In any case, if Tiberius and the Scipios had been politically opposed, any existing alienation ended with Tiberius' subsequent marriage to the young daughter of Africanus, Cornelia. The sources are inconsistent on whether the betrothal and marriage took place before or after Africanus' death, so that any connection between veto and betrothal remains unclear.[29] Attempts to dissociate the two go back to Plutarch who, writing centuries after the event, says that Cornelia's betrothal was decided upon, not by her father, but by his relatives after his death. In this conclusion Plutarch claims to be following Polybius, but the surviving passage of Polybius in which he discusses the betrothals of the Corneliae suggests that Plutarch is making an unnecessary inference.[30] Polybius, who certainly ought to have known, does indeed imply that Cornelia's marriage to Tiberius took place after

27. Pace Geer, "Scipios and Father of the Gracchi," p. 387.

28. See, for example, Livy xxxviii.54.1; Plut. *Cato mai.* 15.1–2; Gell. iv.18.7; cf. Dio frag. 65. See Geer, "Scipios and Father of the Gracchi," pp. 384–386, who argues convincingly that while Dio frag. 65 suggests some measure of political cooperation between Cato and Gracchus, Val. Max. iii.7.7, and particularly the phrase *ad multum odium,* is precisely what might be expected from the censor "towards one who had once supported him and had gone over to the enemy."

29. For the uncertainty see Livy xxxviii.57.2–5; cf. Gell. xii.8.1–4. For the marriage occurring after Africanus' death, see Polyb. xxxi.27. For the betrothal occurring after his death, see Plut. *TG* 4.3. Dio (frag. 65) seems to believe the betrothal was Africanus' work. Both Carcopino (*Autour des Gracques,* pp. 61–62) and Geer ("Scipios and Father of the Gracchi," p. 381) believe the betrothal took place after Africanus' death and insist that there can have been no close connection between it and the intervention. Cf. Münzer, s. v. Cornelia (407), *RE,* 1592.

30. Compare Plut. *TG* 4.3 with Polyb. xxxi.27 and Livy xxxviii.57.2–5.

Africanus' death, for he makes Cornelia's mother Aemilia rather than Scipio Africanus himself pay half their daughters' dowries at the time of their marriages. The betrothal, however, is not mentioned, so that it hardly follows that Africanus had no say in his daughters' betrothals or that there was not a close connection between the marriage and Tiberius' veto. A betrothal could occur years before the marriage was likely to take place, and Polybius, in the same passage, says that Scipio himself set the considerable size of his daughters' dowries. It is not probable that he would have done so without knowing the identity of the intended husbands.[31] Thus, Plutarch's conclusion that the betrothal occurred after Africanus' death may be based on an unnecessary inference from Polybius' statement that the actual marriage occurred then. Even if Plutarch is correct, using some Polybian passage now lost, it does not follow that the betrothal and the veto are not causally connected.

What is incontrovertible is that the man who vetoed the proceedings at the last moment, protesting the while that his action involved no political double-cross since it was a gesture above politics and partisanship, went on to become the son-in-law of the great Africanus, to hold the consulship twice, and to be elected to the prestigious office of censor. Such an access of good fortune leads to a reconstruction of Tiberius' role in the trial of the Scipios on the following lines. In 190 he was not yet an enemy of either Publius or Lucius Scipio. The evidence suggests the opposite. In the years before his tribunate, nevertheless, opposition developed between Tiberius and Africanus on a number of political issues, one of which may have been the role and treatment of the tribunes,[32] which could have encouraged the younger man to

31. On betrothal occurring long before the marriages, see Friedlander, *Roman Life and Manners under the Early Empire*, I, 232–235, and IV, 123–124, for his quotation of supporting sources. Corbett, *The Roman Law of Marriage,* p. 153, speaks of the kind of bargaining that went on between parents and suitors. See also Hopkins, "The Age of Roman Girls at Marriage," pp. 309–327.

32. Even if it is correct to reject Gracchus' speech against Scipio Africanus (Livy xxxviii.56.10–13) as a late Republican invention (see Mommsen, *Römische Forschungen,* II, 502; Meyer, *Caes. Monarchie,* p. 531;

move closer to the Scipios' rival, Cato. Tiberius may even have participated in the early stages of Cato's attack against either or both of them. Once that attack had become public, however, thereby sparking a display of senatorial respect for the prestige of the Scipios, Tiberius revised his earlier estimate of which political alliance would best serve his burgeoning career, and he changed sides. He then distinguished himself by saving Lucius Scipio and thereby ingratiated himself with large numbers of powerful Roman senators.[33] The eight tribunes who refused to respond to Africanus' (or P. Cornelius Scipio Nasica Corculum's) plea to come to Lucius' aid have all been consigned to relative obscurity.[34] Unlike Gracchus, none of the ones whose names we know attained the consulship. Thus the tribunate may be seen as the turning point of Tiberius' political career. He had exploited the office to great advantage, using it to ingratiate himself with one of the most powerful political groups of his day. That it was to prove the terminal point in the careers of both his surviving sons may in some degree be attributed to their excess of zeal in attempting to exploit it as their father had done and so to make family history repeat itself.

In 183, Gracchus *père* was one of three commissioners who founded the important Roman colony of Saturnia in Etruria at the junction of five roads.[35] The next year he became aedile and took advantage of the office to sponsor games that were so lavish as to

---

De Sanctis, "Review of Haywood, *Studies on Scipio Africanus,*" pp. 189–203. Contra, Haywood, *Studies on Scipio Africanus,* pp. 15ff.), it is not only there that we hear of Scipio's rough handling of tribunes. Livy speaks of the tradition in which Africanus is said to have attacked tribunes just before he presents the speech (56.9).

33. Livy xxxviii.57.5–7 whereupon, after the veto, the Senate is said to have urged Africanus to betroth his daughter to Tiberius. Cf. xxxviii.53.6, allegedly after the veto on the proceedings against Publius: "Senatus deinde concilio plebis dimisso haberi est coeptus. Ibi gratiae ingentes ab universo ordine, praecipue a consularibus senioribusque, Ti. Graccho actae sunt, quod rem publicam privatis simultatibus potiorem habuisset."

34. Gellius (vi.19.5) says Africanus; Livy (xxxviii.58.3) Nasica.

35. Livy xxxix.55.9. Salmon, *Roman Colonization under the Republic,* p. 187, n. 184.

prompt senatorial legislation setting a spending limit for future events. His extravagance apparently proved a burden not only to the Italians and the allies of the Latin confederacy but also to the provincials. He thus demonstrated early one of the uses of wealthy provincial as well as domestic clients.[36] The lesson was not lost on his descendants, as we shall see.

He was elected praetor for 180 and was assigned, by lot, to take over the command of the province of Nearer Spain from Q. Fulvius Flaccus. At the beginning of this calendar year, Flaccus had sent his legate, L. Minucius, and two of his military tribunes, T. Maenius and L. Terentius Massiliota, to the Senate. They reported two victories, the submission of the Celtiberians, and the pacification of the province, and then requested that Flaccus be allowed, on his retirement from the province, to take his entire army away with him. Not only was this right, according to Minucius, but it was necessary, for wholesale desertions, or worse, mutiny, might occur if the soldiers were not discharged forthwith. Tiberius, as Flaccus' successor, did not relish the prospect of facing the fierce Celtiberians with an army of raw recruits and opposed the request. He asked rhetorically if Minucius seriously thought he could guarantee the loyalty the Celtiberians had recently pledged. Did he think the province could be held without an army? If he could not give an unequivocal "yes" to these questions, did he not think it a better idea to discharge from Flaccus' army only those veterans who had completed their full term of military service? Experienced soldiers might in this way be mingled with green recruits, and Rome could avoid attracting a barbarian revolt with an army of fledglings. These people had shown themselves fierce and rebellious: what did the claim of having pacified the province really mean? A few cities in the neighborhood of Flaccus' winter quarters were said to be completely under control, but what of the Celtiberians in more remote parts who were still under arms? Would it not, therefore, be more sensible to leave the province in the hands of the tried and proved veteran army that partially occupied it already? Finally, the praetor threatened that, if Flaccus were al-

36. Livy xl.44.10–12. Badian, *FC,* p. 161.

lowed to bring the legions back, he would confine his activities to the pacified districts around his winter quarters. "I will expose no raw recruits to a most warlike enemy."

Flaccus' legate wisely declined to prophesy. No one could predict what the Celtiberians would do, but the advantages of a veteran army had to be weighed against the disadvantages of one that was likely to be mutinous. Thereupon the Senate intervened with compromise. The consuls were instructed to enlist a new legion for Tiberius with an unusually large cavalry contingent. Further, they directed that when Tiberius and his new recruits arrived in Spain, Flaccus could discharge only those of his soldiers, Roman and allied, who had been in the province since at least 187 and those who had distinguished themselves for valor in his two battles with the Celtiberians.[37]

As it happened, the Celtiberians revolted before Tiberius arrived, and Flaccus had to deal with them on his own, though the transfer of troops that the Senate directed seems to have gone off easily and without incident afterward. The Senate renewed Tiberius' *imperium,* and he remained in his province until 178.[38]

His Spanish campaign was very successful and, although the sources disagree about the precise number of cities and towns he took, they concur that there were many.[39] As a military commander Tiberius proved competent, even imaginative, though he is said to have given credit for his successes to his "excellent army." [40] His most remarkable accomplishment, however, lay in imposing on Nearer Spain a settlement that kept the peace in this turbulently hostile province for the next quarter of a century. It would indeed be interesting to know by what political skills this was achieved, especially given the nature of the people and the

37. For the entire incident see Livy xl.35.10–36.5 and 8–12.

38. Livy xl.39.1–40.15, 44.4–5.

39. Livy xl.49.1; Polybius and Posidonius in Strabo iii.4.13; Flor. i.33.9; Oros. iv.20.33. Estimates range roughly between one and three hundred towns, though in regard to Polybius' quotation of the latter figure, Posidonius is said to have gibed that the historian was not very discriminating about the sort of settlement he was willing to call "a city."

40. Frontin. *Str.* ii.5.3; cf. Livy xl.48; Frontin. *Str.* ii.5.14; App. *Iber.* 43; Livy xl.47.7.

history of the area before and after his tenure there. The Celtiberian tribe, the Belli, themselves quoted the settlement with approval to the Senate in 153, and no doubt it was an asset to his son in his successful treaty negotiations with the Numantines over the release of a captured Roman army in 137.[41] Unfortunately, however, the details of the peace arrangements are sparse. Some of the tribes had agreed to pay a tribute and to furnish the Romans with military contingents, but even if Tiberius' assessments were mild and fair, his measures must have gone further than this to have the effect of pacifying the province.[42] The one substantial clue on which to base speculation as to their nature comes from a tantalizing passage in Appian that mentions that in one area Tiberius "gathered the poor together into a community and distributed land to them." [43] No other facts survive. On its own, though, this one hints at a policy of conciliation whose success— there was peace in Spain for the next quarter of a century— contrasts sharply with the repeated failures of the aggressive and treacherous policies that replaced it. The device of settling the poor on the land in order to maintain civil equilibrium also might have provided inspiration for the agrarian measures of the legislation proposed by the tribune of 133.

After founding the town of Gracchuris in Spain (an interesting anticipation of the naming policy later followed by the Roman emperors), Tiberius returned to Italy to celebrate an impressive triumph, whereupon the Roman electorate rewarded his military accomplishments with election to the consulship.[44]

The year before Tiberius took up his office, the praetor in charge of the province of Sardinia reported an insurrection there. Two tribes were wreaking havoc in the province, and the praetor's army, recently devastated by disease, could not withstand them. An embassy of local Sardinians confirmed the account, claiming that they had already abandoned their fields in despair and imploring the Senate to help them defend their towns. Consideration of the matter was postponed for the brief interval until the new

41. App. *Iber*. 44. See, for example, Plut. *TG* 5.3–4.   42. App. *Iber*. 44.
43 App. *Iber*. 43: τοὺς δὲ ἀπόρους συνῴκιξε, καὶ γῆν αὐτοῖς διεμέτρει. Cf. 42.
44. Livy xli.7.1–3.

administration began, but the day after the consuls took office on the Ides of March 177, the province of Sardinia passed into Tiberius' hands, by lot we are told, though, because his grandfather had originally brought the island under the Roman yoke, the assignment may not have been coincidental.[45] Tiberius left with two legions and shortly after his arrival defeated both Sardinian tribes in a pitched battle. He then proceeded to subdue the other cities that had joined the insurgents and to pacify the province. He enslaved large numbers of the vanquished and brought them back to Italy, producing an enormous increase in slave labor on Italian soil.[46] So the father contributed to the problem that the agrarian law bearing the family's name and proposed by his son would seek to ameliorate. In addition, previous tributaries had their taxes doubled while the newly conquered communities were compelled to make grain contributions.[47] His task done, Tiberius requested permission to return from the province with his army, no doubt anticipating a triumph, only to find his request opposed by M. Popillius Laenas, the praetor who was to succeed him. The alleged reason was that such a transfer of commanders at that time would not be administratively sound, but conceivably behind this was retribution for Tiberius' earlier opposition to Q. Fulvius Flaccus' return from Spain.[48] At any rate, the Senate granted Popillius' request and Tiberius, against his will, had his command prorogued and his stay in Sardinia prolonged for another year.

He got his triumph on returning to Rome in 175, however, and in 169 attained the highest regular office in the Roman system, that of censor. His earlier colleague as consul, C. Claudius Pulcher, was elected to the other censorship. The immediate problem facing

45. Polyb. xxv.4.1; Livy xli.6.4–8 and 8.4. There seems, however, to be some confusion in Livy for at 8.2 he claimed that the island had been assigned to the praetor, L. Mummius. It is certainly possible that, under the circumstances, the island was deliberately given to Tiberius because of his demonstrated military ability or because of the previous connections the Sempronii Gracchi must have had on the island as a result of his grandfather's expedition, or for both reasons.

46. Auct. *Vir. Ill.* 57.2.

47. Livy xli.12.4–7, 17.1–3; cf. Flor. i.22.35.   48. Livy xli.15.6–9.

the state at the time they assumed office was the military draft
for the Macedonian war. The consuls had complained to the
Senate that they were having difficulties with the levy because
men of military age were not presenting themselves for conscription. Two of the praetors, however, accused the consuls of playing politics by conducting a biased levy, and they volunteered to
complete the draft. The Senate accepted their offer while, at the
same time, in a stiff pronouncement, the censors set the tone for
the remainder of their censorship: they required a general oath
from each citizen giving details of his military eligibility and
guaranteeing his presence, if eligible, at conscription proceedings.
At this time also, owing to slack discipline by commanding officers,
many of the legionaries who had been serving in Macedon were
turning up on Italian soil, discharged before their formal military
obligations had been fulfilled. Gracchus and Pulcher accordingly
proclaimed that those soldiers in Italy who had been enrolled for
legionary service in the Macedonian campaign in 172 should
appear before the censors within thirty days and return to their
province. Whenever investigation disclosed that the premature
discharges resulted from favoritism, re-enlistment would be ordered. Reportedly, an embarrassingly large number of men responded to the summons.[49]

The censors' severity continued. After reappointing Marcus
Aemilius Lepidus "princeps senatus," they expelled seven members of the Senate.[50] They then turned their attention to the equestrians in general, and the "publicani" in particular. They expelled
many men from the equestrian order and rubbed salt into publican
wounds by declaring that no one who had farmed the public revenues or received a public works contract in the last censorship
(174) would be eligible to bid, or be partner to a bidder, when
they auctioned the public contracts. Unfortunately, the sources do
not elaborate on the scandals connected with the earlier contracts
that must have provoked this action. A furor arose, and some of
the more established publicans sought to persuade the Senate to
limit the censors' power. When the Senate declined and instead

49. Livy xliii.14.   50. Livy xliii.15.6.

supported the censors, the publicans managed, as a final resort, to recruit to their cause one of the tribunes, P. Rutilius, who apparently joined the publican side because of his own grudge against the censors for their treatment of one of his freedman clients.

Rutilius introduced a bill before the tribal assembly proposing to void the public works and revenue contracts Tiberius and Claudius had let as censors and directing that the contracts be auctioned anew without the restrictions on bidders. Tempers flared, and the conflict grew. Both censors came to speak against Rutilius' proposal, and while Gracchus was given a courteous hearing, the arrogant Claudius was greeted with jeers. He thereupon demanded that the herald bring the session to order. Rutilius nevertheless protested that the meeting had been taken out of his hands so that his prerogative as tribune had been infringed, and he promptly withdrew. The next day the dispute exploded. Rutilius now came forth and dedicated Tiberius' property to the gods, charging that he had violated a tribune's right of veto (*intercessio*) when he had fined and sent agents to secure bonds for the client that he, Rutilius, had tried to protect. He demanded that Claudius be tried for taking over the meeting and announced that he judged both censors guilty of treason (*perduellio*), presumably for their violations of the tribune's power. Their trial for *perduellio* was set by the urban praetor, C. Sulpicius, to take place before the centuriate assembly on September 23 and 24. Claudius pleaded his case first, but when eight of the first twelve equestrian centuries as well as many other centuries of the first class voted to condemn the censor (we are nowhere told how the remaining six voted), the elder statesmen of the Senate and Tiberius himself had to intervene to save him. Gracchus, trading on his high popularity with the electorate, swore publicly that if Claudius were condemned he would not await the outcome of his own trial, but would accompany his colleague into exile.[51] His threat seems to have worked, but narrowly, for it was a near thing in the end, with only eight centuries lacking for condemnation. Once Claudius was acquitted, however, Rutilius dropped the charges against Ti-

51. Livy xliii.16.15: "cum clamor undique plebis esset periculum Graccho non esse."

berius.⁵² In revenge, the censors expelled Rutilius from the equestrian order, removed him from his tribe, and disenfranchised him.⁵³

Undeterred by their recent battle, the censors acted next against certain freedmen. In 179, by an act of the censors, freedmen who had both a son and landed property and also those who possessed thirty thousand sesterces worth of land were for the first time permitted to enroll in a rural tribe. Part of the privilege may have been revoked in the subsequent censorship of 174, and one scholar has inferred that by 169 it belonged only to those who owned land worth more than thirty thousand sesterces, though the new legislation was not retroactive and freedmen fathers placed in rural tribes in 179 could stay there. Again, without invoking the principle of retroactivity, Gracchus proposed withdrawing all the earlier concessions and more; he prevailed upon a reluctant Claudius to consign all freedmen to just one of the four urban tribes, thereby minimizing their potential political influence. The Esquiline tribe was selected by lot and Gracchus announced to a grateful Senate and to the distant applause of Cicero that henceforth all former slaves would regularly be deposited by the censors in an urban tribe.⁵⁴

With some of the funds decreed him by the Senate, Tiberius purchased properties and had a Basilica Sempronia constructed, whose remains have been found under the Basilica Iulia in the Roman Forum.⁵⁵ He and Claudius asked that their term of office

52. On this incident see Livy xliii.16; Cic. *Rep.* vi.2; Val. Max. vi.5.3; and the discussion in Badian, *Publicans and Sinners,* pp. 39–47. For the expulsion of senators and equestrians from their respective orders, see Livy xlv.15.8.

53. Livy xliv.16.8.

54. Livy xlv.15.1–8. This is a very difficult passage and I have, for the most part, followed the interpretation of McDonald, "The History of Rome and Italy in the Second Century B.C.," pp. 134–138, esp. n. 96. See also Taylor, *VDRR,* pp. 139–140; Toynbee, *HL,* II, 372; Treggiari, *Roman Freedmen during the Late Republic,* pp. 43–47; Staveley, *Greek and Roman Voting and Elections,* pp. 139–141. For Cicero's approval see *De Orat.* i.9.38; cf. Auct. *Vir. Ill.* 57.2.

55. Livy xliv.16.10–11.

be prorogued so that they might see to the customary building repair and inspect the public works for which they had already contracted, but the tribune Cn. Tremellius vetoed the request, allegedly because he was still angry that the censors had not chosen him for the Senate.[56]

In 165, Tiberius led an important embassy to investigate the state of affairs in Pergamum, Cappadocia, Syria, and Rhodes. In each case he brought back to the Senate a positive report that provided the basis for future dealings between the Romans and these eastern powers.[57] The reports probably constituted a "beneficium" that placed the leaders of those countries reported on in Gracchus' debt. His foreign *clientelae* must have gained significantly thereby. In 133, Tiberius' eldest son threatened to appropriate, against the wishes of the Senate, the estate of King Attalus Philometer of Pergamum—who had in his will bequeathed his kingdom to the Roman people—for the purpose of implementing his agrarian reform program. That the Pergamene ambassador stayed at the house of the Gracchi while in Rome is evidence for the extension of the father's influence abroad a generation earlier.[58]

Gracchus' second consulship, for 163, began with a strange episode that reveals him as a devious politician. His colleague, M'. Juventius Thalna, died in office while in his province, Corsica, shortly after learning that the Senate had decreed him a *supplicatio* for his successes there.[59] Gracchus was to replace him in Corsica and Sardinia, but first had to supervise the consular elections for the coming year.[60] During the proceedings, the official who de-

56. Livy xlv.15.9.
57. For Pergamum, Polyb. xxx.30.7–8. For Cappadocia, Polyb. xxxi.3.4; Diod. xxxi.28. For Syria, Polyb. xxx.27.1–4, 30.7–8; Diod. xxxi.17. In spite of the impression both Polybius and Diodorus deliberately try to create that Tiberius was taken in by Syria's shrewd king, Antiochus, future events suggest that, on the contrary, he read his man very well indeed. See Mørkholm, *Antiochus IV of Syria,* pp. 99–101. For Rhodes, Polyb. xxx.31.19–20; Cic. *Brut.* 79.
58. Badian, *FC,* pp. 173–174.
59. Val. Max. ix.12.3; Pliny *NH* vii.182.
60. Cic. *QF* ii.2.1; Auct. *Vir. Ill.* 57.2.

clared how the first century had voted, while in the act of an-
nouncing the electoral results, suffered a stroke and died. Gracchus, only marginally taken aback, carried on with the election. His
nonchalance at this patently inauspicious omen seems to have
caused a stir among the people so that he referred the matter to
the Senate, which in turn passed it to the haruspices. They pronounced that Tiberius "had not been in order," a judgment that
enraged the consul, who had some unkind words for Etruscan
soothsayers before he sent them packing.[61] Thereafter, P. Cornelius Scipio Nasica Corculum (Gracchus' brother-in-law) and
C. Marcius Figulus duly assumed the consulship, received their
respective provincial commands, and left Rome, Marcius for Gaul
and Scipio for Corsica, the latter presumably on his way to replace Tiberius Gracchus.[62]

At this point, Gracchus, who was himself an augur, while in
Sardinia chanced to discover through a close study of the sacred
books, what he had not remembered before, that the haruspices
had been right and he wrong. He had indeed "not been in order."
There had been a small irregularity. He had set up his augural
tent, then crossed the boundary (*pomerium*) of the city on his way
to a meeting of the Senate, and when he crossed the *pomerium*
again on his return, he had forgotten to take the auspices. Therefore, he concluded, the consuls had not been duly elected. He informed the augural college of this unhappy fact in a dispatch from
Sardinia, and they brought it to the attention of the Senate. The
Senate decided the consuls would have to resign; they did, and
promptly returned from their allotted provinces.[63] Some allegedly
applauded Tiberius' action as that of a man who was not afraid to
admit his mistake when the interests of the state were concerned.[64]
The duly elected consuls for 162 were not likely to have been
among them. Cicero slyly remarks in a letter to his brother Quintus
that the island of Sardinia seems to be curiously restorative of

61. Cic. *Nat. Deor.* ii.10–11.   62. Val. Max. i.1.3.

63. Cic. *Div.* i.33, ii.74; Plut. *Marc.* v.1–3; Gran. Lic. 28.5; Auct. *Vir.
Ill.* 44.2.

64. Val. Max. i.1.3; Plut. *Marc.* 5.1–3.

memory, and elsewhere suggests that something was fishy, for the invalidating rationale had nothing to do with the official's untimely demise and the haruspices were hardly in a position to know about Tiberius' augural tent or his movements to and fro across the *pomerium:* in sum, an example of divination in the employ of political expediency.[65] One scholar has suggested that Tiberius may have been trying to oust his Scipionic brother-in-law from an area he considered his own preserve.[66] Perhaps there was unfinished business that required more time: he may have desired to consolidate his Sardinian *clientela.*

Whatever prompted Tiberius' unorthodox behavior, the task did not detain him for long. He was back in Rome before the end of the year, in time for appointment as head of yet another important legation, this time sent to examine the condition of Greece after the escape of Demetrius I, Soter, king of Syria, from Rome to Syria.[67] Afterward the legation went to Asia to ascertain the effects of Demetrius' actions on other foreign kings, and finally to settle disputes between those kings and the Galatians. Polybius says that Gracchus was chosen because he had personal knowledge of the conditions involved. Indeed, as we have seen, there is good reason to believe that Tiberius had useful connections in all these areas, and this series of reports to the Senate, like the last, would have strengthened the ties he enjoyed with foreign clients, ties to be bequeathed one day to his son.[68] E. Badian has suggested that the foreign connections of Tiberius Gracchus *père* in Macedonia and Greece, in Asia and the kingdoms of the East, in Spain and Sardinia, made him one of the most powerful men of his age, and that the *invidia* created by his possession of this vast *clientela* might have helped precipitate the downfall of the tribune of 133.[69]

This ambassadorship was the last public post Tiberius held for the Roman state. The year before, his son and namesake had been

65. Cic. *QF* ii.2.1; Cic. *Div.* ii.74.   66. Scullard, *RP,* pp. 226–227.
67. Polyb. xxxi.27.7–16.
68. Polyb. xxxi.15.9–12, 32, 33; Diod. xxxi.28.
69. Badian, *FC.,* pp. 169, 173. Cf. Scullard, *RP,* p. 220; Astin, *SA,* p. 35.

born and presumably the next ten years or so of his life, which were to be his last, were spent at home with Cornelia, his wife, and with his children.

Such, then, were the achievements of Tiberius Gracchus' immediate ancestors, culminating in those of his extraordinary father. The son was expected to equal or surpass them, thereby upholding the tradition. The father's path to success would have provided a model for his sons. It would be surprising if, under the guidance of their mother, they did not emulate to some degree his approach to politics and learn from his experiences.

Cornelia was born probably sometime between 195 and 190.[70] As the younger daughter of the great Scipio Africanus and of Aemilia, sister of Aemilius Paullus, victor at Pydna, she was connected with the foremost families in Rome. Besides being Aemilius Paullus' niece, she was the natural first cousin, as well as later the mother-in-law of Scipio Aemilianus. There is some controversy about the date of her marriage to Tiberius Gracchus, but it probably took place somewhere near the middle of the 170s when Cornelia would have been in her mid-to-late teens.[71] Tiberius' age can also be only roughly estimated. He held his first consulship in 177, and the minimum legal age for the office may have been officially set at thirty-six by the *lex Villia Annalis* of 180. He must therefore have been around forty when he married.[72]

The memory of their father's brilliant career must surely have had a profound influence upon the values and ambitions of his two controversial sons. Their formal education, however, was almost exclusively in the hands of their mother. Tiberius may have spent some years at his father's side and under his tutelage, but the boy was probably only about ten years old, his brother Gaius an

70. For the ages of Cornelia and her sons I have followed the rough estimates of Carcopino, *Autour des Gracques,* chap. 2, "Le Mariage de Cornélie," pp. 47–83; though I do not accept his dating of Tiberius' (the father's) birth to 208.

71. *Ibid.,* pp. 61–67. Contra, see Mommsen, *Römische Forschungen,* II, 489–491.

72. See Astin, *The Lex Annalis before Sulla,* pp. 31–46; cf. Mommsen, *Röm. Staats.,* I³ 564–567; Pliny *NH* vii.122.

infant or just about to be born, when their father died. Cornelia's passionate commitment to the upbringing of her two sons became proverbial.[73] When Tacitus, for example, writes of a mother's role in the education of her son, Cornelia is the first example he cites.[74] Plutarch remarks that Cornelia raised her two sons with such scrupulous care that they were thought to owe their virtues more to education than to nature.[75] She was widowed comparatively early, losing her husband when she was probably still in her thirties. Though she had the opportunity, she chose not to remarry. Only three of her children, the two tribunes and Sempronia, who became the wife of Scipio Aemilianus, survived from a marriage that produced twelve children in all. Add to these facts the tradition of greatness the daughter of Scipio Africanus would inherit, and a husband's remarkable achievements, which convention dictated should be matched or exceeded by his sons, and we may begin to understand Cornelia's zeal in their training. She appears to have dedicated herself entirely to them, a commitment that must have made the already heavy burden of the paternal example all the heavier for them to bear.

There is even a story that Cornelia was in the habit of cruelly prodding her young sons with the taunt that she was growing bored at being known as the mother-in-law of Scipio Aemilianus, and not as the mother of the Gracchi.[76] Possibly the tale is apocryphal, though it has the ring of truth about it, intensified by a subsequent irony: Cornelia was to have her title but lose her sons in the process. A statue of her was eventually erected in the capital bearing the inscription, "CORNELIA, AFRICANI F. GRACCHORUM."[77]

Unfortunately, the nature of the surviving evidence makes the real Cornelia difficult to discern. Two of the records from which later authors draw are her own letters and those of her younger son, Gaius—hardly the sort of testimonials likely to present an

73. Cic. *Brut.* 104, 211; Quint. i.1.6.   74. Tac. *Dial.* 28.
75. Plut. *TG* 1.5.   76. Plut. *TG* 8.5.
77. Pliny *NH* xxxiv.31; Plut. *CG* 4.3; *Inscr. Ital.*, XIII, fasc. iii (Elogia) p. 53 = *CIL* VI.31610.

unbiased picture.[78] The frequent tragedies of her life—she survived at least eleven of her twelve children and lived through the murder of both her sons by members of the Roman Senate—must have surrounded her portrait with the distorting halo of martyrdom. That she was obsessively ambitious for her two surviving sons' advancement can readily be accepted, but much of the available information depicts her after the loss of her sons as an indefatigable spirit, abused by fortune but never overcome.[79] In assessing her influence over her sons, we are more concerned with a younger Cornelia, and through the strident encomia for this long-suffering mother emerge suggestions that she was not loved by all.

Undoubtedly many saw her as the woman behind her two young men, and hatred of them must have implied hatred of her. Some accused her of driving her son Tiberius to take up the agrarian problem and of playing an active part in Gaius' seditious activities, even hiring men secretly and sending them into the city in his support disguised as harvesters.[80] Others claimed that she intervened on behalf of the deposed Octavius in 123 and saved his political career by persuading her son to withdraw legislation designed to end it.[81] Contemporary opinion, however, was clearly divided. Gaius on occasion invoked his mother's good name on his own behalf for rhetorical effect, yet at times he was called upon to defend it.[82] Some even accused the ruthless Cornelia of

78. For the letters of Cornelia see Cic. *Brut.* 211 and the almost certain forgeries preserved in Nepos, frag. 1. See now, Instinsky, "Zur Echtheitsfrage der Brieffragmente der Cornelia, Mutter der Gracchen," pp. 177–189. For Gaius' letters see Cic. *Div.* ii.62; cf. Plut. *TG* 8.7.

79. Val. Max. iv.4.1; Sen. *cons. ad Marc.* 16.3; *Sen. cons. ad Helv.* 16.6; Plut. *CG* 19.1–3; Oros. v.12.9.

80. Plut. *TG* 8.5; Plut. *CG* 13.2.

81. Plut. *CG* 4.1. The rogation provided that if the People deprived any magistrate of his office he should not be allowed to hold office a second time, a measure more probably designed to warn off any would-be Octavius in 123 from obstructing the legislative program Gaius intended to implement than to wreak vengeance on an already humiliated tribune. Cf. Diod. xxiv.25.2.

82. Sen. *cons. ad Helv.* 16.6; Plut. *CG* 4.4.

involvement in the suspicious death of Scipio Aemilianus in 129.[83]

When the time came to provide her sons with their formal education, Cornelia turned to Greece, choosing Diophanes of Mytilene as their tutor. This action has been interpreted as an indication of the intellectual predispositions of the household. The father of the Gracchi, as we have seen, had powerful connections in the Hellenistic East. That he had delivered a speech in Greek at Rhodes sometimes leads to the inference that he was an enthusiastic philhellene, whatever that means.[84] More interesting is that fact that the name of mother as well as son would later have high stature in the Greek world. Not only would it stand Tiberius in good stead for the implementation of his agrarian scheme with Pergamene funds, but the reigning Ptolemy in Egypt sought Cornelia's hand in marriage, albeit without success.[85] When Cornelia selected a Greek as tutor, she may well have been seeking to prepare the young Tiberius for his station and his inherited *clientela* in the East rather than displaying a commitment to things Greek.[86]

Before we can assess the influences on Tiberius of his tutors, the question of their identity calls for re-examination. What little is known about Diophanes suggests that Cornelia's choice of him was obvious and natural. Strabo lists him as one of Mytilene's most famous men, and Cicero says he was accounted the ablest Greek speaker of his day.[87] Blossius of Cumae, however, did not have similar stature, though he is assumed by many to be another of Tiberius' tutors, probably because Plutarch throws him together with Diophanes as possible instigators of Tiberius' later conduct.[88] The assumption that he was a tutor is not necessary or even likely, and there is not a scrap of evidence to indicate that Cornelia had

83. App. *BC* i.20.   84. Cic. *Brut.* 79.   85. Plut. *TG* 1.4.
86. Cic. *Brut.* 104.   87. Strabo xiii.2.3; Cic. *Brut.* 104.
88. Plut. *TG* 8.4–5, 20.3–4; cf. Cic. *Amic.* 37: "non enim paruit ille Ti. Gracchi temeritati, sed praefuit, nec se comitem illius furoris, sed ducem praebuit." See, among others, Last, "Tiberius Gracchus," pp. 20–21; Greenidge, *A History of Rome 133–104 B.C.*, I, 104; Marsh, *A History of the Roman World 146–30 B.C.*, p. 322; Münzer, s.v. Diophanes, *RE*, V.1048–1049; Bloch and Carcopino, *Histoire romaine*, II, 186; Ferguson, *Utopias of the Classical World*, pp. 138–139, who uncritically accepts Cicero's hostile allegation.

anything to do with selecting him. Indeed, the Campanian Blossius would have been an extraordinary choice for Cornelia to make, for he had politically tainted ancestry.[89] In fact, Blossius enters the Gracchan picture toward the end of the tribune's life, as far as we can tell, and we know of Tiberius' association with him because he became implicated in the fatal activities of the tribunate. After the tribune's assassination, Blossius was hauled before the special consular *consilium* established by the Senate, though unlike many he was eventually allowed his freedom, possibly, as has been suggested, through the intervention of P. Mucius Scaevola at whose house he had once been a *hospes*.[90] Blossius' dialogue with the court before his dismissal hardly reflects a teacher-pupil relationship. When queried about his own activities he pleaded that he had acted in obedience to his friend Tiberius' instructions. Pressed by Laelius and the consuls, he eventually admitted that, had Tiberius ordered him to set fire to the Capitol, he would have obeyed because, he explained, had the tribune commanded such an act it would most surely have been right—an impressive loyalty, if intellectually shallow.[91] A clear picture thus emerges of a follower-leader relationship, and Blossius' subsequent flight to Asia to join the emancipatory rebellion of Aristonicus gives the impression that he was something of a revolutionary camp follower, committed to the cause of the oppressed masses whenever and wherever the call came.[92] He may have learned of Tiberius' reforming intentions from Scaevola, and his subsequent attachment to Aristonicus indicates that he was not motivated simply by per-

89. See the suggestion of Dudley, "Blossius of Cumae," p. 95, that he may have been a descendant of the Marius Blossius who was a member of the party that urged collaboration with Hannibal (Livy xxiii.7.8–9) and of the "Blossii fratres" who led a conspiracy to set fire to the city, were arrested, and executed (Livy xxvii.3.4–5). Laelius' question to Blossius about arson on the Capitoline gives Dudley's case added plausibility. The Blossii were also a byword for arrogance and luxury. See Cic. *Leg. Agr.* ii.93; Livy xxiii.7.8, xxvii.3.4.

90. Cic. *Amic.* 37. See Dudley, "Blossius of Cumae," p. 97; Africa, "Aristonicus, Blossius, and the City of the Sun," p. 118.

91. Cic. *Amic.* 37; Val. Max. iv.7.1; Plut. *TG* 20.3–4.

92. Badian, *TGBRR,* p. 679, n. 28.

sonal loyalty or anti-Roman, Italian nationalist sympathies. But because we have no knowledge of Tiberius' attitude toward him, his attachment to the Gracchan cause cannot shed light on the tribune's motives and intentions. Nothing save the hostile allegations in Cicero and Plutarch supports the conclusion that Blossius of Cumae had any influence on Tiberius' development, intellectual, moral, or political.[93] What we know of Blossius' association with Tiberius Gracchus tells us far more about the Campanian philosopher than about the Roman tribune.

Unfortunately, the sources provide almost no information about Diophanes' sympathies. His position as Tiberius' tutor of rhetoric cost him his life but this was not the first time that the sins of the pupil were visited upon the teacher, nor would it be the last. His death may be an unhappy fact, but it is not a very helpful one.

It is to attempt to build on sand, therefore, to argue, as one scholar has recently done, that an ideological rift now separated the Scipionic and the Gracchan camps, ultimately traceable to a doctrinal dispute between two Stoic philosophers.[94] According to this theory, the Scipionic group derived its social and political ideologies from Diogenes through Panaetius, who was a member of their intellectual circle. Tiberius, on the other hand, is supposed to represent a more orthodox brand of Stoicism derived directly from Antipater of Tarsus and learned from his tutor, Blossius of Cumae. In view of the slender, not to say invisible, intellectual connection between the tribune and his alleged teacher, not much faith can be placed in such an explanation of the origins of Tiberius' ideas.

Other general theories taking a similar direction are no more convincing.[95] Is it really necessary to search in the writings of the Stoics, or among less specific philosophical theories said "to

93. Plut. *TG* 8.4–5. See Taeger, *Tiberius Gracchus,* pp. 68–69.

94. Smuts, "Stoïsyne Invloed op Tiberius Gracchus," pp. 106–116.

95. See, for example, Nicolet, "L'inspiration de Tibérius Gracchus," pp. 142–159; Brown, "Greek Influences on Tiberius Gracchus," pp. 471–474; Katz, "The Gracchi: An Essay in Interpretation," pp. 65–82; Becker, "The Influence of Roman Stoicism upon the Gracchi's Economic Land Reforms," pp. 125–134.

have been in the air," for the political and social philosophy that
may have inspired Tiberius' law to redistribute the public land?
Surely, circumstance, the observable fact of significant numbers of
citizens displaced from their farms, is sufficient to explain how a
reformer, with whatever ultimate intention and from whatever
motive, came to seek allotments of land for the rehabilitation of
a growing number of dispossessed rural dwellers. Specific details of
Tiberius' legislation may have been patterned on previously successful agrarian practices inside or outside Italy. Nevertheless, the
alleged Stoic, or socialist, or democratic ideals that some claim to
have seen in Tiberius' public speeches may have derived less from
ideological commitment than from the practical need to advance
his reform program. They ought not to be taken as the unchallenged bases for the politician's action. A certain amount of skepticism ought to go into evaluating a politician's professed intentions,
for public speeches intended to persuade are not the most reliable
evidence of a man's true inspiration. If indeed Stoic concepts or
any others that can be identified with a known school or can be
demonstrated to have been current are presented publicly in support of his legislative program, why not suppose that this is a
case of ideology in service to Tiberius rather than the other
way around? Intellectuals who write histories are more likely to be
impressed by abstract philosophical ideas than are politicians, who
tend to use such ideas for their own practical purposes.

The search for the tribune's inspiration, at least in his scheme
to distribute land to the indigent of the Italian peninsula, should be
conducted much closer to his Roman home. We have no reason to
doubt Appian's report that the father of the Gracchi gave land
to some of the Spanish poor in his settlement of the province of
Nearer Spain. Cornelia's zeal as well as the customary practices of
Roman education would have ensured that the young Tiberius was
acquainted with the details of his father's accomplishments and
methods. The first of his lessons on the value of distributing land
to the poor would much more likely have come from his father's
experience in Complega than from Campania via Blossius of
Cumae or from Greece through Diophanes of Mytilene. The
military implications of a declining peasantry could hardly have

escaped a Sempronius Gracchus, heir to a proud military tradition, whose great-uncle had had to face the Carthaginian armies of Hanno with contingents of slaves and criminals and whose father, after insisting upon veterans for his praetorian province of Nearer Spain, then credited his military success there to his excellent army. The tribune's father, in his capacity as censor, also had to deal with the difficulties of the consular levy in 169 and the illegal discharge of some of the Macedonian legionaries in that same year. The son would have been especially sensitive to the underlying causes of such problems, whose symptoms were even more patent a generation later.

Many of the central issues raised by the tribune in 133 may be seen prefigured during the career of his father. The shortage of free manpower available for military service and the consequent difficulties of conducting the levy continued to plague Roman statesmen in the decades after 169 so that the younger Gracchus could raise the question of the maintenance and extension of empire when defending his legislative program. Nor was that all. The father had played a conspicuous role in worsening the social and economic conditions of the peasantry by importing vast numbers of Sardinian slaves into Italy. Later he championed the legislation of 169, during his censorship, that restricted the freedman vote to a single urban tribe, indicating his awareness of the possibility that thousands of manumitted slaves might disrupt established voting patterns in the tribal assembly. Then again, father like son had had his tribunician troubles, when he was charged by Rutilius with *perduellio* for ignoring the tribune's right of *intercessio*. Within the context of Roman society, it was to be expected that his father's experience in a brilliant career should be a prime influence on Tiberius Gracchus when he came to legislate in 133.

The study of Tiberius Gracchus' early career must be approached with a feeling for who he really was, for how he was perceived by contemporaries, and for what would be expected of him. We have seen how his father, ambitious, opportunistic, and successful, raised his family's fortunes to their height. Not only was he adept at the intrigues necessary for political advancement in the Roman capital, but he had also extended the influence of his family well beyond the shores of Italy, amassing a large foreign *clientela* that made him one of the most powerful men of his day. This he bequeathed to his two sons, the only surviving male heirs of his marriage to Cornelia, the younger daughter of Scipio Africanus. Those who wished him well must have hoped for great things from the young Tiberius Gracchus, but those who were differently inclined would keep a nervous eye on the house of the Sempronii Gracchi.

2 The Early Career: Tiberius, Scipio, and the Spanish Fiasco

Nam Ti. Graccho invidia Numantini foederis, cui feriendo, quaestor C. Mancini consulis cum esset, interfuerat, et in eo foedere improbando senatus severitas dolori et timori fuit: eaque res illum fortem et clarum virum a gravitate patrum desciscere coegit.

—Cicero, *De Haruspicum Responsis,* 43

ἀλλ᾽ αὕτη γε πρὸς οὐδὲν ἀνήκεστον οὐδὲ φαῦλον ἐξέπεσε. δοκεῖ δ᾽ ἄν μοι μηδαμῶς περιπεσεῖν ὁ Τιβέριος οἷς ἔπαθεν, εἰ παρῆν αὐτοῦ τοῖς πολιτεύμασι Σκηπίων ὁ Ἀφρικανός.

—Plutarch, *Tiberius Gracchus,* 7.4

Had the plebian consul for 177 lived long enough to see his eldest son pass from adolescence into early manhood, he would have had every reason to be pleased. Even by the criteria of aristocratic Roman society, Tiberius Gracchus the younger looked like a man to be reckoned with. His reputation for competitiveness can probably be concluded from a story, spread later, that he first took up the explosive agrarian problem to outdo one who had been a teenage rival, the obscure Spurius Postumius.[1] This man had stolen a march on him as an advocate after Tiberius had come of age and temporarily left the forum for the field to follow in his father's military footsteps. The way to his other traits must be cut through the usual tendencies of the ancient sources toward a standard idealization. The picture that results, clear in outline, is of an exceptionally well-tutored though not particularly brilliant young man, quietly earnest and apparently, perhaps actually, dependable in his dealings both public and private—in short, a young man whose demeanor would be an asset in the preservation of his awe-

1. Plut. *TG* 8.6.

some *clientela*.[2] When Tiberius spoke upon the rostra, for example, he remained on a fixed spot and did not indulge in the
wild gesticulation, the shouting, and the histrionics that came to
be associated with his younger brother. Tiberius' public bearing
suggested a cool constancy and a *gravitas* matched by both his life
style and his manner of speech, which were said to be simple. His
straightforwardness as an orator won him the approval of his contemporaries, though Cicero, who claims to have read some of
Tiberius' speeches, found them thoughtful and acute but in no way
startling.[3] Finally, though commentators do not remark upon it at
this stage, the young Tiberius must have possessed courage, both
physical and moral, in an uncommon degree. That courage and his
earnestness help to explain his rise to prominence, but they also
played a part in his early undoing.

Tiberius' public career began, as his father's had half a century
before, in a Scipionic camp. The son served in the army and shared
the tent of his brother-in-law, Scipio Aemilianus, before the
walls of Carthage. With them were C. Laelius, Scipio's right-hand
man and *consigliere,* who was later to propose an agrarian law
anticipating Tiberius' by some years, and C. Fannius, probably the
future consul for 122, who first supported then opposed Tiberius'
ill-fated younger brother, Gaius. Although only seventeen or eighteen at the time, Tiberius, according to Fannius who witnessed the
scene, distinguished himself by being the first to scale the enemy's
wall. Thus Tiberius performed up to the standard expected of a
young Roman noble making his military debut. The soldiers in
Scipio's camp reputedly thought highly of him and missed him
greatly when he left.[4]

2. Plut. *TG* 1.5: ὥστε πάντων εὐφυεστάτους Ῥωμαίων ὁμολογουμένως γεγονότας
πεπαιδεῦσθαι δοκεῖν βέλτιον ἢ πεφυκέναι πρὸς ἀρετήν.

3. On the character and personality of the young Tiberius Gracchus, see
Cic. *Har. Resp.* 41; Vell. ii.2.2; Quint. i.1.6; Plut. *TG* 2–4, 8; App. *BC*
i.9. For the judgment on the quality of his oratory see Cic. *Brut.* 103–104.

4. App. *Lib.* 126; Plut. *TG* 4.5. Against this identification with the consul
of 122 see Fraccaro, "Sui Fannii dell' età Graccana," pp. 656–674; Fraccaro,
"Ancora sulla questione dei Fannii," pp. 153–160; reprinted in *Opuscula* II,
103–117, and 119–123, respectively. For the identification see Münzer, "Die
Fanniusfrage," pp. 427–442.

It would be interesting to know what opinion the new conqueror of Carthage had of Tiberius during this period, what sort of terms they were on, and what in general was Scipio's attitude to the ambitious house of the Gracchi. The sources suggest that the relationship between Scipio and Cornelia was anything but constant. A convincing case has been made that tensions existed during the 160s between Aemilianus and both Corneliae, his aunts (Scipio Africanus' two daughters; the elder was wife of P. Cornelius Scipio Nasica Corculum).[5] Polybius tells us that when Aemilia, their mother (she was also Aemilianus' natural aunt for she was the sister of his father, Aemilius Paullus) died in 162, the adoptive head of the household, Scipio Aemilianus, inherited from her a huge fortune consisting of the expensive, ornate paraphernalia Aemilia had displayed on solemn occasions of state. All these valuable possessions, her wardrobe, her baskets and cups, her sacrificial utensils, even her carriage with all its appointments, Scipio dutifully turned over, not to Aemilia's own two natural daughters, but to his mother, Papiria, the long-estranged wife of Aemilius Paullus.[6] Thereafter, Papiria would attend the public sacrifices decked in Aemilia's finery, much to the admiration, we are assured, of the other ladies of Rome, who envied her her devoted son. The two Corneliae might be expected to have envied her, not for her son, but for her heirlooms. They might more easily have accepted the loss of that inheritance had Scipio sold it and kept the proceeds for himself, but if he was giving it away he should have given them preference where their mother's possessions were concerned. Scipio's filial generosity must have dimmed any affection the Corneliae might have had for him. Yet there was worse to come. Two years later, when Papiria died, Scipio bestowed the entire inheritance on his natural sisters who, even Polybius is forced to admit, had no legal claim to it whatever.[7] All cannot have been well between him and his aunts.

The year Aemilia died, 162, another instance of bad blood between the two branches of the family occurred, for by electoral sleight of hand the father of the Gracchi deprived his brother-in-

5. Astin, *SA*, pp. 19–21, 35.   6. Polyb. xxxi.26.
7. Polyb. xxxi.28.8–10.

law, Scipio Nasica, of the consulship to which he had been elected.[8] Late in this same year, or perhaps very early in the next, a third event occurred that strengthens the impression that Scipio Aemilianus had little affection for the house of the elder Tiberius Gracchus.

Scipio Africanus had settled on both his daughters a dowry of fifty talents. After his death his wife had paid half of this to the two husbands, but when she died the rest was outstanding. Scipio Aemilianus was expected to produce the considerable balance. According to Roman law, the two twenty-five-talent sums had to be rendered within a three-year period in equal annual installments, the first due ten months after Aemilia's death. Scipio Aemilianus, however, instructed his banker to pay both men the whole sum when only the first third was due. When Gracchus and Nasica received the money, Polybius tells us, they went together to see Scipio, claiming to be solicitous of his interests and pointing out to him that he surely must have made some mistake in paying off the full debt prematurely. Scipio informed his two uncles that he was fully aware of his legal rights and that no mistake had been made. Polybius tells us that the young man answered (with irony?) that he only observed the letter of the law with strangers, not with friends and relatives, and that Tiberius and Nasica went away astonished and embarrassed. The story is presented by Polybius to illustrate the new magnanimity of the young heir of the Scipios, but his aunts and uncles must have concluded that he desired to be free of any debt to them as quickly as possible, in fact, more quickly than was proper. In a society where friendship was born of obligation such behavior would have seemed a particularly daunting assertion of independence and certainly a rebuff. No doubt the husbands of the Corneliae were happy to receive their money

8. This action might be expected to have aroused Nasica's bitter resentment against Gracchus. Sometimes in this regard it is noted that Nasica's son and namesake incited the riotous assembly in 133 in which Gracchus' son and namesake was murdered (see, for example, Plut. *TG* 19.3; App. *BC* i.16; Earl, *Tiberius Gracchus,* p. 65). Yet Polybius (xxxi.27) clearly portrays these two men associating with each other within the year, at a stage when Nasica's wounds ought still to have been fresh and painful. I confess I can see no explanation for this apparent inconsistency.

early, but Scipio's message cannot have been lost on either of them.[9]

What occasioned Scipio's frosty attitude toward his aunts and uncles? One scholar has invoked, plausibly, Polybius' famous report of his conversation with Scipio, probably in 166, when the latter expressed his unhappiness over what he claimed was the current opinion that he was an unsuitable leader for his great family.[10] "Evidently you [Polybius] have also the same opinion of me that I hear the rest of my countrymen have. For, as I am told, I am believed by everybody to be a quiet and indolent man, with none of the energetic character of a Roman, because I do not choose to speak in the law courts. And they say that the family I spring from does not require such a protector as I am, but just the opposite." If the Corneliae and their husbands were among those so disposed toward him, or if he believed them to be, his conduct toward them is easy to understand. There could, of course, have been other, more concrete, perhaps more serious reasons for Scipio's aloofness which our sources have chosen not to record or of which they were ignorant.

The betrothal of Sempronia, the daughter of the younger Cornelia and Tiberius Gracchus, to Scipio Aemilianus sometime in the next decade probably represents an attempt to quiet troubled waters. The marriage took place before Scipio set off for Carthage in 147.[11] It must have been arranged by Scipio and Cornelia (and by Tiberius Gracchus the elder if he was still alive) for it is unlikely to have been the result of personal inclination. Sempronia, we are told, was physically unlovely, deformed in fact, and the marriage was notoriously unhappy. Some alleged, probably falsely and certainly maliciously, that the wife had a hand in her husband's unexplained death in 129.[12] Whatever the terms on which the couple eventually lived, the marriage was almost certainly an

9. Polyb. xxxi.27.

10. Polyb. xxxi.23.5–24.12. The scholar is Astin. See him also for the date of the conversation, *SA*, p. 245 and n. 6.

11. Cic. *Amic.* 101; Livy *Per.* lix; Val. Max. iii.8.6; Plut. *TG* 1.5, 4.4; *App. BC* i.20; Schol. Bob. 118 Stangl; Auct. *Vir. Ill.* 73.4.

12. Livy *Per.* lix; App. *BC* i.20; Schol. Bob. 118 Stangl.

attempt to create *amicitia,* rather than the symbol of an existing alliance, and not all such attempts succeed. An uncertain truce where old resentments still prickle is not firm friendship, even when both parties think it best to bury the past. During the campaign against Carthage, however, the young Tiberius Gracchus shared his commander's tent, was, as the Romans called it, Scipio's *contubernalis,* though this might have reflected the automatic acceptance of family obligation in Roman society more than special favor. Tiberius' coming of age coincided almost perfectly with Scipio's assumption of the African command; the general had a duty to take his first cousin and brother-in-law with him.

That this new alliance did not work out, that Cornelia remembered Scipio's earlier snubs, or that she sought to extend her influence to other circles is clear from her approval of the betrothal of Tiberius to Claudia, the daughter of Scipio's archrival, Appius Claudius Pulcher, *princeps senatus.*[13] Hopes for close cooperation between the Cornelii and the Sempronii Gracchi must have faded quickly.

Tiberius and Claudia probably married in 143. An attempt to connect alleged hostility between the younger Tiberius and Scipio with events in Numantia and Rome in 137 and 136 has sought to date the marriage later, to sometime after 138, and to depict it as a direct result of a hypothetical conflict between Scipio and Tiberius in Rome in 136. Before that date relations were good; after it they were strained past the breaking point.[14] The study demonstrates only that earlier arguments for placing the marriage in 143 are highly probable rather than indisputable; to date it after 138 requires the acceptance of several improbable assumptions as the arguments for 143 do not. Even if the wedding took place after 138, the betrothal might have occurred earlier, so that Scipio and Cornelia could have been at odds before the events in Nu-

13. Cic. *Brut.* 108; Cic. *Rep.* i.31; Cic. *Pro Scaur.* 32; Plut. *Apophth. Scip.* 9–10; Plut. *Aem. Paull.* 38.2.

14. Earl, *Tiberius Gracchus,* pp. 67–70. Contra, see Fraccaro, *Studi,* p. 42, n. 4; Münzer, *Römische Adelsparteien und Adelsfamilien,* pp. 268f., and the discussion of the relative merits of the arguments by Astin, *SA,* pp. 319–321, whose conclusions I have followed in the text. The relevant ancient sources are: Val. Max. ix.7.2; Gell. ii.13.5; Schol. Bob. 81 Stangl.

mantia. Plutarch does not connect the betrothal with the trouble in Spain, but rather with Tiberius' entrance into the College of Augurs, which we know occurred when he was very young, quite likely soon after he had come of age.[15] All things considered, Tiberius' marriage to Claudia in 143 does not conflict so much with what we know of the inconstant relationship between Scipio and the Sempronii Gracchi as to require a departure from the clear line the sources take.

At this stage, with Tiberius' career auspiciously begun, the so-called Mancinus affair intervenes, drastically affecting the young man's smooth rise to the political eminence of his ancestors. In 137, Tiberius was a quaestor in the consular army of C. Hostilius Mancinus, which was sent to the province of Nearer Spain. The Numantines captured the army; Tiberius conducted negotiations that resulted in a treaty guaranteeing release and safe-conduct. When Tiberius returned to Rome the following year, the Senate repudiated the treaty as a disgrace. Although Tiberius was spared his commander's fate of being turned over to the enemy, his political career suffered a setback that could have been fatal. The events of these two years must be seen in the historical context of the Roman involvement in the Iberian peninsula. The Mancinus affair was only the culmination of a remarkable series of Roman treacheries and defeats.

Roman governors first arrived in the two provinces that were to be called Nearer and Farther Spain (Hispania Citerior and Hispania Ulterior) in 205.[16] Rome had acquired her territories in the Iberian peninsula as a direct result of her conquest of Spain in the course of the Hannibalic War. When the Carthaginians were expelled, the inhabitants of the Iberian communes exchanged their Punic yoke for a Roman one, and thus began one of the most disreputable chapters of Roman provincial history. We have already

15. Plut. *TG* 4. This is likely to have occurred just before Tiberius' departure for Carthage or at the very latest immediately after his return. It seems inconceivable that the betrothal should have occurred in the wake of Tiberius' humiliation as a result of the Mancinus affair.

16. App. *Iber.* 38. For a complete narrative of the events in Spain between 153 and 133, see App. *Iber.* 44–98.

seen how the elder Tiberius Gracchus ended the war against the Celtiberians, which had lasted from 181 to 179 in Nearer Spain. His settlement kept peace there for the next quarter-century, but in 153 trouble began to spread to the east from Farther Spain, where the tribe of the Lusitanians, controlling the area that roughly coincides with modern Portugal, had been successfully raiding Roman territory. They had defeated L. Mummius, the future destroyer of Corinth, and killed some nine thousand of his troops. Their leader, one Caesaurus, sent the Roman standards he had captured to the Celtiberians in the hope of rousing them to join his rebellion.

He succeeded, at least temporarily, for the Belli, a Celtiberian tribe, began to fortify their city, Segeda. When they refused to obey the Senate's order to stop, the consul Q. Fulvius Nobilior marched against them with thirty thousand men, beginning the Numantine War (*bellum Numantinum*). The Belli, joined by the Arevaci, inflicted a serious defeat on the Roman army beneath the walls of Numantia.[17] After a winter of fighting a losing battle against disease and the elements, Nobilior was succeeded by the experienced general Claudius Marcellus, who had been consul three years before and was legally ineligible for the consulship. Events in Spain were serious enough to justify a special dispensation enabling him to become consul now. He proved more effective than his predecessor, arranging a peace treaty with the Arevaci, Belli, and Tithi by renewing the terms earlier made by Gracchus. Despite Marcellus' urgings, the Senate refused to ratify the peace terms he had negotiated, yet peace with Numantia prevailed de facto for the next eight years.[18] This settlement in the east did not help the cause of the Lusitanians in Farther Spain; Mummius recovered after his defeat, and he and his successor, M. Atilius, achieved some temporary and minor progress.

At this point, in 151, L. Licinius Lucullus took the command in Nearer Spain. His second in command was Scipio Aemilianus, who on this trip avoided Numantia, but would one day return to be its conqueror and destroyer, adding the appellation "Numantinus" to

17. Polyb. xxxv.4.2; App. *Iber.* 45–47.
18. Polyb. xxxv.2–3, 4.3; Livy *Per.* xlviii; App. *Iber.* 48–49.

"Africanus." Where these two men found peace, they made war.[19] First, Lucullus moved into the western part of the province and attacked a Celtiberian tribe, the Vaccaei. They surrrendered to him their city, Cauca, on the basis of his promise of friendship, but when he gained possession of the town, he sacked it and massacred all the adult males. After failing in his attempts to take the cities of Intercatia and Pallantia, where he understandably met determined resistance, he joined forces with Servius Galba, M. Atilius' successor as the commander of the Roman forces in Farther Spain.[20] Galba had arrived to find the Lusitanians once more in open revolt and besieging some of Rome's subjects. The year was 150, and the Lusitanians, with the armies of both Lucullus and Galba on their soil, approached the latter to renew a treaty they had earlier concluded with Atilius but had betrayed. Galba feigned sympathy and concluded the truce on condition that the Lusitanians disarm. Then he encircled his unarmed enemy with a ditch and butchered them all, in retribution, it was explained, for their earlier violation of the treaty with Atilius. A few Lusitanians escaped the massacre, among them Viriathus, later his nation's leader, and from this moment one of Rome's most inveterate enemies.[21]

In 147, Viriathus destroyed a praetorian army in a battle that cost the Roman commander his life.[22] The next year he inflicted a crushing defeat on C. Plautius Hypsaeus, with the result that the humiliated general was prosecuted for *perduellio* and forced into exile.[23] His successor for 145, the consul Q. Fabius Maximus

19. Livy *Per.* xlviii; App. *Iber.* 49.
20. For Lucullus' activities in Spain see Polyb. xxxv.3–5; Livy *Per.* lxviii; Flor. i.33.11; App. *Iber.* 51–55, 89; Auct. *Vir. Ill.* 58.2–3; Oros. iv.21.1–2. For Scipio's see also Vell. i.12.4; Val. Max. iii.2.8; Pliny *NH* xxxvii. 4.9; App. *Iber.* 49.
21. For Galba's activities in Spain see Cic. *Brut.* 89; Nepos *Cato* 3.4; Livy *Oxy. Per.* xlix; Livy *Per.* xlix; Val. Max. viii.1.2, 8.1, ix.6.2; Suet. *Galba* 3.2; App. *Iber.* 59–61; Ps.-Ascon. 203 Stangl; Oros. iv.21.10.
22. Livy *Per.* lii; App. *Iber.* 61–63; Oros. v.4.1–2.
23. For his defeat see App. *Iber.* 64; Livy *Oxy. Per.* lii; Oros. v.4.3. For the prosecution see Diod. xxxiii.2. For the debate over whether the charge was *imminuta maiestas* or *perduellio* see Broughton, *MRR*, I, 466, and

Aemilianus, Scipio's brother, also suffered reverses, but had his command prorogued at his brother's urging. He was able to return to Rome claiming some successes to his credit, though none was decisive.[24] They nevertheless sufficed to induce Viriathus to seek Celtiberian allies against his enemy and, like Caesaurus before him, he managed to detach the Arevaci, Tithi, and Belli from their Roman truce. Thus the *bellum Numantinum,* quiescent since 151, flared up anew in 143, and the Romans faced war simultaneously against the Lusitanians and the Celtiberians.

In the east a procession of Roman commanders went down to ignominious defeat. The consul Q. Caecilius Metellus Macedonicus, sent to Nearer Spain on the outbreak of war, had his command prorogued for another year. He subdued the Arevaci, but failed to capture the city of Numantia.[25] His successor, Q. Pompeius, proved an incompetent general and a treacherous negotiator. After he besieged Numantia, he sought to enhance his reputation by moving against the city of Termantia, which he expected to be an easier mark, but was not. After some minor successes against smaller targets, he returned to his seige of Numantia. Arms having failed, he decided to try negotiation and apparently offered the war-weary Numantines peace and independence for a face-saving thirty talents of silver. They paid, but for nothing: when his successor, M. Popillius Laenas, arrived, Pompeius denied that the transaction had happened, thus joining Lucullus and Galba in infamy.[26]

Bauman, *The Crimen Maiestatis in the Roman Republic and the Augustan Principate,* pp. 16–22, who believe it was *maiestas.* See Zumpt, *Das Criminalrecht der römischen Republik,* I.2, 345; Gruen, *RPCC,* p. 29, and Garnsey, "Review of Bauman, *Crimen Maiestatis,*" p. 283, for *perduellio.*

24. For Fabius' activities in Spain see Livy *Oxy. Per.* lii; Vell. ii.5.3; Flor. i.33.17; App. *Iber.* 65. For the prorogation of his command see Val. Max. vi.4.2.

25. Livy *Per.* liii; Livy *Oxy. Per.* liii; Val. Max. ii.7.10, iii.2.21, v.1.5, vii.4.5, ix.3.7; Vell. ii.5.2–3; Frontin. *Str.* iii.7.3, iv.1.23, cf. i.1.12, iv.7.42; Flor. i.33.10; App. *Iber.* 76; Eutrop. iv.16; Auct. *Vir. Ill.* 61.3.

26. Cic. *Font.* 10.23; Cic. *Off.* iii.109; Cic. *Fin.* ii.54; Livy *Per.* liv; Livy *Oxy. Per.* liv; Diod. xxxiii.17.1; Val. Max. viii.5.1; Flor. i.34.4; App. *Iber.* 76–79, 83; Dio frag. 77; Oros. v.4.13, 4.21; Vell. ii.1.5, 90.3; Eutrop. iv.17.

Events in Farther Spain had been following a similar scenario. A consular army that arrived in 141 under a relative of Scipio— Fabius Maximus Servilianus, adoptive brother of Fabius Maximus Aemilianus—suffered a series of defeats and was finally surrounded by Viriathus, who could have put the whole army to the sword. Instead he bought a peace treaty by allowing Servilianus and his soldiers to withdraw in safety. But he did not buy peace.[27] Though the treaty was formally ratified in Rome, the consul for 140, Q. Servilius Caepio, arrived in Farther Spain in 139 and renewed the war against Viriathus allegedly on his own initiative.[28] Because the campaign went as badly for him as for his predecessors, he had to surrender his position to M. Popillius Laenas, but first hit on a plan to end the war against the Lusitanians in a single stroke. He bribed three of Viriathus' intimates to assassinate him, and with the execution of the deed in 138, Rome's war in Western Spain soon came to an end.[29]

The Celtiberian war, however, raged on. Pompeius' successor, Laenas, made no headway in an attack on the Lusones and was routed by the Numantines.[30] In 137 he was relieved by the consul C. Hostilius Mancinus, who brought with him, as quaestor, Tiberius Sempronius Gracchus.

From the outset the new commander fared badly. He had the worst of several encounters with the Numantines, and after an especially sound thrashing his nerve seems to have failed him utterly. When rumors ran round his dispirited force that the Cantabri and Vaccaei were coming, the Roman general decided to withdraw, to conceal his army in a deserted spot where Nobilior had once pitched his camp. The Roman legions extinguished their fires and passed the night in darkness, hiding from their enemies. The attempt at concealment was not successful: at daybreak the

27. For Servilianus' activities in Spain see Livy *Per.* liii–liv; Livy *Oxy. Per.* liii–liv; Diod. xxxiii.1.3–4; Val. Max. ii.7.11; Frontin. *Str.* iv.1.42; App. *Iber.* 67–69; Oros. v.4.12.

28. For Caepio's renewal of the war see Diod. xxxiii.1.4; App. *Iber.* 70.

29. For Caepio's activities in Spain see Livy *Per.* liv; Val. Max. ix.6.4; Vell. ii.1.3; App. *Iber.* 70, 74–75; Dio frag. 78; Eutrop. iv.16; Auct. *Vir. Ill.* 61.3.

30. Livy *Per.* lv; Livy *Oxy. Per.* lv; App. *Iber.* 79.

unfortified camp awoke to find itself completely surrounded and
at the mercy of the Numantines. There is no word of the presence
of either Cantabri or Vaccaei. After several frantic but futile attempts to flee, Mancinus realized that he could not possibly force
his way through and sent heralds to the Numantines to propose a
truce and peace negotiations.[31]

Considering previous events, it is astonishing that the Numantines agreed to negotiate with the Romans. Roman commanders
like Lucullus and Galba had consistently gone back on their agree-
ments and committed atrocities in the wake of their deceits. Even
if the Numantines had forgotten the fate of their Celtiberian and
Lusitanian neighbors—which is, of course, extremely unlikely—
they would still have been smarting from their own recent experience with Pompeius, which should have taught them how
thoroughly a Roman noble might dilute his integrity to gain personal advantage. The impulse for revenge must have been strong;
Roman arms had been spilling Spanish blood for the past fifteen
years. An eloquent case could have been made for butchering the
lot, and we may be certain there were those who made it. Yet,
incredibly, the Numantines not only negotiated with the Romans,
but agreed to a peace pact with Mancinus in which they released
his army unharmed. Why? Undoubtedly they were war-weary;
what else could explain the bizarre agreement with the unsuccess-
ful Pompeius whereby they believed themselves to be buying peace
for thirty talents of silver? They may also have believed, perhaps
correctly, that the destruction of Mancinus' army would bring them
only a temporary respite from the siege of their city and that fresh
legionaries would replace the fallen. These possibilities, taken separately or together, are insufficient to explain why the Numantines
released a Roman army in return for a peace that past experience
indicated would not be honored. They must have been persuaded
that this time there was some reasonable chance that Rome would
stand by its agreement. In fact, the presence of Tiberius Gracchus
saved this Roman army. Plutarch records that the Numantines said
they trusted no Roman except the son of their benefactor and

31. Plut. *TG* 5.1–3; App. *Iber.* 80.

moreover, obviously did not feel inclined to spare
eputation as they had Fabius'. The factional affiliations
magistrates are not needed to explain the ignominous
eral would suffer. The contrast often made (by Cicero
y others) between Mancinus' condemnation and Pom-
ittal can be misleading.[44] Some have used *amicitia,* the
tical loyalty, to explain the apparent discrepancy. "He
appealed to the case of Q. Pompeius who for equally
deeds had escaped punishment three years before. But
it seems, had had support within the chief magistracy
ie. Mancinus saw no friendly faces in 136."[45] No doubt,
his deeds equally disgraceful? Patently not, as Mancinus
e known as well as anyone. To be sure, Pompeius de-
had betrayed the agreement he had made with the Nu-
, but this would hardly have startled the Senate, which as
ad done the same. Pompeius' betrayal might have created
difficulties for later Roman negotiators, such as Man-
ut whatever his military position when he sat down to
e with his enemy, at least he had extracted from the Nu-
s a payment of thirty talents of silver for a hypothetical
Pompeius disclaimed ever making the treaty, and he never
he Senate to honor it—disgraceful behavior, of course, but
comparable in Roman eyes to Mancinus' abject capitula-
e had hidden from the enemy. He had allowed his unforti-
sition to be surrounded while he cowered in darkness. He
egotiated not merely from a position of weakness, but of
ete collapse, for he had his soldiers give up their armor,
ns, and personal possessions as plunder. Finally, he con-
d a dishonorable peace. Pompeius' crime was deceit, Man-
cowardly incompetence. It is obvious which was more
ful to an imperial power and which the Romans would have
idered more contemptible.

ancinus and his lieutenants probably did not expect the Senate

. Cic, *Rep.* iii.28; Cic. *Off.* iii.109; cf. Vell. ii.90.3: *turpe Q. Pompei
us turpiusque Mancini.* Flor. i.34.4–5; App. *Iber.* 83; Eutrop. iv.17;
. v.4.20–21.
. Gruen, *RPCC,* pp. 40–41.

patron.[32] Within the year, however, their confidence in Tiberius'
ability to make Rome stand by his word was totally undermined.

Unfortunately, the sources give little information about the bar-
gain Tiberius made. The Numantines apparently insisted upon
making the treaty on equal terms, not as subordinates;[33] they
were to keep as plunder all the property they had captured from
the Roman camps;[34] the terms of the peace applied not only to the
Numantines but to the peoples of some of the other Celtiberian
cities as well.[35] According to Plutarch, Tiberius got the Numantines
to accept some conditions; in Dio a proponent of ratification claims
that Rome was to retain all her possessions in Spain.[36] Beyond
these details, the ancient sources assure us only that, from the
Roman point of view, the treaty was an unmitigated disgrace,[37] as
it must have been, given the likely effect of Rome's past treachery
and the desperate circumstances from which the agreement sprang.
Tiberius can have been granted only the flimsiest of face-savers;
any retention of Roman possessions in Celtiberian Spain must have
been virtually or even wholly nominal.

After the army was on its way home, Tiberius realized that
among the property being held by the Numantines were the ledgers
he had kept containing the records of his official expenses as
quaestor. In order to recover them, he turned back toward the city
with three or four of his companions. He explained to the
Numantine magistrates with whom he conferred that he required
his ledgers so that he might be able to fight his enemies at Rome
if they accused him of taking bribes to accept the Numantine
terms. He retrieved his tablets, but at great cost. He was required

32. Plut. *TG* 5.3. Appian does not mention Tiberius' role in the negotiations.
33. App. *Iber.* 80.   34. Plut. *TG* 6.1; Flor. i.34.6.
35. Appian tells us (*Iber.* 80) that the consul, M. Aemilius Lepidus, who
was sent to replace Mancinus, falsely accused the Vaccaei of supplying the
Numantines with provisions during the war, ravaged their country, and
laid siege to their principal city, Pallantia, which had not violated the
treaty. The clear implication is that the Vaccaei were included in the treaty.
36. Plut. *TG* 5.4; Dio frag. 79.
37. Val. Max. i.6.7, ii.7.1; Vell. ii.1.4–5, 90.3; Plut. *TG* 7.1; App. *Iber.*
80, 83; Flor. i.34.7; Eutrop. iv.17; Oros. v.4.20.

to proclaim his personal friendship for his country's enemy, an enemy that had just humiliated the army of which he was quaestor and had plundered its camp. Plutarch, or the partisan source he was following, perhaps Tiberius' younger brother Gaius, attempts to justify the quaestor's conduct by explaining that he desperately needed the ledgers back and that he feared to exasperate the Numantines with any show of distrust.[38] Yet he also accepted a meal and the return of his frankincense, thrust on him, Plutarch explains, by the Numantines.[39] The episode is fascinating, both for what it reveals of Tiberius' character and for the light it sheds on events in Rome the following year.

Tiberius' father had been the Numantines' *patronus:* his son was behaving more like their *cliens,* forced into a compromising intimacy with and indebtedness to his country's enemy. Romans might forgive the demeaning negotiations because they saved the lives of twenty thousand soldiers, but they would find it harder to understand why a Roman officer would allow himself to be humiliated for some quaestorial ledgers. Tiberius naturally wanted the return of his financial records, particularly if he anticipated a charge of bribery, but his decision to return to Numantia was impetuous, revealing a clear failure of judgment. That trip must have done incomparably more damage to his reputation than any unsubstantiated charges of bribery could have done. That the story had reached Plutarch, and that it is couched in apologetic terms, suggests that the episode was not to Tiberius' credit and compromised his defense when he stood trial in Rome the following year.

The inevitable storm greeted Mancinus on his return to Rome. The war in Spain was now seventeen years old. The *bellum Numantinum* alone had dragged on for seven frustrating years, which must have seemed to those at home an inexcusably long time for an insignificant barbarian city to keep Roman might at bay. Constant campaigning in the Iberian peninsula was helping to impoverish, even reduce the numbers of the rural citizenry. Their massive discontent was having a disquieting political effect in Rome. Senate and people must have felt their patience pushed past

38. Plut. *TG* 8.7. See Badian, *FC*, p. 172, n.7.   39. Plut. *TG* 6.1–3.

the breaking point so that th[...] some quarters have bordered [...] had to be made at Rome, s[...] those who wrote about them. [...] peace agreement that Mancin[...] concluded with the enemy; s[...] those who had concluded it?

Tiberius' treaty can have st[...] the Senate. The pusillanimous [...] jeopardized the sole tangible R[...] carious peace with the Lusitan[...] thanks to the assassination of Vi[...] would show these old enemies t[...] prevail against the Romans and [...] the fruits of military victory by rev[...] that had apparently lost the will to [...] One year later L. Aemilius Paul[...] that "to abandon the war would in i[...] practically involve the breaking away[...] despised the Romans for cowards." [40] may have been leaderless, but the [...] crushed.[41] What would be the effect if [...] were now sent to them as they had bee[...] iberians sixteen years earlier, a rallying[...] Rome for Spanish autonomy? That the [...] act quickly and could not afford to sho[...] ness explains why they did not resort to [...] the case of Servilianus of ratifying the t[...] Even temporary capitulation might have i[...] delicate was the situation that when the [...] arrived in Italy to receive the Senate's deci[...] mitted to enter the city.[43]

40. App. *Iber.* 81.   41. App. *Iber.* 71–75.
42. Astin (*SA*, p. 150) wonders why the Rom[...] expedient. Perhaps also it would have been harder n[...] a Fabius than that of a Hostilius Mancinus.
43. Dio frag. 79.

to ratify and honor the compact Tiberius had negotiated for them. The best they could realistically have hoped for was the kind of temporary confirmation Servilianus' surrender had received earlier. Military necessity, on the one hand, and disgust at military ignominy, on the other, deprived Mancinus even of that gesture. Dio, nevertheless, presents us with arguments that he claims Mancinus and his associates advanced on behalf of ratification. An examination of those arguments shows that Dio is probably confused and that the treaty makers were arguing on behalf of their own necks, not their treaty. They claimed that the compact they had made was necessary to save the lives of the soldiers and pleaded with their countrymen to view the pact in its desperate context rather than in the secure atmosphere of the present. They urged that deliberations center on what could have been done, not what should have been done.[46] These are not arguments urging ratification, or even, strictly speaking, arguments of any kind. They are excuses, explanations of why the treaty had been made in the first place, that were advanced to defend its authors from the accusations of cowardice and incompetence.

In the end Mancinus alone was convicted. Tiberius and the other officers were let off, thanks, we are told, to the efforts on their behalf of Scipio Aemilianus, a fact that curiously is often ignored.[47] The line of argument that led to Tiberius' acquittal and Mancinus' conviction is not hard to imagine. The general points reported by Dio would have constituted Tiberius' main defense of his share in what had happened. His cause gained support from the survivors' families, who came to lobby on behalf of their relatives' saviors.[48] The opposition could, and undoubtedly did, point out that the agreement would not have been needed had the commanders prevented the army from getting caught, vulnerable and cringing, and the point would have to be conceded. But Mancinus alone, as commanding general, bore responsibility for that, not Tiberius and the other officers. This part of the case was indeed so clear that Mancinus had the dignity and the belated courage not

46. Dio frag. 79. For the view that the treaty makers genuinely hoped for ratification, see Crawford, "*Foedus* and *Sponsio*," pp. 1–7.

47. Plut. *TG* 7.3.   48. Plut. *TG* 7.1.

only to submit stoically to his fate, but to support the legislation against himself.[49] Therefore, he alone stood, bound and naked, before the gates of Numantia, a symbolic offering in compensation for yet another repudiated Roman treaty.[50] The offering was rejected by the Numantines, surely not out of human decency as one scholar has supposed, but because they were infuriated and intended to do nothing that could in any way be interpreted as countenancing this latest example of Roman treachery.[51] When Mancinus then returned to Rome and entered the Senate house, Publius Rutilius ordered him out. A legal debate ensued over whether the Numantines' rejection of him entitled Mancinus to resume his previous status as citizen and senator.[52] Even though the most eminent lawyer of the day, P. Mucius Scaevola, argued against his case, it looks as though the pro-Mancinus legalists had their way.[53]

A prosopographical study has argued that Scipio was the moving force behind the prosecution and conviction of Mancinus. Scipio allegedly had been irritated by one of Mancinus' cousins, L. Hostilius, who ten years earlier had exaggerated his own role in the taking of Carthage. Scipio Aemilianus therefore used the Spanish disgrace to avenge himself on a Hostilius. This conclusion is buttressed by the claim that the consul who conducted the trial proceedings in 136, L. Furius Philus, was an intimate member of the Scipionic circle and so must have been working on behalf of the man who gave the group its name.[54] Any truth in this inter-

---

49. Cic. *Rep.* iii.28; Cic. *Off.* iii.109; cf. Vell. ii.1.5.

50. Cic. *Caec.* 98; Cic. *Off.* iii.109; Livy *Per.* lvi; Vell. ii.1.5; Flor. i.34.7; Eutrop. iv.17; App. *Iber.* 83; Dio frag. 79; Oros. v.4.21.

51. Gruen, *RPCC*, p. 41. Vell. ii.1.5: "Quem illi recipere se negaverunt, . . . dicentes publicam violationem fidei non debere unius lui sanguine."

52. Cic. *Caec.* 98; Cic. *De Orat.* i.181 and 238, ii.137.

53. On Scaevola's position see Dig. xlix.15.4; 1.7.18. See also Bernstein, "Prosopography and the Career of Publius Mucius Scaevola," p. 43. On the final outcome see Cic. *Caec.* 98.

54. Gruen, *RPCC*, pp. 41–42. For Furius and Scipio see Cic. *De Orat.* ii.154; Cic. *Rep.* iii.5; Cic. *Brut.* 258; Münzer, s.v. Furius (78), *RE*; Rawson, "Scipio, Laelius, Furius and the Ancestral Religion," pp. 161–174.

pretation can be only a small part of the story. The names of Scipio and Furius are often associated in intellectual contexts in the sources, and Scipio may not have loved Hostilii, but these associations can have been only secondary factors in the conviction of Mancinus. The exigencies of the Spanish situation and the general's conduct in itself make it doubtful that anyone could have saved him. Mancinus' political life was not wrecked by Scipio; he alone was responsible, and his final self-condemnation intimates that he would have admitted as much.

The sources suggest that even saving Tiberius was not an easy task, complicated as it was by Tiberius' incriminating familiarity with his captors.[55] Yet Plutarch says that Tiberius was unhappy with Scipio for not saving Mancinus and for failing to get his pact ratified.[56] If this is true, Tiberius was either appallingly naive or unreasonable. To be sure, he had good cause for unhappiness. Within the context of the disaster they faced, Tiberius must have felt it a real achievement to have saved the Roman legionaries, and he probably returned from Numantia in this frame of mind. He most likely arrived in Rome anticipating considerable if restrained praise for his intervention and willingness on the part of the Senate to preserve his good name by honoring his treaty for a decent interval.[57] He failed, of course, to view the circumstances and his action in the wider context of Rome's political problems in Spain. Upon his return he saw, to his horror, his reputation as a man of authority dishonored in the eyes of the clients his father had bequeathed him. This ambitious young man, who had had reason to think he was doing all things right, must have been agonized to face the prospect that his public career might end here in disgrace when it had hardly begun. Cornelia cannot have been pleased. Cicero's comment springs to mind: "The unpopularity he gained

On the political insignificance of Furius' appearance as an interlocutor in Cicero's *Republic* see Zetzel, "Cicero and the Scipionic Circle," p. 174.

55. Plut. *TG* 7.1–2; Dio Frag. 83.2: ἀλλὰ καὶ προσεκινδύνευσεν ἐκδοθῆναι. Cf. Vell. ii.2.1; Quint. vii.4.12–13; Flor. ii.2.2.

56. Plut. *TG* 7.3.

57. Dio's statement (frag. 83) that he was expecting a triumph on his return is manifestly absurd.

from this, together with the uncompromising attitude of the Senate in withholding their assent from his treaty inspired him with resentment and apprehension, a combination of circumstances which compelled that gallant and distinguished man to sever himself from the lofty policy of the Fathers." [58]

If Tiberius' fury and frustration came to focus temporarily on Scipio, it was probably because the wily Aemilianus had behaved with formal correctness but had done the minimum for his *adfinis*. Scipio could not properly or profitably have allowed his young brother-in-law to suffer Mancinus' fate. To have done so might have redounded to Scipio's own discredit. Besides, as we have seen, Tiberius' cause was apparently popular, and Scipio's backing for it would be expected in quarters that provided much of his own political support.[59] Scipio had saved this Sempronius Gracchus from Mancinus' fate, but had stopped short of proclaiming his innocence. The coolness that must have ensued between these two men should not be exaggerated or transformed into vendetta. Plutarch writes: "This disagreement certainly resulted in no mischief past remedy. In my opinion Tiberius would never have met with his great misfortunes if Scipio Africanus had been present at Rome during his political activity." [60] This is a perfectly reasonable conclusion.

58. Cic. *Hars. Resp.* 43.   59. See Astin, *SA*, pp. 26–34.
60. Plut. *TG* 7.4.

3 The Changing World of Italy

Ita quod in advorsis rebus optaverant otium postquam adepti sunt, asperius acerbiusque fuit. Namque coepere nobilitas dignitatem, populus libertatem in lubidinem vortere, sibi quisque ducere, trahere, rapere. Ita omnia in duas partis abstracta sunt, res publica, quae media fuerat, dilacerata.

—Sallust, *Bellum Iugurthinum,* 41.4–5

Rome's military misfortunes in Spain at this time, as in Sicily, were symptoms of a social crisis in Italy that constitutes the setting for Tiberius' next political appearance after the Mancinus affair. The disgrace and punishment of Mancinus did not improve the fate of the Roman legions in Nearer Spain. The next two consular commanders came and went without a sign that any lesson had been learned from their predecessor's experience. First M. Aemilius Lepidus Porcina, then Q. Calpurnius Piso, suffered defeats at the hands of the Numantines; and when he returned to Rome, Aemilius was fined for his lack of success. Repeated humiliations by the Spanish barbarians now called for extraordinary measures.

Scipio Aemilianus, the man who had ploughed over Carthage, though legally ineligible, was granted a special dispensation to run for the consulship of 134. He was elected, given the Spanish command, and set off for his province with some four thousand volunteers and clients, none of whom was on the active service lists. They bolstered the demoralized and slackly disciplined army already there.

Scipio spent the remainder of the year drilling his troops into shape and devastating the surrounding countryside in preparation for the siege of Numantia. He was joined in his winter quarters by a Numidian contingent under Jugurtha, who later became leader of his people in a protracted war against Rome. Scipio then established two military camps close to Numantia, one under his own command, the other under that of his brother, Q. Fabius

Maximus Aemilianus. They would blockade the city until they starved its inhabitants into unconditional surrender. In the course of these activities, Scipio discovered that a contingent of young hotbloods in the neighboring town of Lutia were urging that their city aid Numantia. He threatened to invade and thereby intimidated the elders into turning over to him four hundred young men. He cut off their hands and was back in his camp the next day to continue, undisturbed, his siege of Numantia. The Numantines surrendered after having been reduced to cannibalism. Scipio selected fifty of the survivors for his triumph and sold the rest into slavery. He razed their city to the ground. At last a Roman commander had managed to dispose of this persistent enemy. The barbarians had been defeated by a power more ruthless than they. The year was 133.[1]

The period between Mancinus' defeat by the Numantines and Scipio's destruction of them also saw the Roman legions beaten in a series of encounters with an even more despised enemy. The agricultural slaves who worked Sicily's large estates had risen in revolt. The news must have shocked Rome: slave revolts were rare in antiquity, and the location of this one in Sicily, the source of Rome's grain supply, threatened the city with starvation. The leader of the revolt, a Syrian named Eunus, is reported to have collected some sixty thousand followers who laid waste Sicily's towns and fortresses.[2] In 137, and again in 136, his men defeated the praetorian armies the Senate sent against them.[3] In 134 the problem was thought so urgent that the command was given to Scipio's consular colleague, C. Fulvius Flaccus. There are no reports of his progress against the insurgent slaves, but it is unlikely to have been spectacular.[4] One of the consuls for 133, L. Calpurnius Piso Frugi, succeeded him, and had to restore the discipline of the Roman armies before proceeding to capture Murgantia and

1. See App. *Iber.* 80–98 for the events at Numantia between Mancinus' defeat and Scipio's victory.

2. Cic. *Verr.* ii.3.125; Livy *Per.* lvi; Diod. xxxiv/xxxv.2.20–23; Flor. ii.7.19; Obsequ. 27; Oros. v.9.7.

3. Frontin. *Str.* iii.5.3; Flor. ii.7.19.

4. Livy, *Per.* lvi; Obsequ. 27; Oros. v.9.6.

to attack Enna, a town near the center of the island, where the slaves had their base.[5]

Some of the slaves in Italy apparently caught the fever from their southern counterparts, though their revolt did not meet with similar initial success. Four hundred and fifty slaves were crucified at Minturnae, a city on the Campanian border at the mouth of the Liris, in Latium. At Sinuessa, a Latin colony also in Campania, a rebellion involving four thousand slaves was also crushed.[6]

Piso, meanwhile, continued to reverse Roman fortunes in Sicily. He captured a town, probably Messana, and killed eight thousand rebel slaves.[7] But not until 132, when the command passed to the consul P. Rupilius, was the Sicilian slave war finally brought to an end. He besieged both Tauromenium, on the east coast, and Enna. Employing the tactics that had served Scipio so well the year before in Spain, he confined the rebels and starved them into cannibalism. When they finally surrendered he butchered more than twenty thousand of them.[8]

This litany of degrading defeats, ending in equally degrading victories, stands in strong contrast to the preceding century of successful warfare (264–146) that had seen the Carthaginians' power exterminated and the surviving states of the Hellenistic world brought under Rome's hegemony. How had the nation that vanquished Hannibal and the advanced civilizations of the East so soon found itself struggling to prevail against barbarians and slaves?

The extension of the Roman *imperium* during the first half of the second century accompanied a gradual yet eventually catastrophic domestic transformation. The political revolution of the first century resulted largely from the social and economic upheaval of the second. The demands and even the profits of incessant war had long strained the economy of Italy, and fissures had appeared in the peninsula's social structure. A central cause of the Roman

5. *CIL* I².2.847; Val. Max. ii.7.9, iv.3.10; Frontin. *Str.* iv.1.126; Oros. v.9.6.

6. Obsequ. 27b; Oros. v.9.7.   7. Oros. v.9.7.

8. Cic. *Verr.* ii.3.125; Diod. xxxiv/xxxv.2.20–23; Val. Max. ii.7.3, vi.9.8. ix.12. ext. 1; Oros. v.9.7.

revolution was created with the widespread displacement of the small farmer, backbone of Italy's yeoman economy and of Rome's legions.[9]

During the final quarter of the third century, many of Italy's rural proletariat had found themselves temporarily displaced from the land they tilled by Hannibal's devastation of great tracts of the peninsula.[10] Many others whose farms were not destroyed nevertheless could not continue to cultivate them because of obligatory service in the war against the Carthaginians. After the Roman victory, the Senate did not allow the small farmers, who formed the bulk of the peninsula's free population, to return and refurbish their deteriorating acreage. On the contrary, its foreign policy, insisting on total security and therefore on the submission of all competitive or potentially competitive foreign powers, immediately embroiled them in a war with one of the powers across the Adriatic. The conflict with Hannibal had ended in 201, leaving Italy with an abundance of fertile land badly in need of cultivation. Unfortunately, it left also a shortage of farm labor and of small freeholders with sufficient capital to put the land to productive use.[11] In 200 such difficulties worsened when the Senate persuaded a reluctant citizenry to declare war on the Carthaginians' passive ally, King Philip V of Macedonia,[12] and thus initiated another half-century of wars. These, waged in Macedonia, Greece, Asia, Africa, and Spain, kept great numbers of citizens of Rome and the allied communities on campaign away from their farms for prolonged periods. Private sacrifice for public dominion impoverished and eventually decreased the size of this social class.

To be eligible for conscription into a legion, a Roman citizen had to be of *adsiduus* status, that is, he had to possess a certain

9. Brunt, "The Army and the Land in the Roman Revolution," pp. 69–86.

10. The long-term effects of Hannibal's devastations are sometimes exaggerated. See, for example, Toynbee, *HL*, II, 9–105. A useful corrective can be found in Brunt, *IM*, pp. 269–277.

11. Yeo, "The Development of the Roman Plantation and Marketing of Farm Products," pp. 323–326.

12. Livy xxxi.3–8, 11.

minimum of property.[13] During the course of the second century, and even before, the qualifying figure was lowered several times. This, in what was almost certainly a period of inflation, indicates dramatically the economic strain of Rome's growing military commitments, as well as the impoverishment of the class being called upon.[14] That class probably consisted almost exclusively of the rural proletariat, Roman citizens, the majority of whom normally earned their living by tilling the soil. An *adsiduus'* military obligation could amount to an astonishing sixteen (possibly even twenty) of the years between his seventeenth and forty-sixth birthdays.[15] The information available does not permit exactness about the actual time a man might serve, but while few Roman citizens ever had to fulfill their maximum legal terms of service uninterruptedly, the average citizen farmer who met the required property qualification could expect to spend six of his prime years continuously away from his farm in a legion; he might even be recalled to serve again, now especially valued because of his previous experience.[16] The same pattern of military obligation and economic dislocation must have marked the allied peasantry: their military contingents invariably accompanied Rome's citizen legions into the field. While

13. *Proletarii,* however, might be called upon to serve in the legions in times of emergency, and both they and freedmen regularly rowed in the fleet.

14. For the downward trend in the property qualification see Livy i.43.8 (following Fabius Pictor), who gives the minimum rating at 11,000 *asses,* Polybius vi.19.2 who knew it to be 4,000, and finally Cicero who, in the *De Republica* ii.40, the dramatic date of which is 129, has it set at 1,500. For the significance of these reductions see Gabba, "Le origini dell'esercito professionale in Roma," pp. 184–187. For the likely dates of the reductions, Brunt, *IM,* pp. 403–404 seems to take the evidence as far as is proper. See also Crawford, *Roman Republican Coinage,* II, 621–625, for the final decrease occurring in ca. 141 when the denarius was revalued at 10 instead of 16 *asses.*

15. Polyb. vi.19. See Brunt, *IM,* p. 399.

16. See the calculations of Afzelius, *Die römische Kriegsmacht während der Auseinandersetzung mit den hellenistischen Grossmachten,* pp. 48–61, and the reservations of Smith, *Service in the Post-Marian Roman Army,* pp. 6–10. See also Toynbee, *HL,* II, 79–80; Brunt, *IM,* pp. 399–402.

the ratio of Romans to allies under arms fluctuated considerably throughout the century, there were usually more allies in combat than Romans. More allies also, however, lived in the peninsula, so that proportionately the burden of military service in the long run bore down about as ruinously on them as on the Romans.[17] Many of those conscripted—Romans, Latins, and Italians—would die in the field.[18] They at least would be spared the struggle for

17. The Romans called up their allied contingents in accordance with the *formula togatorum* (see De Sanctis, *Storia dei Romani*, II, 453, n. 1, for a full citation of the relevant title from the *lex agraria* of 111 B.C.). Toynbee (*HL*, I, 424–437) believes that the *formula togatorum* fixed for all time the maximum number of men the Romans were legally entitled to demand from allied cities that had not concluded *foedera aequa* with Rome (see Beloch, *Der italische Bund unter Roms Hegemonie*, pp. 201–210). Brunt (*IM*, pp. 545–548), on the other hand, believes that each ally (whether or not it had a *foedus aequum*) was bound to put out its entire levy on demand and that the *formula togatorum* was merely an administrative device that operated as a sliding scale designating the number of allies to be conscripted for each Roman legion in the field, while allowing the number to vary from year to year, at Rome's pleasure, as Polybius (vi.21.4) suggests. Toynbee (*HL*, II, 132–135) believes that the burden of military service in the first quarter of the second century weighed disproportionately on the allies, but that when it became clear that the strain was greater than their manpower could bear, Rome redressed the imbalance so that from 178 onward this was no longer cause for allied dissatisfaction. Brunt (*IM*, pp. 677–686) thinks that the ratio of allies to Romans varied, not only during the second century as a whole, but over quite short periods, for different armies and in different years. He traces a broad trend in which the percentage of allies to Romans bearing arms declined during the Hannibalic War owing to defections to the Carthaginians, rose sharply thereafter when the Romans penalized the traitors, but then moved toward parity, reaching it in about 170. By the end of the century, however, apparently two allies were being conscripted for every Roman because of citizen discontent with the draft and the decline of *adsidui* qualified for legionary service (cf. Gabba, "Ricerche sull'esercito professionale romano da Mario ad Augusto," p. 190, n. 2; cf. "Le origini dell'esercito professionale in Roma," p. 200). This may not have been as inequitable as it at first appears if Brunt's estimate (*IM*, p. 84, for the year 225) that there were 640,000 adult male allies but only about 300,000 Romans in the peninsula is near the mark.

18. For some very tentative estimates of the casualties suffered see Frank, *ESAR*, I, 110; Toynbee, *HL*, I, 473–477, II, 65–72; Brunt, *IM*, pp. 65, 419, 694–697.

existence which many of the survivors had to begin when they returned home.

A peasant's livelihood is usually precarious, but in the decades before Tiberius' tribunate many a family, deprived for years of its full complement of manpower and therefore of its full earning power, must have found itself unable to carry on. Both conscription and the results of war profiteering brutally increased the pressures normally involved in a marginal agrarian existence. The financial opportunities created by war produced various social effects. Wealth flooded in, the practice of usury increased, a luxurious life style developed, instances of discontent and lack of discipline in the army became more frequent, a middle class made up of people owning medium-sized estates arose, the number of slaves climbed steeply, and cash-crop farming became more common. All of these effects benefited some of the population, but together they drove the rural proletariat into a cycle familiar in preindustrial societies: debt, forfeiture, and displacement, poverty and sometimes death.

The influx of wealth from conquered territories in the East was distributed unevenly among the peninsula's inhabitants. Not all the spoils remained in the hands of Rome's generals and ruling aristocracy, as Sallust, for example, would have us believe.[19] The second century brought unmistakable signs of nonsenatorial speculators operating on a grand scale as well as indications of Italy's growing economic imbalance.

As early as 196, for example, fines exacted from only three graziers tried before the People sufficed to cover the cost of building a temple to Faunus.[20] Three years later two porticoes were constructed and gilded shields were set upon Jupiter's temple, again with money gained from the illegal activities of more graziers.[21] The violators may have trespassed on public land they had not

19. Sall. *Jug.* 41.7–8: "The generals divided the spoils of war with a few friends." Though an exaggeration, the statement was not entirely without foundation. The tribune M. Philippus could claim in 104 (Cic. *Off.* ii.73) that "there were not 2,000 citizens in the state who possessed property." Several decades later Cicero himself (*Verr.* ii.50.126) wrote, "all the money of all nations has come into the hands of a few men."
20. Livy xxxiii.42.10.   21. Livy xxxv.10.11–12.

leased, or on *ager compascuus;* they may have exceeded the legal number of cattle to be grazed on the public land or failed to pay their tax per head of cattle.[22] Whatever their violations, presumably the offenders were wealthy men, not only because large-scale animal husbandry required substantial amounts of capital, but also because they were obviously able to pay the heavy fines imposed upon them. All this provides vivid illustration of Cato's famous dictum that the three most profitable uses to which land could be put were "pasturage, pasturage, and pasturage." [23]

In this same period the increased activities of usurers reveal the difficulties of the newly impoverished against the background of the increasing affluence of some. In 193 the Roman laws of usury had to be extended to cover transactions in which a Latin or Italian had dealings with a Roman citizen.[24] Not content with legal rates of interest, Roman moneylenders had been employing allied agents to obtain greater returns on their loans than Roman law allowed. In the following year the many successful prosecutions brought by the curule aediles against usurers yielded fines that again paid for impressive building enterprises.[25]

Only the successful prosecutions of illegal activities have come down to us. Many graziers must have either escaped detection or pastured their considerable flocks within the limit of the law.

22. For the legal limit on the number of cattle to be grazed on public land, see App. *BC* i.8. For taxation per head of cattle owned, see the *lex agraria* of 111 B.C., line 14 in Bruns, *Fontes Iuris Romani Antiqui,* pp. 77 and 82. *Ager compascuus* was municipal *ager publicus* possessed by autonomous communities within the Roman body politic. Use of *ager compascuus* was restricted to the citizens of the particular *municipium* in question. See Zancan, *Ager Publicus,* p. 76.

23. Cic. *Off.* ii.89. Cf. Plut. *Cato mai.* 21.5; Pliny *NH* xviii.29–30. There need be no contradiction between what Cicero reported that Cato said and what Cato says about the primacy of the vineyard in his own treatise on agriculture, for in the latter (i.7) he is discussing the best use to be made of a hundred-*iugera* (roughly sixty-acre) tract. See Yeo, "The Overgrazing of Ranch-Lands in Ancient Italy," pp. 275–307, for a discussion of the effects of large-scale grazing. See also Trapenard, *L'Ager Scriptuarius,* p. 107; Tibiletti, "Lo sviluppo del latifondo in Italia dall'epoca graccana all'impero," p. 265.

24. Livy xxxv.7.   25. Livy xxxv.41.9–10.

Again, if some were desperate enough to pay illegal rates of interest to Roman moneylenders, far more must have been driven into debt and eventually forced to forfeit their acres as a result of legal loans that were not recorded in the sources. Finally, the graziers and usurers who were exposed and punished probably were not members of the senatorial order. Their number, their anonymity, and the success of the prosecutions against them indicate the opposite.

In the next decade riches continued to flow into the peninsula, bringing with them the disruptive fruits of conquest.[26] During his censorship, in 184, Cato proposed new measures to combat what he considered to be the creeping evils of the new, luxurious life style. He imposed a 3 percent tax on ornaments, women's clothing, certain vehicles, and highly skilled, therefore costly, slaves, and made statues and other art objects, obviously the by-products of Rome's eastern interventions, liable to a luxury surtax.[27] Many of those affected by Cato's restrictions would have been senators, but some outside that order also enjoyed the material benefits of military conquest and might even have become wealthy enough to be affected by the censor's legislation. Even before the second century, in 210, extremely wealthy nonsenators contributed substantially to the Roman war effort in the famous affair of the *trientabulum,* to mention only the most conspicuous instance.[28]

26. Pliny *NH* xxxiii.138; cf. Livy xxxix.22.8.

27. Livy xxxix.44; Plut. *Cato mai.* 18; Nepos *Cato* 2.3. See also Mommsen, *Röm. Staats.* II, 395, n. 7, and Scullard, *RP,* p. 156, n. 1, who points out that since the normal price of a slave was about 5,000 *asses,* and since Cato's tax applied only to slaves worth more than 10,000 *asses,* its intention cannot have been to help the small farmer by checking the spread of slave labor, but rather to limit the influx into Roman households of highly trained Greeks.

28. In 210 a number of voluntary contributions had been made to the war effort, initially by the nobility, but later by members of the equestrian order and the populace as well (Livy xxvi.36). In 204 the moving force behind these contributions, M. Valerius Laevinus, urged that the money be repaid to the donors (Livy xxix.16.1–3). The Senate accordingly decreed that it should be paid in three installments, the first immediately and the others three and five years hence. The final payment fell due in 200, but in that year the treasury was burdened with the new war against Macedonia, and no

Now, however, not only generals, but some fortunate and prudent officers and soldiers emerged from their terms of service with capital to invest.

In this period we hear a good deal about discontent among Rome's military rank and file. At the very end of the 190s, a praetor was unable to restrain his troops from plundering Phocaea after the city had surrendered, and the next year a Roman commander could not prevent his men from plundering a Gallic camp and keeping the booty.[29] In 187, Cn. Manlius Vulso was rumored to have ruined the military discipline of the troops he took over from Scipio "by permitting every kind of license" among his soldiers. On the incident Livy comments, "the beginnings of foreign luxury were introduced into the city by the army from Asia. They, for the first time, imported into Rome couches of bronze, valuable robes for coverlets, tapestries and other products of the loom, and what at that time was considered luxurious furniture—tables with a single pedestal and sideboards. Female players of the lute and harp and other festal delights of entertainments were incorporated into our banquets and the banquets themselves began to be planned both with greater care and at greater expense. At that time the cook, to the ancient Romans the most worthless of slaves, both in their judgment of values and in the use they made of him, began to have value, and what had merely been a necessary service came to be regarded as an art. Yet those things which were then looked upon as remarkable were hardly

payment was made (Livy xxxi.13). Despite wartime conditions, the creditors appealed to the Senate and a compromise was worked out. Then creditors claimed that had they been paid what was owed them they naturally would have invested the money in land that was currently available. The reasonableness of their argument was accepted, and the creditors received choice *ager publicus* within a fifty-mile radius of Rome, though a token rent of one *as* per *iugerum* was charged to testify that this land was still part of the public domain. The land was called *trientabulum* because it was allotted in discharge of one-third of the debt.

29. Livy xxxvii.32.11–14. For similar difficulties earlier in the decade see Livy xxxii.3.2–7; Malcovati, *ORF*, 3d ed., Cato, frag. 17–18; Livy xxxiv.56.1–2, xxxviii.23.4.

even the germs of the luxury to come"[30] (Loeb translation, slightly modified).

The period is punctuated by instances of discontent in the army, particularly on campaigns in the West—in Liguria, Spain, Istria, and Sardinia—where the spoils of war were probably less abundant and less attractive than in the East.[31] One expedient for alleviating such trouble apparently was to allow the soldiers, when possible, to loot freely, which may explain, at least partially, some of the more blatant atrocities committed by the Roman legions in Spain.[32] When writing of the levy in 171, Livy mentions voluntary enlistments induced by the rich rewards brought back by those who had served in Macedonia and in Asia against Antiochus.[33] The practice of awarding donatives to discharged veterans, not spectacular sums, but enough to help the former legionary refurbish his failing farm, may have represented another, though probably not as attractive, means of compensating the soldiers in part for the excessive, often ruinous, length of their military service.[34]

Some of those fortunate enough to take part in the looting of a wealthy city and prudent enough to hold onto the cash obtained from the sale of their loot—probably on the spot to a camp-following speculator—or from the ransom of a prisoner might return to Italy with considerable assets. They could maintain their neglected farms and even invest afresh in the profitable new cash-crop farming that flourished in mid-century in certain sections of the Italian peninsula, especially the districts around Venafrum and Casinum. These investors may eventually have formed a consider-

30. Livy xxxix.6; cf. Pliny *NH* xxxiii.53.

31. For Spain see Livy xxxix.38.6–12; for Spain, Liguria, Istria, and Sardinia see Livy xl.1.4, 16.9, 35.7, 39.4, 40.14, 41.8–11, xli.10.6–10.

32. For instances of looting and the disposal of booty generally see Polyb. ix.10.7–13, x.16, xi.3.2, xi.25; cf. Livy xxviii. 25.15; Polyb. xi.28.5–6, xiv.6.5, 10.2, xviii.27.3, 38.7, xxi.30.9, xxii.14, xxxi.25.5, xxxix.2. See also Shatzman, "The Roman General's Authority over Booty," pp. 177–205.

33. Livy xlii.32.

34. For the awarding of donatives see Livy xxxiv.52.11, xxxvii.59.6, xxxix.5.17, xl.43.7, 59.2, xli.7.3, 13.7–8, xlv.40.5, 43.7. See McDonald, "The History of Rome and Italy in the Second Century B.C.," p. 133, n. 56.

able part of the audience of middle-sized estate owners farming the olive and the vine for whom Cato composed his famous handbook on agriculture.[35] They, as well as the landowning magnates, played a part in ruining the peasantry, as we shall see.

Thus the familiar textbook picture of the mammoth Italian plantations, the *latifundia,* gobbling up the peasants' small farms during this period, and of the wholesale displacement of staple grain farming by the new cash crops, is probably overdrawn. Archaeological discoveries, as well as careful investigations of the literary sources, indicate that the oft-quoted statement of Pliny the Elder that "the *latifundia* have been the ruin of Italy" grossly oversimplifies the situation even for the period when it was written; certainly it does not apply properly to ours, as has often been supposed.[36] Indeed, the word *latifundia* appears in no text before the first century of the Christian era and is then used vaguely, for only a short span of time.[37] The real picture of second-century agrarian conditions is more complex, allowing for regional variation in size of farm, composition of the soil, kinds of crops produced, and types of labor employed. Agriculture in Italy at this time will not fit into a few neat propositions.

Where and when they did exist, the *latifundia* were single estates of hundreds of acres and normally fell into two categories.[38] First, there were ranches comprised of extensive tracts of pasture lands

35. See Yeo, "The Development of the Roman Plantation and Marketing of Farm Products," pp. 459–461; White, "Latifundia," p. 72.

36. Pliny *NH* xviii.35. For other contemporary uses of the term see Seneca, *Epist.* lxxxviii.10, lxxxix.20; Petronius 77. See also Siculus Flaccus, p. 121 and p. 125, a "gromaticus" of uncertain date. For a detailed picture of the complexities of the agricultural conditions in Italy see White, *Roman Farming,* with Brunt, "Review of White, *Roman Farming,*" pp. 153–158 and Frederiksen, "The Contribution of Archaeology to the Agrarian Problem in the Gracchan Period," pp. 342–347, 355–356.

37. See Earl, *Tiberius Gracchus,* pp. 29–30, and p. 30, n. i; White, "Latifundia," pp. 63ff., esp. pp. 65 and 73. White thinks *latifundia* (which never occurs in the singular) may simply have been a colloquial term used by small holders to refer to the great tracts of wealthy magnates and that its nearest English equivalent is "broad acres."

38. See White, "Latifundia," p. 76–77. See also Dohr, "Die italischen Gutshöfe nach den Schriften Catos und Varros," pp. 29–41.

for herds and flocks: this type was most common in southern Italy, especially in Calabria, where the terrain was suitable. Second, there were large-scale mixed farms, on which many acres might be unproductive, set aside for the customary pleasures of country gentry. An economically important class of such estates, found most notably in Campania, produced not only great quantities of wine but also the pots and jars in which it was marketed. Some of this Italian wine was exported to the Hellenistic East, probably via the island of Delos, where the archaeologists have unearthed Italian wine jugs dating from as early as 167.[39] A Gallic market flourished also. An old Greek ship laden with Campanian table-ware and about ten thousand jars of wine, some Greek but some red Latian from the Sabine hills, foundered among a group of deserted islands just south of Marseilles in about 230.[40] Posidonius, who was probably born just a few years before Tiberius' tribunate, claimed that wealthy Gauls were so fond of the Italian wine transported to them on navigable waterways that they were willing to exchange a slave for a six-gallon jug of it. That slave, very probably, would become a unit in the production of future jugs.[41] Most wine produced during the middle of the second century was consumed not by Greeks and Gauls, but by Italians, especially residents of the growing cities.

With cheap land readily available, with expanding markets both at home and abroad, and, as we shall see, with an inexpensive labor force at hand, Italy after the Hannibalic War must have been as

39. See Yeo, "Development of Roman Plantation," pp. 337–338, for the archaeological and inscriptional evidence. Pliny *NH* xiv.87: "Among these topics, however, it occurs to me that while there are in the whole world about eighty notable kinds of liquor that can properly be understood as coming under the term 'wine', two thirds of this number belong to Italy, which stands far in front of all the countries in the world on that account; and further investigation going into this subject more deeply indicates that this popularity does not date back from the earliest times, but that the importance of the Italian wines only began from the city's six hundredth year"—that is, in 154 B.C.

40. See Cousteau, "Fish Men Discover a 2,200-year-old Greek Ship," pp. 1–36.

41. Diod. v.26.3; cf. Cic. *Font.* 19; Athen. iv.152 C.

much a paradise for the entrepreneur with sufficient capital for investment as it was a purgatory for the defenseless and impoverished peasant whose acres were coveted by the new and old capitalists alike. The evidence suggests that the landowning magnates were often not the ancient analogues to the "latifondisti" of, say, modern Sicily, but men who exploited the favorable economic circumstances by accumulating numbers of medium-sized estates, These would be *fundi* rather than *latifundia,* one or two hundred acres, not very different from the ones Cato describes or those unearthed in archaeological excavations around Pompeii. A single owner might have several estates in one area or spread over Italy. Such multiple ownership frequently comes up in the literary sources for the first century and was probably a common way of accumulating land in the second as well.[42] There were undoubtedly economic advantages to owning several estates in different parts of the peninsula, the obvious one being that drought or other natural disasters in one part of Italy would cause a financial setback rather than a collapse. It must also have been pleasant to have varied scenery and climates for jaunts away from the hurly-burly of Rome. Finally, a magnate with political interests might wish, for electoral purposes, to be able to exert economic pressure on dependent peasant voters in more than one of the rural tribes.

Landholding relations in consequence became quite complicated with tenants and sharecroppers, seasonal and migrant laborers, fortunate or persistent peasant proprietors, and successful entrepreneurs ensconsed side by side in the country. A prospering landowner in expansive mood had a fair variety of maneuvers at his disposal through which to separate a smaller neighbor from his surplus or actual subsistence: forced sale, forfeiture of a debt, and, quite commonly, violence.[43] An example of what probably hap-

42. See Yeo, "The Economics of Roman and American Slavery," pp. 446–454, for a description of the finds of the villas around Pompeii, pp. 459–460, for multiple ownership. See also Frederiksen, "The Contribution of Archaeology to the Agrarian Problem in the Gracchan Period," pp. 356–357.

43. See, for example, Hor. *Carm.* ii.18; Livy xxxiv.4.9; Sall. *Jug.* 41.8; Juv. xiv.140; Columella *De Re Rust.* i.3.6; Flor. ii.2.3; Seneca, *Epist.* xc.39; Mart. x.79; App. *BC* i.7. Brunt, *IM,* pp. 551–557.

pened comes to us from Juvenal, writing during the early empire. He tells of the greedy grazier who, wishing to coerce a grain-farming neighbor reluctant to sell, would let loose by night his herd of lean and hungry cattle. These would feast upon the poor man's produce so that by morning there was nothing left of his crop. It was as though, we are told, it had been meticulously sickled to the ground.[44] Legal redress was difficult, if not impossible, for the humble to obtain. Occasionally the Senate might balk at the more blatant excesses of a zealous land accumulator: in 173 a consul was sent to Campania to check on the activities of some large landowners who had imprudently infringed, not on small private properties, but on the public domains.[45] On the whole, though, second-century administrators of justice seem to have been unconcerned and rather shortsighted about the protection of the poor and powerless. Indeed, not just the administrators but the system itself barred the way to legal redress. Roman law provided no adequate mechanism for ensuring the presence of the defendant at his own trial. A law proclaimed that the plaintiff could use force to bring the accused before the court. If the defendant refused to attend, as well he might under the circumstances, a second law proclaimed his refusal illegal, though this law was as unhelpful and unsatisfactory as the first since, again, the responsibility of coercing attendance for the second violation fell to the same aggrieved plaintiff.[46] Needless to say, few peasants would be able to muster the physical force necessary to bring a powerful neighbor before a Roman court of law, a neighbor who had committed his offence in the first place because he was strong enough to get away with it. In fact, if not in theory, the principle that might makes right was institutionalized by the legal system of Republican Rome.

44. Juv. xiv.145–149: "And if no price will persuade the owner to sell, you will send into his green corn by night a herd of lean and famished cattle, with wearied necks, who will not come home until they have put the whole new crop into their ravenous bellies; no sickle could make a cleaner job."
45. Livy xlii.1.6.
46. See Kelly, *Roman Litigation,* pp. 1–30; Lintott, *Violence in Republican Rome,* pp. 22–34; for the concept of self-help, see pp. 125–131.

This bleak picture of the hardships faced by Italy's rural proletariat was bleaker still because they had to contend with another
bitter fruit of Rome's military success, the flood of slaves brought
into Italy. In the first half of the second century as many as a
quarter of a million prisoners of war arrived on the peninsula as
slaves: men, women, and children exploited at almost every con-
ceivable level of economic activity, but especially in agriculture.[47]
The latest demographic study of ancient Italy tentatively estimates
that the slave population was about six hundred thousand in 225
and had risen by the time of Augustus' death to three million,
despite the rapid manumission of slaves for which the Romans were
famous.[48] How did this vast increase affect the native peasantry?
Certainly it must have restricted brutally any new opportunities for
employment that might have been afforded by the increase in
cash-crop farming.[49]

This brief survey has given some indication of the complexity
and severity of the economic pressures bearing down upon the
struggling small farmer. How, then, did those who managed to
survive do so and what demographic changes accompanied the
economic upheaval? How were oligarchic governance and the
Roman political system affected?

According to a frequently accepted theory, the small farmer
facing destitution abandoned his ancestral way of life and sought
salvation in the city. A great rural exodus occurred; significant
numbers of peasants displaced by the pressures just described
emigrated to Rome in search of work or of other means of subsistence. This migration is supposed to have been fairly constant

47. For the extensive use of slaves during this period see, among others,
Cato *De Agr. Cult.* 2.2, 5.1, etc.; Diod. xxxiv/xxxv.2.27, 32, 34; Plut. *TG*
8.4; App. *BC* i.7; Brunt, *IM,* p. 122; Toynbee, *HL,* II, 340. For nonagri-
cultural employment of slaves, see, among others, Polyb. x.17.9–16; Livy
xxvi.47; Westermann, "Industrial Slavery in Roman Italy," pp. 149–163, esp.
pp. 151–157; Gummerus, "Industrie und Handel," *RE,* IX, 1454–1455;
Frederiksen, "Republican Capua, A Social and Economic Study," pp. 112–
113.

48. Brunt, *IM,* pp. 121–130, 347. For the manumissions of slaves see
Treggiari, *Roman Freedmen during the Late Republic,* pp. 34–36.

49. App. *BC* i.7.26–32; Plut. *TG* 8.3–4.

during the first half of the century but especially dynamic in the decade or so before Tiberius Gracchus' tribunate, as people were lured by the extensive building activities that seem to have begun in earnest in about 145. It was becoming, so the theory goes, increasingly difficult to keep down on the farm penurious peasants who had been exposed while on campaign to the joys of the urban East. They were attracted to city life in general, and the great metropolis of Rome in particular, which now conveniently needed their labor.[50] If correct, this demographic schema would seem to have important political implications. Many of those who accept it see the presence of the rural proletariat in the capital as disruptive of the Roman oligarchy's traditional methods of controlling the vote. Because of their numbers and their nearness to the polls, displaced peasants from the outlying areas, who were still registered in one of the thirty-one rural tribes but now resided in Rome, are assumed to have confounded the customary Roman electoral and legislative procedures. Thus the election of magistrates, control of their official actions, and the passing of legislation began to slip from the oligarchy's grasp.[51]

As early as the first decade of this century the great Italian scholar Guglielmo Ferrero warned his European and American colleagues not to impose contemporary urban conditions, resulting from the Industrial Revolution, anachronistically on the ancient city.[52] A number of more recent scholars have also dissented from such an interpretation.[53] The sources contain clear evidence that the crisis that came to the boil in 133 was at heart rural rather than urban and that it was not, therefore, affecting the oligarchy's control over voting and legislation in the tribal assembly (*comitia*

50. See Boren, "Numismatic Light on the Gracchan Crisis," pp. 140–155; Boren, "The Urban Side of the Gracchan Crisis," pp. 890–902; Boren, *The Gracchi*, pp. 41–53.

51. Carney, "Rome in the Gracchan Age," pp. 38–42.

52. Ferrero, *Grandezza e decandenza di Roma*, II, 534.

53. See, for example, Gabba, *Appiani, Bellorum Civilium Liber Primus*, p. 41; Brunt, "The Army and the Land in the Roman Revolution," pp. 69–83; Lintott, *Violence in Republican Rome*, p. 178; Nagle, "The Failure of the Roman Political Process in 133 B.C." (1970), pp. 372–394, (1971), pp. 111–128.

tributa) or the centuriate assembly (*comitia centuriata*) in the way often supposed.[54] To be sure, the Roman republican oligarchy was, in this period, losing some of its control over electoral and legislative processes, but not, apparently, because of pressures from a displaced peasantry resident in Rome. The effect of any such people on the decisions of the *comitia centuriata* would, of course, be infinitesimal; presumably, they were landless and in that body therefore put together in a single century that might never be called upon to vote.[55] On the other hand, such a drastic movement of population to the capital might have had an important effect on the activities of the more popularly controlled *comitia tributa*. An increasing number of legislative proposals were being brought before it, a fact that betokens growing discontent with traditional governance.[56] Yet, if proponents of the urban thesis are right about the nature of the political crisis caused by recent demographic changes, the challenge could surely have been met quite simply. The censors, who held office every five years for a period of eighteen months, ought to have reregistered the propertyless migrants, now living in Rome, in one of the four urban tribes. They would thereby minimize if not nullify the newcomers' effect on the activities of the *comitia tributa* and ensure that the wealthy senatorial landowners could continue to manipulate that body. Since these migrants would no longer own property or reside in a rural tribe, there would be ample justification for such reregistration. It is hard to believe that shrewd Roman politicians would not have resorted to so obvious an expedient, especially since this was the method they had used to deal with the freedman problem when the elder Tiberius Gracchus, father of the Gracchi, was censor. He

54. For the rural nature of Tiberius' supporters see Diod. xxxiv/xxxv.6.1; Plut. *TG* 8.7; App. *BC* i.10, 13, 14.

55. Dion. Hal. iv.20.5, 21.1, 21.3.

56. See Taylor, *RVA*, pp. 100–106. The centuriate assembly had been the major lawmaking body of the state, but by 218 most legislative proposals had been transferred to the tribal assembly. As Taylor notes, we know of only one law passed in the centuriate assembly between 70 and 49—that proposed by the consul Lentulus Spinther to recall Cicero from exile in 57.

had reregistered all of them in a single urban tribe.[57] The sources do not mention such reregistration of the rural masses at this time, nor do they say anything about the effects of the urban crisis. The absence of evidence for tribal reregistration is inconclusive. It might suggest that the ruling oligarchy did not think of resorting to such a corrective; more probably, it suggests that they never needed to. If urban conditions were so critical that the ruling classes were beginning to lose their control over the elections of the lower magistrates and the passage of the laws, why do we not hear of any measure in this period explicitly designed to remedy a situation that must have been intolerable?

This is not to assert that in the decades before Tiberius' tribunate no Roman farmers, driven from their lands, came to the capital in search of work. Some, especially among the younger generation, may have come seeking a new livelihood, anticipating no future in small farming. We simply do not know that there were many of them, or that they took up permanent residence in the city. In fact, the line that divided the urban from the rural proletariat might not have been at all clear, since seasonal workers and even marginal and tenant farmers might have drifted between country and city as their agricultural commitments and the opportunities for urban employment dictated. When his rural supporters failed him in his bid for a second tribunate, Tiberius is said to have "had recourse to the residents of the city, going around asking each one separately to elect him tribune for the coming year on account of the danger he was incurring on their behalf." These men may have been either inhabitants of the rural tribes who lived so near Rome that they might be described as residents of the city or rural voters who had migrated to Rome. The phrase "each one separately" could mean that Tiberius canvassed people individually but did not canvass them all, or that he did indeed seek out every eligible rural voter in the city.[58] The latter meaning would imply the presence of some rural voters resident in Rome, but leads to the conclusion that their number cannot have been great.

57. Cic. *De Orat.* i.9.38; Livy xlv.15.1–8; Auct. *Vir. Ill.* 57.2. See above, p. 38.

58. App. *BC* i.14. See Taylor, *VDRR,* chaps. 7, 8, and 9.

An extensive building program was in progress in Rome in the 140s but this, in itself, does not entail the conclusion that large numbers of peasant migrants did the work. Native artisans, perhaps some of them migrants from the other cities of Italy, and most of all slaves, would have occupied permanently the positions former peasants might otherwise have sought.[59] The slaves in particular would make the free man's labor expendable in the city as they had done in the country. Under such circumstances, the free man would have no reason to think the city offered him a better chance of finding work than he would have at home, where he at least had the advantage of possessing the appropriate skills. The ancient literary sources do emphasize the employment of slaves in agriculture precisely because it was a source of grievance among the free inhabitants of the countryside and because the practice ran counter to Rome's long-term interest, but this emphasis does not indicate that prospects in the city were such as to tempt the peasants to pull up roots. Nor does it exclude the possibility of increased use of slave labor in the cities, too, and in the building programs of the capital in particular. Slaves brought to Italy from the cities of the East probably possessed skills that would qualify them admirably for urban employment. Such slave manpower must have been used outside the cities in the "enormous number of contracts throughout the whole of Italy . . . which [were] given out by the censors for the construction and repair of public works." [60] Slaves who normally worked as farm laborers might have been hired out in slave gangs during the off season for public works in both the country and the city. That is implied in Cato's warning to the prospective purchaser of a farm that an overseer doing work for a farmer with his slave gang is apt to plead the responsibilities of a public works contract as an excuse for his failure to complete a satisfactory amount of work on the farm.[61]

59. Brunt (*IM,* p. 345) thinks that the craftsmen of the provincial cities may have suffered as a result of the large estates' movement toward self-sufficiency and their employment of slave craftsmen.

60. Polyb. vi.17.2–4. Said to apply to circumstances ca. 150 by Walbank, *COP,* I, 692.

61. Cato *De Agr. Cult.* 2.2.

Inscriptional and literary evidence, moreover, creates the strong impression that the majority of urban inhabitants, especially those engaged in trade and the crafts, were eastern slaves or freedmen who arrived in Italy with the requisite skills.[62] When the great influx of slaves began with a vengeance in the second century, it was probably channeled into industrial labor and domestic employment even before it was directed to agricultural pursuits.[63]

The real danger of viewing the crisis that exploded in 133 solely in urban terms is that it can lead to mistaking a possible symptom for the cause and that it diverts attention from the basic area of trouble—the countryside. The main effect of the economic crisis in the first half of the second century was to allow the Roman *patroni* to pay ever less for the maintenance and loyalty of their impoverished *clientes,* so that the poor man's lot was becoming intolerable. The system of clientship did not, however, collapse altogether, and it is clear that some of those hardest hit in the economic crisis did stay on the land and survive there. That they did so was due to their usefulness: large Roman landowners gained certain political advantages from employing free Roman citizens rather than slaves, from allowing an indebted farmer to eke out some form of existence—as a tenant on the small tract he had previously owned or as a laborer or odd-job man on a larger estate. Expediency advised throwing him some crumb, albeit a smaller one than before, to hold him in the region and keep him politically obedient to his niggardly benefactor, rather than evicting him altogether. Naturally, upper-class Roman families involved in the political struggles of the Forum sought to manipulate as many votes as possible in the Roman assemblies; that was how oligarchic governance was maintained. In the tribal assembly particularly, with its thirty-one rural and only four urban tribes, the country voter clearly had value, even if he was propertyless. How many clients could a Roman *nobilis* support by means of his urban properties? Indeed, how many *nobiles* at this date had investments

62. See Treggiari, *Roman Freedmen,* pp. 32–36, 91–106; Brunt, *IM,* pp. 95–97; Brunt, "The Army and the Land," pp. 69–70; cf. Duff, *Freedmen in the Early Roman Empire,* pp. 107ff.
63. See above, n. 47, esp. Westermann.

permitting employment of former peasants as, say, craftsmen, shop-keepers, and shop assistants, building superintendents and janitors? We do not know, but we can assume that the prudence and con-servatism of the Roman aristocracy might have inclined them to put economic investments in service to political ambitions and thus to pursue the proved methods of controlling voters in the tribal assembly.[64] On the other hand, the newly rich landlords earlier described would have been concerned more with maximizing profits than with the political implications of their choice of labor force. In this regard, they probably did more to aggravate the conditions of the peasantry in the first half of the second century than did the more politically involved senatorial land magnates.

Roman oligarchs may have taken steps to keep their clients in the countryside, often as their tenants. Mommsen surmised that tenant farming was as old as the Roman state, and although some consider the practice a late Republican and early imperial develop-ment, both our sources nearest the Gracchan Age, Cato and Terence, refer to tenancy.[65] Cato mentions it in connection with grain farming, while Terence in his *Adelphi* has Demea ask Micio to turn over to Hegio one of his tenant farms near Rome.[66] In 134, when the Senate refused either to allocate to Scipio Aemilianus funds for his campaign against the Numantines or to allow him to levy fresh troops, he took volunteer contingents sent him by cities and kings on account of their personal relationship to him; in addition, he enrolled a personal bodyguard of five hundred clients

64. For Roman citizens receiving patronage in the capital see Sall. *Cat.* 37; Cic. *Leg. Agr.* ii.72; Varro *De Agr. Cult.* 2.3; App. *BC* ii.120. For the system of clientship in general see Premerstein, "Clientes" in *RE*, IV, 23–55; Mommsen, *Römische Forschungen,* I, 319–325; Badian, *FC,* pp. 1–14.

65. Mommsen, "Decret des Commodus für den Saltus Burunitanus," p. 408. See also Clausing, *The Roman Colonate: The Theories of Its Origins,* pp. 258–261. Contra see Brunt, "Review of Westermann, *Slave Systems,"* pp. 166–167.

66. Cato *De Agr. Cult.* 136, cf. 137; Terence *Adelphi* 950–955. References to *coloni* (tenant farmers) for the Republic have been gathered by Bolkestein, *De Colonatu Romano ejusque Origine,* Caput II, pp. 82–118, who has found nearly one hundred and fifty of them, though often the word *colonus* simply means "cultivator."

and friends. These latter were not on the lists of men eligible for active service and so some of them may not have owned sufficient property to qualify for *adsiduus* status. Certainly they were Scipio's dependents, possibly his tenants, and might once have been eligible for legionary service, or have actually served, but their absence from the lists of those liable for military induction meant they must now have farmed land they no longer owned.[67] Similarly, Pompey, in 83, just before the return of Sulla to Italy, raised from the district of Picenum a substantial army filled with his father's clients, men who might have come under Pompeian aegis in the Gracchan Age or shortly therafter. Some of those now recruited on behalf of Sulla seem to have come from local towns, which might explain why they were not on active duty, but others may have been, like Scipio's bodyguard, agrarian dependents, below *adsiduus* status because they were tenants or landless rural workers resident in the area.[68]

The fuller sources for the first century refer frequently to the practice of tenancy, often on a grand scale, and no compelling evidence indicates a change in the economic conditions over these two centuries that would cause the practice to arise suddenly. Sallust, for example, reports that in 63 part of Catiline's army consisted of his tenants, while during the Civil War, Domitius Ahenobarbus not only manned his ships with his own tenants, but delivered a speech to his army promising to provide each soldier with four acres of land out of his own properties.[69] Surely men who would serve their *patroni* in the field during wartime would serve them in the Forum in peacetime. The former practice may have been extraordinary; the latter would call for no special mention. The works of Cicero are dotted with references to tenants, both the author's and those of others. He says that even the municipalities found it profitable to lease land to tenants in order to

67. App. *Iber.* 84, cf. 89; Sall. *Jug.* 7.2; Cic. *Reg. Deiot.* 19; Livy *Per.* lvii; Vell. ii.9.4; Schol. Clun. p. 272 Stangl. See De Sanctis, *Storia dei Romani,* IV, iii, 260–263 with references.

68. Vell. ii.29; Plut. *Pomp.* 6; App. *BC* i.80. Cf. Polyb. ii.21.7–8.

69. Sall. *Cat.* 59.3 for Catiline. Caes. *BC* i.34 and 56 for Domitius Ahenobarbus manning his ships with his tenants; i.17 for his promise of four acres of land to each of his troops from his own possessions.

raise revenue for public expenditure.[70] This being so, many a large landowner must have employed the device as well. Horace used tenants to cultivate his estates, and the juridical texts for the first century contain several references to the practice.[71] Indeed, L. Cincius, a first-century author, reports that the ninth month of the year was called Mercedonius because it was then that the tenants paid the rents (*merces*) to their landlords. Whatever we make of his etymology, it indicates that such payments must have been an old custom, so that a sizable segment of the rural population in the second century would have consisted of impoverished tenants.[72]

Tenant labor was indispensable in farming. Since grain growing was not easily adaptable to the use of slaves, as the American in addition to the ancient experience has shown, free men were probably preferred to cultivate it.[73] Although in the second century the

70. Cic. *ad Att.* xiii.9.2 with Heitland, *Agricola,* p. 216, n. 1; Cic. *Leg. Agr.* ii.30; Cic. *Cluent.* 175, 182; Cic. *Caec.* 17, 57, 94; Cic. *Verr.* ii. 3.12–15, 53–55, 228; cf. Cic. *Off.* ii.73. A passage in a letter to M. Junius Brutus, written by Cicero in 46 (*ad Fam.* xiii.11.1), alludes to the municipalities' practice of leasing their lands to tenants to raise money for public expenses. He is speaking of his own *municipium,* Arpinum, and he claims that the towns' "entire income and resources, which enable them to keep their temples and other public buildings in repair, depend upon the rents which they own in the province of Gaul." Capua owned land in Crete (Vell. ii.81) and Atella owned land in Gaul (Cic. *ad Fam.* xiii.7.1), but lands belonging to the *municipia* were usually in the immediate vicinity (Tyrrell and Purser, *The Correspondence of M. Tullius Cicero,* IV, 278, n. 1). If tenants were also leased such lands, they may have been among those to whom Appian (*BC* i.10) refers when he writes that "a great number of others, composed of colonists or inhabitants of the free towns, . . . flocked in and took sides with their respective factions after Tiberius proposed his agrarian law."

71. Hor. *Sat.* II.2.115, 7.118; cf. Hor. *Epist.* i.14.1. For the references to the juridical texts see Brunt, "The Army and the Land," p. 71, n. 31; Ser. Sulpicius *Dig.* xix.1.13.30, 2.15.2, 2.35.1 (?); Alfenus Varus xv.3.16 (slave *quasi colonus*), xix.2.30.4; Aelius Tubero xix.1.13.30; Labeo vii.8.10.4, xix.2.60.1 and 5, xx.6.14, xxxiii.2.30 (?), 2.42 (?); 7.12.3 (slave *quasi colonus*), xxxix.3.17 (?) (mentioning *reliqua colonorum*), xxxix.3.5.

72. Cited by Lydus *Liber de Mensibus* iv.144.92, p. 164 Wuensch. See also, Coulanges, *Recherches sur quelques problèmes d'histoire,* p. 11.

73. See Yeo, "Economics of Roman and American Slavery," pp. 468–472; I am following his arguments and conclusions concerning the use of free and slave labor for the cultivation of the vine, the olive, and grain.

city of Rome was largely supplied by the Sicilian grain tithe, provincial grain more than likely had little effect on local inland grain markets, areas not readily accessible by waterway. The cost of overland transportation in the ancient world was almost always prohibitive. Cereal production, therefore, in most places outside the immediate vicinity of Rome, must have remained the most popular and conceivably even the most profitable crop.[74] Aside from what Cato says about tenant farming and grain production, the ancients in general seem to have believed that grain was better cultivated by free workers than by slaves. Both Columella and Pliny the Elder denounce strongly the use of slaves on a grain farm.[75] The objections arise from two economic facts of life. First, the growing season for grain lasted a relatively short time, only some forty days per year, leaving a long period of idleness between harvest and planting and preventing the uninterrupted employment needed to make profitable a permanent slave labor force that must be fed, clothed, and housed year round. Second, a single worker was able to cultivate twenty or thirty acres of grain on his own. Thus the farmhands would scatter over a wide area, and when

---

74. For the difficulties of overland transport see Cato De Agr. Cult. i.3; Varro, De Agr. Cult. i.16.6; Columella De Re Rust. i.2.3, i.3.3, vii.8.1, vii.3.22. For the costliness of land transport, see Westermann, "On Inland Transportation and Communication in Antiquity," pp. 364–387. From Varro we learn that exporters kept droves of pack donkeys to carry "even cereals" as well as wine and oil from the Ager Brundisinus and from Apulia to the water's edge (ii.6.5), but the distances were very short. While Cato recommends that his farmers produce their own grain, the archaeological evidence indicates that his advice was not always followed (Yeo, "Development of Roman Plantation," pp. 450–451). When larger farms did produce their own grain (Columella De Re Rust. i.2.4; Varro De Agr. Cult. i.45, 48, 53) it was only for home consumption and seed (Varro De Agr. Cult. i.69.1) and not for sale. The grain crop on Cato's wine and oil farms produced five hundred and forty bushels for bread to feed the slaves (Cato De Agr. Cult. ii.5, x.3–4, xi.4, lvi; cf. Gummerus, "Der römische Gutsbetrieb," p. 33) and was to be sold only when a surplus existed (Cato De Agr. Cult. ii.5, ii.7; cf. Weber, "Agrarverhältnisse im Altertum"). Brunt, "Review of Westermann," p. 169, believes that while wine and oil may have been the best cash crops, grain almost always covered the largest acreage.

75. Columella De Re Rust. i.7.6; Pliny NH xviii.7.36.

those farmhands were slaves working with little or no incentive, they would require the constant supervision of overseers; the cost would make the employment of slaves to produce grain still less attractive economically.[76] Provincial as well as Italian employment practices support the conclusion that farming grain with a slave labor force was avoided whenever possible.[77]

The tendency to overemphasize the displacement of free labor by slave, and so to expect the rural proletariat to be relocated in the city, probably originates in Cato's *De Agri Cultura,* which is our sole surviving second-century treatise on agriculture.[78] The work is not, however, a handbook describing contemporary agricultural conditions throughout Italy; it addresses itself to a limited audience, the prospective farmer of the vine and the olive in the Campanian area. These crops provide ideal conditions for the employment of slaves. Both necessitate labor all year round because they require frequent ploughing and constant digging in spring, summer, and autumn to conserve moisture in soil and plants throughout the growth period. Slaveowners therefore suffered a minimum of loss through the occasional idleness of their full-time labor force. In addition, both crops lent themselves to routine, so that the unskilled could easily learn to cultivate them, and they were suited to production in relatively small areas, so labor could be grouped in easily controllable units, thereby reducing problems of cost and supervision. Obviously, the *De Agri Cultura,* with its strong regional and class bias, and dealing almost entirely with

76. Cf. Weber, "Agrarverhältnisse," pp. 296–297.

77. Polyb. xv.18.1; Justin xxi.4.6. Haywood, "Roman Africa," *ESAR,* IV, 28, 45, esp. 89–94; Scramuzza, "Roman Sicily," *ESAR,* III, 316–317; Johnson, "Roman Egypt," *ESAR,* II, 277–278.

78. Also, the urban plebs were an important factor in the later stages of the Roman revolution. Cicero said that "urbanam plebem nimium in re publica posse; exhauriendam esse" (*Leg. Agr.* ii.70 delivered early in 63). Even then, though, their power showed itself physically rather than electorally or legislatively. If, indeed, Gaius Gracchus paid them more attention than did his older brother, he may have been seeking their support not as much for the votes they would cast as for his personal safety: Cic. *Off.* ii.21.72; Cic *Tusc. Disp.* iii.20.48; Cic *Sest.* 103; Livy *Per.* lx; Diod. xxv.25; Vell. ii.6.3; Plut. *CG* 5; App. *BC* i.21; Schol. Bob. p. 135 Stangl; Oros.v.12.

the cultivation of vine and olive, provides a poor basis for generalization on Italian agriculture as a whole, diverse as it was.[79]

Finally, to argue that most peasants who survived the new economic crisis of the second century did not exchange their rural for an urban existence is not to diminish the hardship they experienced, which was the cause of Italy's new political crisis.

Legislation proposed and passed around the middle of the century creates the impression that, as a result of the upheaval in rural conditions, oligarchic governance was no longer functioning smoothly. Small landowners from the countryside or propertyless citizens still living outside Rome apparently would come to the capital on occasion and disrupt the normal machinery of aristocratic government. Certain laws support the view that Roman conservatives feared the threat to the established order presented by the votes of the rural population and that they took what they believed to be precautions against it.

Just before Tiberius Gracchus' tribunate, perhaps within a decade of the passing of the *lex Sempronia agraria,* a provision of the *leges Aelia et Fufia* made it illegal to propose and pass a law around the time of the elections,[80] specifically the period beginning with the first (of three) proclamations of the coming elections, when the candidates made their declarations (*professiones*), and ending with the elections themselves. This period, the *trinundinum,* covered at least eighteen days (though it might be as long as twenty-four) and allowed for the announcement of the names of the candidates for office on three days designated for meetings of the *comitia* (*dies comitiales*).[81] The object of the provision must have been to prevent popular laws from being proposed to and passed by the tribal assembly at precisely the moment when Rome was crowded with disgruntled country folk who had come or been

79. See the precautionary remark of Aymard ("Les Capitalistes romains et la viticulture italienne," p. 257), and of Frederiksen ("The Contribution of Archaeology to the Agrarian Problem in the Gracchan Period," p. 335).

80. For the problems of dating the Aelian and Fufian legislation see Appendix B.

81. Schol. Bob. p. 148 Stangl; cf. Macrob. *Sat.* i.16.4. See Lintott, "Trinundinum," pp. 281–285, and Michels, *The Calendar of the Roman Republic,* pp. 197–206 with n. 13.

summoned for the elections, presumably to support their patron's candidates.[82]

The ties that held many a rural *cliens* to his *patronus* by now must have become sufficiently tenuous that under certain circumstances rural votes could be difficult to control. Such clients would be present in the capital in great numbers during the *trinundinum*, but their obligation, their *officium,* to the great Roman *patroni* was liable to be undermined by a piece of legislation they found particularly attractive. In fact, the client's *officium* to his former patron might have been undermined through provision of a liberating *beneficium* from another; C. Laelius' abandoned agrarian proposal might have done this, and Tiberius Gracchus' proposal for redistributing the public land certainly did it. Of course, the Roman system of *clientela* never ran perfectly. Throughout Roman history voters would have had conflicting obligations and loyalties, and there must always have been mavericks. During the course of the second century, the deteriorating economic conditions of the peasantry must have loosened the structure of the patron-client system. The smaller the *beneficium* a patron conferred, the less he

82. As Taylor has argued, "Forerunners of the Gracchi," p. 23; cf. Taylor, *RVA,* p. 68. Astin ("Leges Aelia et Fufia," p. 437) thinks this explanation inadequate and has argued, "If it is true that the legislative process was liable to interfere seriously with canvassing, the proposers of legislation must normally have avoided this time in any case; for they would hardly have risked angering candidates at the very time when these latter had their maximum *clientelae* mobilized and present, and most fully under control." Hence his belief that this clause of the Aelian and Fufian laws was designed to prevent the kind of last-minute legislation that would grant a normally ineligible candidate a special legal exemption and allow him to run for the office from which he would normally be debarred. The evidence for such a conclusion is sparse, but whatever truth the explanation has must be only part of the story. Mommsen thought that a formal *professio* was not, at this time, necessary for election to office (*Röm. Staats.* I[3], 471–474, 501–504. Contra, see Astin, "*Professio* in the Abortive Election of 184 B.C.," pp. 252–255). After all, if a Marcellus or a Scipio wished to run for an office for which he required a special legal dispensation, and so wanted to skirt the Aelian and Fufian legislation, he would need only to have a tribune agitate for a special dispensation on his behalf before the first announcement of the elections.

could count on the recipient's loyalty when the prospect of an alternative presented itself. This breakdown lies behind the passing of legislation in 181 and 159 designed to curb bribery, which, of course, becomes a serious social problem only with the existence of a sufficient number of independent or would-be independent voters prepared to accept what is offered.[83] Those who could be swayed by bribes might also be induced by promises to neglect their former loyalties and voting habits and to cast their ballots for a particularly attractive piece of legislation or for a candidate who promised to propose one. They might, that is, "vote according to their own preferences, and their preferences could be influenced." [84] The *trinundinum* clause of the Aelian and Fufian legislation, when taken together with the laws introducing the closed ballot that were passed in the 130s, strongly indicates that the significant independent voters were mostly rural residents. No doubt they had some ties to patrons, but the dire economic developments in the Italian countryside had made them dissatisfied with the diminishing returns their political loyalty was securing. The passage of three closed ballot laws in this decade (the *lex Gabinia* of 139, which introduced it for elections, the *lex Cassia* of 137, which made the ballot secret for most judicial decisions, and finally the *lex Papiria* of 131, or 130, which closed it for legislative votes) need not imply that the traditional system of clientship was breaking down because of large numbers of voters without patrons at Rome.[85] It leads rather to the conclusion that clients with valuable rural votes, living in the country under the

---

83. See Astin, *SA,* p. 29. Livy xl.19.11; Livy *Per.* xlvii; Polyb. vi.56.4. Mommsen points out that, as early as the end of the Hannibalic War, the public games of the aediles were having a marked effect on the elections (*Röm. Staats.* I³, p. 532, cited by Astin, *SA,* p. 339).

84. Astin, *SA,* p. 28.

85. For the *lex Gabinia* see Cic. *Leg.* iii.35; Cic. *Amic.* 41; Livy *Per. Oxy.* liv; for the *lex Cassia* see also Cic. *Brut.* 97, 106; Cic. *Sest.* 103; Ascon. p. 78C; Schol. Bob. p. 135 Stangl; Ps.-Ascon. p. 216 Stangl; for the *lex Papiria* see also Cic *De Orat.* ii.170. On the importance of the *leges tabellariae* see Larsen, "The Judgement of Antiquity on Democracy," p. 10; Taylor, *RVA*, pp. 34–58; Wiseman, *New Men in the Roman Senate 139* B.C.–A.D. *14*, pp. 4–6.

thumbs of exploiting landlords and so under economic conditions that they quite reasonably found unacceptable, were now seeking to avoid their patrons' control. If votes for legislation as well as votes for office could be obtained by new methods outside the traditionally closed Roman system of clientship, the factional struggles of the oligarchy would gain an added dimension. *Clientelae* could be padded with voters grateful for suitably popular legislation. The usual inaccessibility of the potentially independent rural voter would have made it difficult to pass laws to his advantage, but he was normally present in the capital at the time of the elections. Appropriately appealing measures would naturally be more difficult to oppose and veto during the *trinundinum*. When large numbers of rural voters were present at Rome, a faction or an individual might be politically embarrassed and even injured if forced to move against a piece of popular legislation. Electoral votes could be won by proposing or lost by vetoing legislation designed to find favor with the rural masses. Thus the purposes of conservative Roman oligarchs would be served by a general ban on legislation during this period.

The most serious objection to this interpretation of the clause of the *leges Aelia et Fufia* under consideration is that the clause could be circumvented by promulgating a bill the day before the first announcement of the elections, by keeping it alive until the elections were held, and then by voting on it on the first comitial day after the elections.[86] This objection would be particularly serious if the majority of the voters were urban inhabitants, but probably the impoverished rural voter would be able to spend only a very limited time in the capital, certainly not as long as the month the process presumes. The longer stay, moreover, might make migrant and seasonal workers, sharecroppers and tenant farmers, especially susceptible to the pressures of their patrons and employers. These latter, having summoned their supposed dependents to Rome for the purpose of the elections, would grow suspicious and might take retaliatory action if the clients insisted upon remaining in Rome after they had served the purpose for which they had been called.

86. Astin, "Leges Aelia et Fufia," p. 438.

Such, then, were the conditions forming the background to the remarkable events of 133. Extended military commitments abroad, the profits of war, the importing of a vast slave labor force, the expansion of cash-crop farming and large-scale grazing, wild land speculation—all combined to create a serious economic crisis that was aggravated by the lack of a system of justice capable of protecting the poor and powerless. Life became a misery for the majority of Italy's rural citizens, and the steady, rapid deterioration of their living conditions resulted first in the military problem of obtaining enough suitable recruits for Rome's legions, then in a more serious political one. As conditions worsened, as the oligarchic system showed itself either unwilling or unable to ensure its citizens the basic necessities for existence, the system began to change. The rules of *clientela,* on which Rome's governance had long depended, were increasingly being broken by both sides of the partnership. The old vertical lines that had previously separated competing political groups within the Roman state began to tilt toward the horizontal. Thus the wretched became a constituency. The possibility of their gaining a champion for their cause, of their becoming finally the *clientela* of a single man or group of men, must have tempted the politically ambitious and troubled farsighted patriots.

4 The Senate and the Sponsors of the *Lex Sempronia Agraria*

Firmamentum autem stabilitatis constantiaeque est eius quam
in amicitia quaerimus fides est.

—Cicero, *De Amicitia, 65*

Despite the political changes in the air by the time Tiberius
Gracchus took his place in the tribunician college, the oligarchic
system was still functioning much as it had for generations. The
important decisions of state in the Middle Republic were made in
fact if not in theory with the consent of the majority of Roman
senators. Throughout the second century, the Senate consisted of
approximately three hundred men. If we knew nothing else about
Roman politics in this era, we should expect that a congress of
such size would divide into and be directed by smaller units for the
purpose of everyday government. Since the body lacked a formal
substructure of what would today be called committees and a
rapid turnover in its membership, such units naturally clustered
round particularly formidable and respected leaders who possessed
in a distinguishing degree the traditional Roman attributes of
dignitas and *auctoritas*. Inevitably, in the absence of defined
political parties, these units had become rivals, struggling with
each other to acquire and maintain supremacy within the body
as well as to control admission to it.[1] Given the nature of Republican society, these groups of politicians might have been expected
to reflect something of that society's clan basis. Indeed, of the
200 consuls who held office in the century before Tiberius

1. Admission to the Senate was controlled by manipulating the elections
of the *comitia centuriata* through the system of patronage and clientship.
See, among others, the discussions of Scullard (*RP*, pp. 12–30), Taylor
(*Party Politics in the Age of Caesar*, pp. 41–49), and Wiseman (*New Men-
in the Roman Senate 139 B.C.–A.D. 14*, pp. 3–6).

Gracchus' tribunate, 159 came from only 26 families, while 99 came from only 10 families.[2]

Roman oligarchic politicians were hardly unique in forming alliances among themselves to procure power, to promote policy, or both. The composition and operation of the alliances, however, reflect some of the features peculiar to Roman society. This does not necessarily mean that the mechanisms of Roman political alliance have no historical parallel, yet one society cannot be used simply as an analogue to explain the functioning of another. Acceptance of any parallels must depend on reasoned demonstration of their accuracy. Mommsen omitted such a demonstration when he used the now-discredited model of the nineteenth-century parliamentary democracies to illuminate the workings of Republican politics, and a similar error is made by those who invoke as guide an ever-narrowing period of eighteenth-century England.[3]

The supporters of what has come to be called the prosopographical thesis find the clue to Roman politics in the web of extended familial relationships and feuds of the period. This approach has by no means won universal acceptance. Major questions about the nature of the senatorial alliances and how they worked remain to be answered, for the most fundamental disagreement persists among the practitioners of the prosopographical method, after years of strenuous debate among themselves and with others in the field. Consensus remains elusive even about what counts as evidence of the existence and composition of the alliances, how they were formed, the length of time they might normally endure, and, most important, the purposes for which they came and remained together.[4] This lack of consensus in vital areas in itself

2. Scullard, *RP,* p. 11.

3. For the inapplicability of the English model for Rome, see Meier, *Res Publica Amissa,* pp. 187–190.

4. A useful and up-to-date survey of recent studies on prosopography as applied to the politics of the Roman Republic occurs in the Foreword (pp. xvii–xxxiii) to the second edition of Scullard's *RP,* where the author attempts to reply to the critics of the first edition. See also the moderate approach of Broughton, "Senate and Senators of the Roman Republic: The Prosopographical Approach," pp. 250–265, and the reservations of Brunt, *"Amicitia* in the Late Roman Republic," pp. 1–20 (reprinted in Seager, ed.,

weakens trust in the usefulness of sociological paradigms as indicators of how the Roman oligarchy functioned.

The role family connections and the *amicitiae* based upon them played in Roman politics has too often been overemphasized and exaggerated. Some studies assume that such bonds alone determined public action. Enthusiastic scholars seeking new ways to solve old problems have narrowed the prosopographical method of investigation and based a dogma on it. In the hands of some, prosopography, from being an aid to historical inquiry, has become its goal. To track down the membership of the alliances, to lay bare the familial structure presumed to underlie Roman political action and change are considered the chief, if not the sole, task of the historian.[5] As a result, it has happened that a scholar will build intricate systems upon the flimsiest evidence, employ criteria that will not bear serious scrutiny, use distant relationships as sole proof of partisan collaboration, or, indeed, accept names alone where no other evidence exists. Roman politicians are thereby assigned to what were once called "parties" but what current practice terms "factions." [6] These acquire an improbable

---

The Crisis of the Roman Republic, pp. 199–218). See also Stone, "Prosopography," pp. 46–79, and Carney, "Prosopography: Payoffs and Pitfalls," pp. 156–179. Most especially, however, see the cautions of the master prosopographer, Gelzer, collected in his *Kleine Schriften,* pp. 186–210. See also Badian, "Review of Weisch, *Studien zur politischen,*" pp. 216–222, esp. p. 219. I should like to thank W. G. Sinnigen and Meyer Reinhold for allowing me to see copies of their comments made at the annual convention of the American Historical Association in 1967 on the subject, "The Uses and Limitations of Prosopography in Roman History." I owe a special debt to Reinhold who has helped to shape my thoughts on the subject.

5. For example, Scullard (*RP,* p. 3) writes, "It is this far-reaching nexus of personal and family relationships and obligations that underlies the basis of Roman public life."

6. See Seager, *"Factio:* Some Observations," pp. 53–58. Through a meticulous examination of the use of the word *factio* in the ancient sources the author shows that they never used it to designate "competing factions of the nobility," that only one *factio* is ever said to exist at any given time, and that even when the state is described as being divided into two groups, the sources do not speak of *factiones.* He cautions against replacing parties with factions. Also on political terminology see Hanell,

permanence that spans not merely generations, but literally centuries. Some of the professedly more moderate advocates of the prosopographical thesis concede a certain dynamism and fluidity in these factions but, unfortunately, often fail in practice to take account of it, treating the assemblages as static.

When prosopography becomes a goal rather than a technique, it usually includes the assumption that the promotion of the interests of the faction, its advancement to power greater than that of its competitors in the arena of Roman politics, was the dominant motivating force behind the public actions of every Roman aristocrat. Other apparent or professed motives are believed only to provide smokescreens and rationalizations for the subtle and covert promotion of the unit. True Roman politicians, it seems, would involve themselves in land distributions, in military reform, in promoting programs to distribute grain to the urban citizenry, in advocating the extension of the full franchise to the Latins and Italians, solely to augment their *clientelae,* that is, to increase the number of voters whose electoral behavior they could control. They would thereby also increase their own and their family's power and so that of their faction. This view sees the Roman oligarchy as a closed system of family units, each seeking power for its own sake and for no other reason.[7]

Dissent from such a rigid approach to Roman aristocratic society does not necessitate wholesale rejection of all the contingent assumptions. Obviously, family traditions had a significant influence on an aristocrat's actions.[8] The important contributions made to our understanding of Roman politics and society through prosopography as judiciously applied by scholars such as Mattias Gelzer, Friedrich Münzer, Sir Ronald Syme, E. Badian, and Lily

---

"Bemerkungen zu der politischen Terminologie des Sallustius," pp. 263–276; Vretska, *C. Sallustius Crispus, Invektiven und Episteln,* p. 64; Hellegouarc'h, *Le vocabulaire latin des relations et des partis politiques suos la république,* pp. 100–109; Smith, *"Factio, Factiones,* and *Nobilitas* in Sallust," pp. 187–196.

7. These seem to be the underlying assumptions of, for example, Earl, *Tiberius Gracchus,* pp. 7–13.

8. See Badian, *TGBRR,* p. 674, n. 16.

Ross Taylor demonstrate that it is a tool the scholar cannot ignore. The apparently open-ended controversy indicates that an aristocrat's actions were indeed powerfully affected by family loyalties and the political alliances built upon them, but that he could also be governed by considerations outside—it is tempting at times to say above—this particular brand of family partisanship. His loyalty to his associates might, on occasion, conflict with obligations to clients, or be tempered by his sense of integrity or of his own dignity, by his devotion to the law, and *mos maiorum,* by his desire for glory rather than power, by his personal feelings about the men he found himself involved with and the way they behaved. Regard for class or the interest of the state, calculation of private economic advantage, his opinion of the propriety of the means being advocated or employed toward some end all could have played a part.

Undoubtedly, Romans formed political alliances, and some might endure for considerable periods of time as the individuals involved sought to acquire power. The desire to further the faction's interests was one purpose of the search, but, of course, power had meaning beyond its usefulness to the factions. Roman politicians of the second century entertained few illusions about its value and were restrained by few inhibitions over its use; that is the inescapable conclusion to be drawn from the Senate's foreign policy in general and from its policies in Spain in particular. Such an attitude toward power must, in part, reflect domestic conditions. In second-century Rome power and its workings had not yet become veiled by a panoply of complex institutions; even the man in the Roman street knew who possessed power and how it might be used to help or hurt him. He would not have hesitated to acknowledge his belief that power, and its concomitant authority, should be feared and respected, certainly not despised. The existence of the system of *clientela* presupposes this attitude, as do the open voting procedures that were only now being challenged, and for economic rather than moral reasons.[9] At the same time

9. Cic. *Leg.* iii.33–39: "The next law takes up the subject of votes which, according to my decree shall not be concealed from citizens of high rank, and shall be free to the common people."

the obligations of the powerful were no less strictly defined than the behavior of others to them. These phenomena do not seem strange in a society that conferred absolute authority, in the form of the *patria potestas,* on the head of every family, who could exercise even the power of life and death (*ius vitae necisque*) over the other members.[10] Family and state had not yet come to exist as separate entities. The family institutions might therefore be expected to have some public analogue, such as there appears to have been, first, in the *potestas* of the annual consular magistrates, second, in the collective *auctoritas* of the senators, who were, of course, called *Patres,* and finally, in the title *Pater Patriae* granted to Augustus but used informally for Marius and Cicero.

Familial authoritarianism provides the background for Roman political affiliation. The political importance of the family structure lies in the intense loyalty it demanded, loyalty incomparably more binding than can be made intelligible through analogy with modern Western societies. Since political affiliations were built upon this family base, they elicited a similarly intense loyalty. The fundamental and peculiar family nature of Roman oligarchic politics and the attitude toward political loyalty it engendered cannot be ignored. Owing to these distinctive features of Roman society, prosopographical researches have, in the past, paid rich dividends when properly applied.

On the other hand, many Roman aristocrats must sometimes have felt the demands of conflicting loyalties, and loyalty itself is unlikely to have been the only imperative that affected their actions. Political alliances cannot always have been so distinct as to eliminate conflict; we have already seen that the young Tiberius Gracchus married the daughter of Appius Claudius, while his sister was Scipio Aemilianus' wife.[11] Loyalty to state, to class,

10. This institution was considered by the Romans uniquely theirs (Gaius *Inst.* i.55). The *ius vitae necisque* had been exercised as recently as ca. 220 when M. Fabius Buteo put his son to death for stealing (Oros. iv.13.18). It was used again when A. Fulvius Nobilior killed his son for participating in the Catilinarian conspiracy (Sall. *Cat.* 39). In both cases, of course, there is no suggestion that such actions constitute a norm.

11. See Cic. *Rep.* i.31. Bicknell (*Studies in Athenian Politics and Genealogy,* Preface) suggests that the marriage ties between the Sempronii

to self, or to some other competing moral principle could compromise a political alliance. To presume that, because Roman
senators were hardheaded and pragmatic, they took no account,
in their actions, of moral considerations would be naively cynical.
Certain traditional moral attributes—a sense of justice, a concern
for fair dealing, pride in a reputation for personal integrity,
courage—played a part in Roman society, though the ruling class
at this stage in its social and intellectual development probably
viewed them through a thick utilitarian lens. When, for example, a
Roman aristocrat acted from integrity he was less likely to do so
because he valued the quality in itself than because he considered
it required of a prudent man of honorable reputation in the conduct of his affairs.[12] This is not to say, of course, that these
Romans, *uomini di rispetto* as they were, valued such virtues any
the less.

   To posit as some do that the world of oligarchic politics lacked
the multifarious pressures that men of public affairs normally face
is to ignore the complexities of reality. Roman society may not
have been as complex as that of the modern industrial democracies,
nor as intellectually sophisticated as that of Classical Athens, but
it was not so simple that its rulers' actions were determined by
only one imperative, factional loyalty. Nor did all Romans seek
power for its own sake and function, in effect, as simple idolators

---

and the Cornelii Scipiones at this time do not betoken conflicting loyalties
because political intermarriage is not always intended to cement alliances.
Sons and daughters of rival families are sometimes married to each other,
"hostages in each other's camps," as Luigi Barzini wrote of modern Italian
families. Bicknell never says whether he believes Sempronia a hostage in
the Scipionic camp, or Tiberius a hostage in the Claudian, and he produces
no evidence, understandably perhaps, in a work on fifth-century Athenian
politics.

   12. Second-century Roman senators would probably have easily compre-
hended and had a good deal of sympathy with Cephalus' definition of justice
(Plato *Rep.*, 331C) as truth-telling and paying one's debts, or with Pole-
marchus' endorsement and explanation of Simonides' definition (*ibid.*,
332A) as helping friends and injuring enemies, or with Thrasymachus'
remark (*ibid.*, 338C) that justice is the advantage of the stronger. There
would have been less sympathy with and comprehension of Socrates' notion
(*ibid.*, 444D, cf. 433B).

of the great god *Potestas*. As in most societies, some undoubtedly were power-hungry and coveted the commodity as an end in itself. The majority of Roman oligarchs, however, were unlikely to be quite so single-minded that they did not, at least sometimes, seek power as a means to some further end. The historian must, then, ask why alliances of Roman senators and politicians formed. He must not view the unraveling of the relationships presumed to bind them either as the totality of his task or even as his main function.

Finally, there is no simple, formulary answer to the question of how long these alliances were meant to endure. Loyalty was highly valued and, not surprisingly, the obligations of friendship were felt so deeply by a few families that they were honored for generations, but the evidence does not support the view that this was true for all or even for most.[13] There must have been many degrees of political affiliation, and often the bonds of friendship would be maintained for as long as the men involved judged that circumstances allowed them to honor their loyalties or until they attained the end for which they had joined together. In troubled times, as new controversies arose to divide influential Romans, pressure would be put on earlier alliances, providing arguments for breaking with old loyalties. In the Gracchan Age instances occurred when a Roman oligarch decided he could no longer cooperate with a group to which he had formerly been tied.[14] Whether his action, under the circumstances, was seen as a betrayal must have varied from case to case.

The interweaving of political and familial relationships and the complexities of individual political motivation lie at the heart of any account of the next stage in Tiberius Gracchus' career. The *lex Sempronia agraria* of 133 has become known as his creation

13. See Gruen, *RPCC,* pp. 279–287.

14. So, for example, C. Papirius Carbo (Cic. *De Orat.* ii.106, 170; Cic. *Amic.* 41; Cic. *Leg.* iii.35) and C. Fannius (Plut. *CG* 8.2–3, 9.2–3, 12.1–2; cf. Cic. *Brut.* 99; Cic. *De Orat.* iii.183; Malcovati, *ORF,* 3d ed., pp. 143–144). Not so for P. Mucius Scaevola, however, of whom Nasica said, "he is prejudiced against everybody" (Cic. *De Orat.* ii.285), implying that he was known to be above partisan loyalties.

for his name is the most conspicuous in the sources, but an inexperienced tribune, unavoidably tainted by the disastrous Mancinus affair, was naturally in no position to initiate and handle legislation of his own devising. The agrarian laws advanced in 133 were in reality the product of men far more powerful than Tiberius Gracchus.[15]

The ancient sources identify the following distinguished Romans as aiding in the drafting or in the implementation of the agrarian legislation: Ap. Claudius Pulcher, consul for 143, censor in 136, and *Princeps Senatus* since 136; P. Mucius Scaevola, consul for 133 and *Pontifex Maximus* from 130 until his death in around 115; Scaevola's younger brother, P. Licinius Crassus Dives Mucianus, consul for 131 and *Pontifex Maximus* from 132 until his death just two years later; C. Papirius Carbo, consul for 120; M. Fulvius Flaccus, consul for 125; C. Porcius Cato, grandson of the censor and consul for 114; and, finally, C. Sempronius Gracchus, younger brother of Tiberius, tribune in 123 and 122.

Plutarch names Ap. Claudius Pulcher, P. Mucius Scaevola, and P. Licinius Crassus Mucianus as having taken part in the actual drafting of the agrarian law.[16] Cicero expresses some doubt about Scaevola's participation, and we know that of the three only he did not serve as an agrarian commissioner.[17] These two circumstances suggest that Scaevola acted only as legal adviser in the early stages. Possibly Tiberius' later unorthodox behavior caused this conservative legalist to refuse any further role in the agrarian program. Whatever the case, the man's reputation and his other actions indicate that his reluctance to involve either himself or the state in Tiberius' riotous final assembly more likely resulted from farsighted and cool-headed statesmanship than from partisan in-

15. See the discussion by Briscoe, "Supporters and Opponents of Tiberius Gracchus," pp. 125–135, for a conflicting view.

16. Plut. *TG* 9.1. For the sources on the careers of Ap. Claudius Pulcher, P. Mucius Scaevola, and P. Licinius Crassus Dives Mucianus, see Münzer, s.v. "Claudius" (295), *RE,* III, 2848; s.v. "Mucius" (17), *RE,* XXXI, 425–428; s.v. "Licinius" (72) *RE,* XIII, 334–338.

17. Cic. *Acad. pr.* ii.13. For the service on the agrarian commission of Ap. Claudius and P. Crassus, see Livy *Per.* lviii; Plut. *TG* 13.1, 21.1; Vell. ii.2.3; App. *BC* i.13; Auct. *Vir. Ill.* 64.4; Dessau, *ILS,* I, nos. 24 and 26.

clinations.[18] He and the two others named as drafters of the law were well suited to their job. The brothers, Scaevola and Crassus, were two of the leading legal experts of the day, and the proposal that finally emerged spoke well for their talents and their efforts, as we shall see.[19]

Carbo, Flaccus, and C. Gracchus all served on the agrarian commission that carried out the actual redistribution of the public land.[20] The persistent loyalty of the younger Gracchus requires no special explanation. There are signs that the support of Carbo and Flaccus antedated their membership on the commission. The sources attest that both belonged to the movement behind the law in the period between the deposition of Octavius and Tiberius' assassination, and their election by the People, as replacements for Tiberius and Ap. Claudius on the commission, indicates that they had worked openly for the program.[21] Finally, in a passage that appears in no way tendentious, Cicero speaks of Cato's support of the tribune, though the precise form of the support is unknown.[22]

18. See Bernstein, 'Prosopography and the Career of Publius Mucius Scaevola," pp. 43–46; Wiseman, "Note on Mucius Scaevola," pp. 152–153; contra, Gruen, "The Political Allegiance of P. Mucius Scaevola," pp. 321–332.

19. For Scaevola, see Cic. *Verr.* i.52; Cic. *Brut.* 108, 239; Cic. *Fin.* i.12; Cic. *Off.* ii.47; Cic. *Leg.* ii.47–57; Cic. *De Orat.* i.212. For Crassus, see Cic. *De Orat.* i.170, 239–240; Cic. *Brut.* 98; Pompon. *Dig.* i.2.2.40; Quint. xi.2.50; Gell. i.13.9–13.

20. For the sources on the careers of C. Papirius Carbo and M. Fulvius Flaccus see Münzer, s.v. "Papirius" (33), *RE,* XVIII, 1015–1020; s.v. "Fulvius" (58), *RE,* VII, 241–243. For their service on the agrarian commission see Livy *Per.* lix; Auct. *Vir. Ill.* 45.4; App. *BC* i.18; Vell. ii.6.4–6; Dessau, *ILS,* I, no. 25.

21. For Flaccus' previous attachment see Plut. *TG* 18.2; for Carbo's, see Cic. *Amic.* 39, 41.

22. Cic. *Amic.* 37. For the sources on the career of C. Porcius Cato see Miltner, s.v. "Porcius" (5), *RE,* XXII, 105. Plutarch (*TG* 11.1) also refers to a consular Fulvius and a consular Mallius who both appealed to Tiberius to submit his dispute with Octavius to the Senate, as, in fact, he did. This Fulvius could have been any one of four Fulvii who had held the consulship since 159. Mallius is usually identified with M'. Manilius, consul for 149 (see, for example, Fraccaro, *Studi,* p. 105; Gabba, *Appiani, Bellorum Civilium Liber Primus,* pp. 35–36), though more recently he has been identi-

Some of the ancestors of the eight men could have collaborated previously, but probably not regularly, and the evidence for any such collaboration is so tenuous as to make it irrelevant to an assessment of the motives and purposes of 133.[23] Far better evidence exists for family alliances formed for the first time in this generation. As we have seen, Tiberius had married Ap. Claudius' daughter, Claudia, and so became the son-in-law of the powerful *Princeps Senatus*. The adoption of P. Mucianus by the Licinii Crassi had established a link between them and the Mucii Scaevolae. Mucianus, in turn, married a Claudia who was probably Ap. Claudius' sister. Finally, C. Gracchus married Licinia, the daughter of Crassus and Claudia. Not all the participants named by our sources, however, shared bonds of marriage or adoption. M. Fulvius Flaccus and C. Papirius Carbo seem to have had no family connections within the group. C. Porcius Cato, a loyal supporter both of the program and of its most conspicuous proponent, was the grandson, not only of Cato the censor but also of

---

fied with A. Manlius Torquatus (Gruen, *RPCC*, p. 53; Astin, *SA*, p. 348), apparently because the consul for 149 was a friend of Scipio's (Cic. *Rep.* i.18, iii.17). Badian, however, still prefers Manilius, tentatively suggesting that the two men (M'. Manilius and a Fulvius related to M. Flaccus) were sent to Tiberius to represent both points of view in the Senate (*TGBRR*, p. 706, n. 116). The identifications are uncertain, however, and the evidence is such that neither name ought to be tied to the proposal or the proposer. Earl ("Calpurnii Pisones in the Second Century B.C.," pp. 283–298) would also like to place the consul for 133, L. Calpurnius Piso Frugi, in this group, but his argument is too speculative. Contra, see Richard, "Qualis Pater, Talis Filius," pp. 53–55, who argues, equally speculatively, that Piso is the author behind a propagandistic tradition hostile to Tiberius that appears in Livy's account of the elder Gracchus' career. Finally, Cicero writes (*Amic.* 37), "Tiberium quidem Gracchum rem publicam vexantem a Q. Tuberone aequalibusque amicis derelictum videbamus" (cf. Cic. *Brut.* 117). This need not imply that the proverbial and fanatical young Stoic (Cic. *Brut.* 117; Cic. *Mur.* 75–76; Cic. *De Orat.* ii.341, iii.87; Cic. *Off.* iii.63; Cic. *Tusc. Disp.* iv.4; Cic. *Fin.* iv.23; Cic. *Acad. pr.* ii.135; Cic. *Rep.* i.14–15; Val. Max. vii.5.1; Sen. *Epist.* xcv.72–73, xcviii.13, civ.22; cxx.19; Plut. *Luc.* 39.3) or any of his anonymous contemporaries had been sponsors or supporters of the *lex Sempronia agraria*.

23. See Earl (*Tiberius Gracchus*, pp. 8–15) for the evidence, which will not bear the weight of his prosopographical conclusions.

L. Aemilius Paullus, so that he was the nephew of Scipio Aemilianus, Ap. Claudius' archrival.

Such family ties as exist between these men do not, then, prove that they became involved in a proposal to redistribute portions of the public land solely, or even primarily, for the purpose of advancing a political coalition of which they were already members. The opposite hypothesis would be equally justified: that they supported the *lex Sempronia agraria* from pure altruism and sought their allies in the most obvious and dependable quarters. Both hypotheses would sacrifice truth for simplicity. Political advantage and the interest of the state were not then, nor are they now, always at variance for the politician.

Because C. Laelius, a political rival of Ap. Claudius, had in the preceding decade proposed a measure similar to the *lex Sempronia agraria,* some have concluded that the politicians of the day supported or opposed land reform according to the dictates of political advantage; land reform was not in itself the unifying issue for any constant group of politicians. Political rivals successively adopted schemes to relocate the displaced peasantry, but the fact may indicate rather that the problem was disruptive and threatening. Disagreement among the ruling classes would therefore center not as much on the desirability of settling the growing problem as on the appropriate and acceptable means of doing so.

Unfortunately, we have no details of Laelius' proposal to distribute lands to the dispossessed in the 140s.[24] All we know is that it provoked opposition intense enough to persuade Laelius to withdraw it. Certainly, high-quality legal minds would not have been needed to draft the *lex Sempronia agraria* of 133 had it been merely a carbon copy of Laelius' earlier effort. Alternatively, the two proposals may have distributed different holdings, in which case they would have challenged vested interests in different ways. Any distribution of land to the indigent would have cut someone's profits, so that the intensity of the opposition to a particular provision may have reflected, at least in part, the cost to the dis-

24. For Laelius' proposal see Plut. *TG* 8.4. He probably advanced it as praetor in 145 or as consul in 140. Astin (*SA,* pp. 307–310) accepts the notion that Laelius intended to distribute *ager publicus.*

senters.[25] The specifics, then, rather than the general intent of Tiberius' agrarian proposal may have been largely responsible for the determined opposition to it. Indeed, the carefully considered, moderate, and elaborate proposal that emerged in 133 may have been molded by a genuine attempt to infringe as little as possible on vested interests while providing grounds for legal justifications where infringements were unavoidable.

The list of eight names that has come down to us leads to a further complication in that we do not know what percentage it represents of the total number of senators who were in some degree committed to the law. The distinction of the names and the incompleteness of the sources make it unlikely that the list is exhaustive.[26] Such names would most probably have carried with them many of the lesser senators whom our sources, concentrating on leaders and active participants rather than passive supporters, leave unmentioned. A group of eight men whose public careers would eventually include six consulships (the only two who did not reach that office were, of course, the Gracchi themselves, who were assassinated), a censorship, two high priesthoods, and a *Princeps Senatus* sounds more like the nucleus than the whole. The eight could have been alone, but, at least at the beginning of the year, and specifically before the deposition of Octavius, many senators might have been sympathetic to the aims of the group and sufficiently impressed with the proposal advanced by Tiberius Gracchus to allow their clients to vote for it. After all, the initial movement for the law would not have appeared to contemporaries in the same light as did the phenomenon into which it was transformed after Octavius' veto: that is, a breakaway fringe group capitalizing, paradoxically, on the very economic and demographic conditions the law sought to ameliorate.

Reasons for opposing the agrarian bill, and reasons for opposing Tiberius himself after he removed from office M. Octavius, the

25. For economic arguments possibly made against the *lex Sempronia agraria* see Gabba, "Motivazioni economiche nell'opposizione alla legge agraria di Tib. Sempronio Gracco," pp. 129–138; cf. Gabba, "Studi su Dionigi D'Alicarnasso," pp. 29–41.

26. Contra, see Briscoe, "Supporters and Opponents," p. 132.

colleague who eventually vetoed the bill, would have differed. We cannot assume, therefore, that the identity or number of the dissenters remained constant. The deposition dramatically changed the issue at hand and the battle lines must have been drawn anew. Only one man definitely fought the proposal before the deposition —Octavius himself. Of course, he did not act only for himself, but exercised his right of *intercessio,* as the sources plausibly assert, on behalf of powerful men who preferred to remain in the background. Who, then, were these men? To posterity they have remained anonymous, being variously called the wealthy (οἱ πλούσιοι), the propertied (οἱ κτηματικοί), and the powerful (οἱ δυνατοί).[27] These words, while certainly not an inaccurate description of Scipio Aemilianus and his associates, do not seem a natural choice for *populares* (men who strengthened their political power by appeal to the *plebs*), who had sponsored the recent proposal for land distribution and persuaded the tribune Briso to withdraw his veto of a piece of closed ballot legislation.[28] These men, however,

----

27. For the men putting pressure on Octavius see App. *BC* i.12; Plut. *TG* 10.2, 12.3. Earl has recently argued that Octavius was working on behalf of an anti-Gracchan alliance of Octavii, Popilii, and Scipiones ("M. Octavius, trib. pleb. 133 B.C., and his Successor," pp. 657–669). His conclusion is unconvincing because it depends on some tenuous prosopographical assumptions. Boren simply assumes that the Scipionic group opposed the land law, and he presents neither argument nor evidence, although the main thesis of his article is that opposition was more the result of Tiberius' methods than of the law's provisions ("Tiberius Gracchus: The Opposition View," pp. 358–369, esp. p. 361). See also Bilz, "Die Politik des Cornelius Scipio Aemilianus," p. 66. On Octavius generally, see F. Münzer, s.v. "Octavius" (31), *RE,* XVII, 1820–1822; Drumann, *Geschichte Roms,* IV, 2d ed., 242; Fraccaro, *Studi,* pp. 93–118; Taeger, *Tiberius Gracchus,* pp. 73–86. For the language used by the sources to describe the men behind Octavius see, for example, App. *BC* i.10 (τοὺς πλουσίους); Plut. *TG* 9.3 (οἱ δὲ πλούσιοι καὶ κτηματικοί), 10.2 (πολλῶν δὲ καὶ δυνατῶν), 10.7 (οἱ κτηματικοί).

28. For Scipio as *popularis* see Astin, *SA,* pp. 26–34. For his support of the *lex Cassia* of 137, which introduced the closed ballot for all popular trials except where the charge was *perduellio,* see Cic. *Brut.* 97: "Tum L. Cassius multum potuit non eloquentia, sed dicendo tamen; homo non liberalitate, ut alii, sed ipsa tristitia et severitate popularis, cuius quidem legi tabellariae M. Antius Briso tribunus plebis diu restitit, M. Lepido consule adiuvante; eaque res P. Africano vituperationi fuit, quod eius auctoritate de

often figure as the *éminences grises* behind Octavius' determined opposition, which is interpreted in factional terms. Scipio undoubtedly would not have enjoyed the prospect of his rival, Ap. Claudius, gaining the credit for the passage of an obviously popular law, yet vetoing that law would have been an embarrassment to a man who had skillfully cultivated a popular image. How, then, can we assume that he or one of his known political allies inspired Octavius' action? Scipio himself was out of Rome for the whole of 133, besieging the hapless Numantines, so that he would have had to direct operations by remote control—not an easy feat at that time. Some of the supporters of the agrarian bill may have favored it as a way of stealing Scipio's thunder on his triumphant return from Spain, if indeed the fall of Numantia could have been anticipated in Rome at this stage. The friends of Scipio looking after his interests at home would in that case have ranged themselves with the opposition to the bill, but it does not follow that they led that opposition and that Octavius was a puppet on their string. Scipio's later denunciations of Tiberius' behavior and his intervention in 129 against the agrarian commission's activities on behalf of the Italian allies are not evidence that he persuaded Octavius to exercise his veto. Too much changed with the removal of Octavius from office, as economic self-interest was swept up in political and constitutional issues touching the interests of class and state. The deposition and Tiberius' subsequent actions must have violently affected Scipio's attitude to his brother-in-law.[29]

---

sententia deductus Briso putabatur"; Cic. *Leg.* iii.37: "nam Cassiae legis culpam Scipio tuus sustinet, quo auctore lata esse dicitur. tu si tabellariam tuleris, ipse praestabis." Badian, however, accepts the picture of Scipio as a *popularis* with reservations (*TGBRR*, p. 698) and doubts whether his persuading Marcus Antius Briso to withdraw his veto constitutes evidence that Scipio was the law's true author. Badian suggests instead that in his action Scipio was following an unwritten constitutional tradition "that the People was entitled to an unhampered power of decision" (p. 699). Scipio may have believed he had constitutional precedent on his side and still have been the bill's author, and the *De Legibus* passage seems to suggest that Scipio's involvement in the law's passage was commonly held to have been deeper than Badian allows.

29. For Scipio's attack on Tiberius' behavior see Plut. *TG* 21.4; Cic. *De Orat.* ii.106; Cic. *Mil.* 8; Livy *Per.* lix; Val. Max. vi.2.3; Vell. ii.4.4; Auct.

Finally, later hostility to Tiberius came not only from Scipio but from an enemy of Scipio, Q. Metellus Macedonicus, but no one has yet suggested that he inspired the veto.[30]

These, then, were the supporters, sympathizers, and opponents with whom Tiberius Gracchus had to deal as he strove to rebuild his reputation by promoting the *lex Sempronia agraria*. His career had suffered a near-fatal blow as a result of his well-intentioned but unfortunate involvement in the Mancinus fiasco. He had been implicated in a disgrace. Although he was legally exonerated from ultimate responsibility for the military disaster of 137, his role as negotiator of the humiliating treaty repudiated by the Senate must have damaged his chances, not just of reaching the eminent position his father had attained, but even of rapid advancement through the competitive *cursus honorum*.[31] What is more, Tiberius had blundered tactically. His conduct under stress had allowed his enemies to show him in a bad light. He had not only weakened his credentials as a fitting heir to the distinguished and previously untarnished military tradition of the Sempronii Gracchi, but he must also have made people wonder whether he had inherited the abilities of that clever politician, his father, who won two consulships and the prestigious rank of censor. Hardheaded Roman senators, scanning the ranks of the younger generation for protégés, and keeping a watchful eye on the house of Cornelia, would have been less than impressed by Tiberius' performance. Some may have excused it as appalling luck and viewed him as a victim of circumstances, but charitable indulgence of failure was not a characteristic response from Roman senators; they more probably shunned Tiberius with the politician's instinctive

---

Vir. Ill. 58.8. For his intervention on behalf of the Italian allies see App. *BC* i.19.

30. For the attack on Tiberius by Q. Metellus Macedonicus, see Cic. *Brut.* 81; cf. Plut. *TG* 14.3; Fraccaro, "Studi nell'età Graccana," pp. 335–336; Malcovati, *ORF,* 3d ed., p. 107. For the enmity between Scipio and Metellus, see Cic. *Rep.* i.31.

31. See Astin, *The Lex Annalis before Sulla,* esp. pp. 19–30, for the actual steps of the *cursus honorum* as set down by the *lex Villia Annalis* of 180.

dread of association with disgrace. This young man of the future suddenly might not have a future; the substantial political capital bequeathed to him by his father no doubt appeared poorly invested. Ap. Claudius Pulcher may have quietly rued the day he enthusiastically and proudly betrothed his daughter Claudia to the promising young augur.

Cicero observed—and many of the other ancient writers agree—that the events in Numantia in 137 and the treatment Tiberius received in Rome in 136 were responsible for his "severing himself from the lofty policy of the Fathers." [32] This assertion deserves acceptance only when sufficiently explained and with the proviso that the break did not occur in 136. Because the sources concentrated on finding an explanation for Tiberius' unprecedented later behavior, they neglected the admittedly less striking reaction to that behavior by the senators. The latter's opinions of Tiberius in 135 and 134, however, are vital for understanding his actions in 133. The Senate's coolness toward him in the preceding years must have affected his decision whether to confront the controversial question of land reform, though for reasons different from those commonly supposed.

The actions that harmed Tiberius in the Senate's eyes probably earned him popularity elsewhere. He was, after all, the savior of many Roman and allied lives. This new source of influence might offset the loss of respect of the senators if exploited to prove to them that he was still a man to be reckoned with. In 134, therefore, Tiberius had reason to feel he still had a stake in the traditional political system. We cannot assume that he sought at this stage to break away from the Senate. His present situation, the chronic economic crisis with all its political and military ramifications, his father's success with land distribution in Spain, the family's strong military tradition and sensitivity to the need for proficient legionaries all suggest that Tiberius adopted agrarian reform with a view to solving at a stroke his country's problems and his own.

If this is true, it would have been natural for him to approach

32. Cic. *Har. Resp.* 43; Cic. *Brut.* 103. See also Vell. ii.2; Quint. vii.4.13; Flor. ii.2; Dio frag. 83.2–3; Oros. v.8.3.

Ap. Claudius Pulcher, his father-in-law and the *Princeps Senatus,* with his scheme, probably not yet carefully detailed, to bring up the controversial issue once again. Tiberius' father, when tribune, had served the powerful Scipios, though he collaborated along the way in Cato's opposition to them. His performance in this office proved to be the turning point in his distinguished public career.[33] If the younger Gracchus still hoped to follow in his father's footsteps, he would have turned to Ap. Claudius instead of Scipio because, Plutarch claims, he was piqued with his brother-in-law's behavior in 136. No doubt he wanted to beat Scipio at his own game, by succeeding where the shrewd Laelius had failed. Alternatively, he may have chosen as he did simply because Africanus was abroad. At any rate, the presence of Ap. Claudius' name on Plutarch's list implies that he gave Tiberius his endorsement, however guarded it may have been. Apparently he was willing to see a second trial balloon go up, this one with his son-in-law at the end of the string.

None of this, though, makes Tiberius any more than a proposing tribune. Behind the law stood senators of senior rank and long political experience. Such men would not have involved themselves in this controversial proposal to distribute portions of public land to the poverty-stricken of the countryside merely or even mainly to boost the faltering career of a plebian tribune still in his twenties.[34] A young man who looked as though he would not scale the heights his father had reached can have been no rarity in Republican Rome. The formidable group backing this political venture would hardly have accepted Tiberius as their leader: surely he served them. Though it is probably unwise and misleading to attach a label to the group who collaborated in drafting and proposing the agrarian bill early in 133, "Claudian" is more apposite than "Gracchan," for the name of Ap. Claudius stands out as *Primus inter Pares,* at least in political influence.

The sources state that Tiberius did not draw up the law on his

33. Pace Richard, "Qualis Pater, Talis Filius," pp. 43–55.

34. Earl (*Tiberius Gracchus,* p. 15) is correct in insisting that, insofar as the bill had the backing of a formidable senatorial group, it cannot have been the work of a revolutionary tribune.

own but sought aid from two leading legal experts as well as from Appius Claudius. A major obstacle to understanding the events of 133 has been the failure to distinguish between the intent of the *lex Sempronia agaria* itself and Tiberius' intention in proposing it. If he did not devise its provisions, as may well have been the case, they cannot be used as evidence of his intentions.

The intentions of the others may not have coincided with those of Tiberius and his father-in-law, who had primarily, though not exclusively, political objectives in turning the proposal into law. As in many a political coalition, the various members may have responded to other factors. Some may have endorsed and allowed their clients to vote for the *lex Sempronia agraria* because they had the foresight to realize that land reform was desirable and necessary in the long run because it would preserve not only Rome's empire but oligarchic governance. Others may have believed that a suffering citizenry that had conquered most of the Mediterranean world for Rome and now maintained her hegemony, deserved better than it was receiving. Perhaps men like Scaevola lent their support because they believed the law regulating the possession of *ager publicus* should be enforced and obeyed. There is no evidence, but some, who had not speculated heavily in acquiring public land, may have supported or sponsored the reforms as a way of attacking enemies who had done so. Of course, some supporters may have fitted more than one of these categories. To reject such possibilities would be to oversimplify, to attribute to the senators behind the land law an unlikely unity of purpose and motivation.

It is only too easy to allow our knowledge of the events of the whole of 133 to determine our conception of Tiberius Gracchus' position early in the year. Contemporaries could hardly have discerned the future importance of this man with a short, inglorious political career; they would not have bestowed upon him the attention lavished by succeeding generations. The historian can get an accurate picture of Tiberius' position late in 134 or early in 133 only by discarding, for a moment, the often distorting lens of hindsight. To this end, let us examine the results for Tiberius' reputation with posterity had the events of 133 gone differently.

Suppose that Octavius had not vetoed Tiberius' proposal but allowed it to pass peacefully into law; that Octavius did veto the proposal but was persuaded or bullied into withdrawing his veto, as had often occurred in the past and most recently in 137 when M. Antius Briso was persuaded to withdraw his veto so that Cassius' *rogatio* became law;[35] that Octavius vetoed the proposal and remained steadfast but that Tiberius had responded by dropping the matter for the year until some other young tribune might guide the proposal through a tribunician college without a vetoing member and so through the *concilium plebis* and into law;[36] that Tiberius, after his legislative victory, had decided against attempting to set in motion the machinery that would provide him with a second tribunate, so that, in all probability, he would not have been assassinated by a senatorial mob. If any of these possible alternatives had happened, more than likely the lives of the Gracchi would not have provided material worthy of Plutarch's authorship, and Appian would have begun his account of Rome's Civil War with a later date. Tiberius might have been just another name in the consular Fasti (if even that), remembered for his association with an interesting but ultimately ineffectual law for redistributing part of the public land, a man who created a few ripples but no great splash in the flow of Roman history. Tiberius in fact made his mark on posterity because certain events in his career as tribune, and especially the end of that career, his assassination, raised crucial issues that were finally resolved only by a long and bloody revolution culminating in the establishment of a tyranny of remarkable duration. In addition, the younger brother's fate has emphasized Tiberius' own and thrown the rest of his career into sharper relief, injecting an apparent premeditation into their public actions that did not exist at the time.

---

35. Cic. *Brut.* 97. Astin (*SA*, pp. 44, 127–130) sees a growing trend of circumventing the tribune's veto and Badian (*TGBRR*, pp. 706–712) has argued that Octavius' refusal to withdraw his veto "was nothing less than a breach of all constitutional custom."

36. For a description of the means that might be employed to prevent the election of a hostile and potentially vetoing tribune to a college in any given year see Jones, "De Tribunis Plebis Reficiendis," pp. 35–39, esp. p. 37.

Only in retrospect can Tiberius be regarded as belonging to a tradition. He was not the first tribune, nor would he be the last, to propose controversial legislation on behalf of more senior and more powerful politicians. As recently as 137, L. Cassius Longinus Ravilla may have introduced some closed ballot legislation on behalf of Scipio Aemilianus, but P. Servilius Rullus is probably the most conspicuous example of the tribune introducing legislation for more powerful forces.[37] Neither Cassius nor Rullus, however, had the lineage of Tiberius Gracchus; neither was son-in-law of the *Princeps Senatus,* neither had Cornelia for a mother, and neither seems to have had Tiberius' degree of ambition. What is more, neither Cassius nor Rullus was immortalized for posterity by falling victim to political assassination at the hands of a furious mob of Roman senators.

37. Cic. *Leg. Agr.* i.22.

5 Lex Sempronia Agraria

ἅπαξ δὲ τοῖς σοφίσμασι τοῖσδε τοῦ Γρακχείου νόμου παραλυθέντος,
ἀρίστου καὶ ὠφελιμωτάτου, εἰ ἐδύνατο πραχθῆναι.
—Appian, *Bella Civilia,* i.27.123

The bill Tiberius Gracchus introduced before the popular assembly proposed to reclaim some of the lands held by the wealthy and to turn them over to the poor. Not all categories of land were to be redistributed, of course. An assault on the sanctity of private property was unthinkable in second-century Rome. The text of this new proposal concerned only public land (*ager publicus*) that was being held in excess of the allowance set by an earlier law.

Public land was originally tracts acquired by Rome during her conquest of the Italian peninsula. She punished communities that had resisted by annexing portions of their territory. Later, in the wake of victory over Hannibal, she chose a similar method of retribution against former allies who had deserted to the Carthaginians. In cases of especially stubborn and costly resistance, as well as of rebellion, the Romans usually seized a third, but sometimes half or even two-thirds, of an offending community's land. Not only did the proportion vary, but the peace treaties concluded sometimes provided for no exactions. In any case, the annexed territories were initially designated public and suffered a variety of fates.

Both citizens and allies were settled in colonies on the conquered territories, while citizens could have plots of such land assigned to them on an individual basis (*viritim adsignatus*). By the Gracchan Age substantial amounts of the public land had become the private property of these settlers. Land that had not passed into private hands belonged to the Roman state, which rented it to individuals and communities. The rent they paid (*vectigal*) entitled them to the usufruct from it, their tenure being called *possessio,* which meant that they could bequeath the land to their heirs and legally defend their title to it against all claimants save the state. In many instances the annexed territory simply changed its legal status without a concomitant change of possessor: the previous allied owners continued to cultivate, as renters, the properties they had earlier owned.[1] A significant proportion of the public land, however, came into the hands of Roman citizens in general and wealthy equestrian and senatorial entrepreneurs in particular, who exploited great chunks of it for farming and large-scale ranching.[2]

According to Livy, the famous Licinian-Sextian legislation of 367 contained a clause that regulated the use of public land, limiting to five hundred *iugera* (roughly three hundred acres) the amount any individual could legally occupy. Livy's reliability here has been questioned, and some have concluded that the limit was not imposed until the beginning of the second century.[3] Scholars

1. App. *BC* i.7; *lex agraria* of 111 in Riccobono, *FIRA*, no. 8, sec. 29. See also Pais, *Dalle guerre puniche a Cesare Augusto*, pp. 563–564; Meyer, "Untersuchungen zur Geschichte der Gracchen," pp. 403–404; Bloch and Carcopino, *Histoire Romaine*, II, 149; McDonald, "The History of Rome and Italy in the Second Century B.C.," p. 126; McDonald, "Rome and the Italian Confederacy, 200 to 186 B.C.," pp. 17–18; Göhler, *Rom und Italien*, p. 82; Afzelius, *Die römische Eroberung Italiens (340–264 v. chr.)*, pp. 313–314; Frank, "Italy," p. 336; Frank, *ESAR*, I, 124; Tibiletti, Il possesso dell' *ager publicus* e le norme *de modo agrorum* sino ai Gracchi" (1948), p. 190; Toynbee, *HL*, I, 166, II, 243–247, 546–554; Brunt, *IM*, pp. 282–283; Badian, "Roman Politics and the Italians (133–91 B.C.)," pp. 398–399.

2. Cic. *Sest.* 103; Livy xxxiii.42.10, xxxiv.4.9, xxxv.10.11; Livy *Per.* lviii; App. *BC* i.7. See also Caspari, "On Some Problems in Roman Agrarian History," p. 193; Katz, "The Gracchi: An Essay in Interpretation," pp. 77–80; Toynbee, *HL*, II, 177, 290; Brunt, *IM*, 28–29; Badian, *Publicans and Sinners*, p. 44.

3. Livy vi.35.5, 42.9–14, vii.16.9, x.13.14, xxxiv.4.9; Varro *RR* i.2.9; Val. Max. viii.6.3; Columella *De Re Rust.* i.3.11; Vell. ii.6.3; Pliny *NH* xviii.17; Plut. *Cam.* 39.5; Plut. *TG* 8; Gell. vi.3.37, xx.1.23; App. *BC* i.8–9; Auct. *Vir. Ill.* 20.3–4. Tibiletti, "Il possesso dell' *ager publicus*" (1948), has argued that the five-hundred-*iugera* limit was not set down by the *lex Licinia Sextia* but was established by a law passed sometime after the end of the Second Punic War. He alleges that Livy is unreliable for this information and that agrarian conditions at this point in the peninsula's history were inappropriate for such a prohibition (cf. Niese, "Das Sogenannte Licinisch-Sextische Ackergesetz," pp. 410–423; De Sanctis, *Storia dei Romani*, II, 203–210;

do agree that by 133 occupation of more than five hundred *iugera* of public land was prohibited by law. Precisely when violations of this law began is not clear, but we have seen how conditions in Italy immediately after Hannibal's defeat offered ideal opportunities for the wealthy speculator.[4] Arable land was abundant, yet free men available to farm it were scarce. As Rome expanded to the Greek East and the Iberian peninsula and prolonged campaigning kept the peasant from his farm, the slaves imported to Italy to fill the labor need facilitated the growth of ranches and large-scale cash-crop farming. Thereby vast amounts of land accumulated in the hands of those wealthy enough to buy slaves to exploit it. The censors, who recorded the disposition of the public lands, seem to have turned a blind eye on the enforcement of the old law in cases where the initial alternative to illegal use was unproductive neglect. In the course of time this permissive policy naturally became difficult to reverse, as past mistakes were compounded in the name of precedent and consistency. By the middle

Beloch, "Römische Geschichte bis zum Ende der Republik," p. 344; Toynbee, *HL*, II, 554–561; Boren, *The Gracchi*, p. 52). Contra, Brunt, *IM*, pp. 28–29, with n. 5, who thinks that the great estates may have been forming in the fourth century (cf. Burdese, *Studi sull' Ager Publicus*, p. 55; Pareti, *Storia di Roma*, II, 797–798).

4. In 167, Cato delivered a speech (frag. 167, Malcovati, *ORF*, 3d ed., p. 65 = Gell. vi.3.37–40) that has led some to conclude that infractions of the Licinian-Sextian legislation governing the possession of *ager publicus* were not much in evidence at this time (for example, cautiously, Earl, *Tiberius Gracchus*, p. 29, and Toynbee, *HL*, II, 555–556). Cato argues in a debate that the Rhodians, whom the Romans suspected of spiritual infidelity, should not be punished. He says that punishment should be exacted for violation, not for the wish to violate, and uses the law on the possession of *ager publicus* to exemplify his point. "Is there any law so severe as to provide that if anyone wishes to do so and so, he be fined 1,000 sesterces, provided that be less than half his property; if anyone shall desire to have more than five hundred *iugera,* let the fine be so much, if anyone shall wish to have a greater number of cattle, let the fine be thus and so. In fact, we all wish to have more, and we do so with impunity." This fragment can be read in two ways. That Cato could use such an example may indicate that his audience did not possess more public land than the law allowed. On the other hand, his words could have carried heavy irony, a reminder to his peers to cast the beam from their own eyes.

of the second century probably little public land went without a claimant. The peasants dispossessed as a result of the changing economic circumstances of the preceding fifty years could only be settled if the state reclaimed *ager publicus* for the purpose. This is what the proposed *lex Sempronia agraria* aimed to do.

A commission of three men was to be elected, probably annually, by the tribal assembly.[5] They would possess the judicial powers necessary for reclaiming the public lands being held illegally in excess of the old Licinian-Sextian allowance—though with some special concessions added. They would be empowered to redistribute the land to the indigent and landless, who would pay the state a rent for its use.[6] The rights the beneficiaries would have over the land bestowed on them were restricted by two provisions. First, the plots were to be inalienable: that is, they could not be sold by their possessors, although the law almost certainly provided that a man could bequeath them to his heirs.[7] Second, they were to be held *in possessione* rather than owned.

Inalienability was an unprecedented concept in Roman land tenure. Some Greek communities during the Hellenistic Age, however, had had recourse to the practice, and it was a feature of the famous Lycurgan system of classical Sparta, at least as Greeks of the third and second centuries envisaged it to have worked origi-

5. Cic. *Leg. Agr.* ii.31; Livy, *Per.* lviii; Val. Max. vii.2.6; Vell. ii.2.3; Plut. *TG* 13.1; App. *BC* i.9, 13. Carcopino has advanced the view (*Autour des Gracques,* chap. 4), based on App. *BC* i.9, that the commissioners were not elected annually but merely rotated their chairmanship once a year. See the reservations of Badian, "From the Gracchi to Sulla (1940–1959)," pp. 210–211; Badian, *TGBRR,* pp. 704–706; and Molthagen, "Die Durchführung der gracchischen Agrarreform," pp. 432–439.

6. For their judicial powers see Livy, *Per.* lviii; cf. Val. Max. vii.2.6. Mommsen (*Gesam. Schrift.* I, 103) in his commentary on line 14 of the *lex agraria* of 111 inferred that the Gracchan land allotments were not more than thirty *iugera* (cf. Clausing, *The Roman Colonate: The Theories of its Origins,* p. 246; Brunt, "Review of Earl, *Tiberius Gracchus,*" pp. 189–190, citing Columella, *De Re Rust.* ii.9.1 for the amount of land needed on average soil with a two-field system). Conceivably the size of the allotment granted to a poor man varied with the land's quality and the use intended for it.

7. App. *BC* i.10, 27.

nally.[8] The plausible, though unprovable, suggestion has been made that inalienability in Sparta served as the model for the drafters of the Sempronian land law.[9] Whether they borrowed the idea or developed it themselves, independent of Greek examples, the consequences of such a restriction are important.

A serious reformer, whatever his motives—social, military, or political—must have realized that inalienability protected his newly reinstated farmers (and/or clients) from again losing their lands precisely as they had before.[10] In fact, as soon as the ban on sale was removed, just over a decade later, that is exactly what happened; the lands returned to their status before 133. Appian tells us explicitly that "not long afterward [that is, after the death of Gaius Gracchus] a new law was enacted to permit the holders to sell the land about which they had quarrelled; for even this had been forbidden by the law of the elder Gracchus. At once the rich began to buy the allotments of the poor, or found pretexts for seizing them by force. So the condition of the poor became even worse than it was before." [11] Naturally, if a reformer prohibits the sale or the transfer of the land he dispenses, he does so to ensure that his beneficiaries stay out of the clutches of wealthy land speculators.

The drafters of the land law of 133 no doubt had this object in mind. They may also have abridged free right of disposal to prevent the land reform program as a whole from being undermined if the wrong kind of poor profited from the assigned allotments in an unintended way. One scholar, believing that the law was meant to benefit principally the urban plebs, considers the possibility that they might not voluntarily re-emigrate to the country, suggesting that they would nevertheless be happy to receive "something for nothing," the "something" being, of course, the sale price of the land.[12] The inalienability clause, however, would have precluded

8. See Finley, "The Alienation of Land in Ancient Greece: A Point of View," pp. 25–32; Nicolet, "L'Inspiration de Tibérius Gracchus," pp. 142–158.

9. Nicolet, "Inspiration," pp. 149–150; Badian, *TGBRR*, p. 681.

10. Brunt, "Review of Earl," pp. 189–190.   11. App. *BC* i.27.

12. Earl, *Tiberius Gracchus*, p. 42.

sale. In making the allotments inalienable, the drafters provided
the clearest bit of evidence that their bill was not merely a demagogic bid for popular endorsement. They were sincere reformers
to the extent that they intended plots to go only to those who
would farm them and therefore rejected the temptation to seek
support for their law from those who would, in fact, have received
something for nothing.

More broadly, the inalienability clause has been criticized as an
"economic absurdity" that would keep in the hands of small farmers lands that might have produced more efficiently if absorbed
into the larger farms of a wealthy estate owner. Land would be
taken from efficient farmers and given to members of the urban
proletariat, which is described as having little interest and less
experience in farming: "There is no point in forcing men to retain possession of land they have no intention of working, nor is
there any economic or moral advantage in doing so." [13] This argument depends partly on the doubtful assumption that the urban
plebs would be the law's main beneficiaries, partly on the assumption that those who did not want to farm the land would receive
plots. The latter is taken for granted despite the overwhelming
evidence that large numbers of Roman citizens strenuously supported the *lex Sempronia agraria* with its inalienability clause.
They forced its passage against fierce opposition within the Senate, deposing a tribune along the way, and many therefore ran
serious risk of economic reprisals from disgruntled *patroni*. Far
from being an economic absurdity, the inalienability clause was an
economic necessity, for the object of the total reform was to re-
establish, as permanently as possible, the rural peasantry. Citizens
who had no intention of becoming farmers had to be prevented
from profiting from the sale of their allotments, since this would
work against the interests of the state.

The proposed law's second restriction on the rights of its beneficiaries—that they could not own their plots outright—raises the
question of how it affected the position of a previously landless
peasant in the census lists, and thus his eligibility for legionary service. Would the censors register inalienable land held *in posses*-

13. Earl, *Tiberius Gracchus,* p. 37; Last, "Tiberius Gracchus," p. 20.

sione, land that could not be converted into currency, among a man's assets? If they did not, the proposed law would not change a citizen's census status or his eligibility for military service.[14] Two sections of the *lex agraria* of 111 provide the basis for the claim that it would not: one is said to indicate that only after the removal of the ban on sale did the censors register inalienable allotments (section 8), the other, that any lands with conditions still attached to them were not entered in the census at all (sections 12–13).

The first reads as follows: *CENSORQUE QUEICOMQUE ERIT FA[c]ITO, UTEI IS AGER LOCUS AEDIFICIUM, QUEI E[x hace lege priuatus factus est, ita, utei ceteri agri loca aedificia priuati, in censum referatur. . . . . . .* "The censor, whoever he may be, is to see to it that these lands, grounds and buildings which by this law have become private, are so set down in the census, just as other private lands, grounds and buildings are." This is taken to mean that all *ager publicus* that had previously been held *in possessione* was to become *ager privatus,* thus qualifying for the first time for registration by the censors. Such an interpretation of the restored Latin is improbable. From the beginning of the Republican era the censors administered the distribution of the public lands, leased *ager publicus* was called *ager censorius,* and not the praetor but the censors adjudicated disputes concerning *ager publicus.*[15] How unlikely, therefore, that the distributions of public lands went unrecorded by the censors, especially since the holders of the lands owed rents to the state. The existence of a legal maximum for holdings of *ager publicus* necessitated a record of the allocations, as the entire Sempronian land reform program would have done. The Latin quoted need not mean that the censors kept no record before the removal of the inalienability clause, but only

14. Bourne, "The Gracchan Land Law and the Census," pp. 180–182, esp. n. 10. Boren takes a similar position (*The Gracchi,* p. 47). He attempts to resolve the difficulty by assuming that these tenants of the state would eventually come to own yokes of oxen and teams of mules whose value would qualify them for legionary service.

15. Mommsen, *Röm. Staats.,* II³, 459–468; Gabba, *Appiani, Bellorum Civilium Liber Primus,* p. 13; Jhering, *Der Besitzwille,* p. 124, n. 1.

that after that the censor registered as private the lands the law of 111 made so. This in turn need not imply that such public properties had not previously counted toward a man's placement in the *comitia centuriata.* The clause could simply be guaranteeing the private ownership of these properties by recording them under the heading *ager privatus,* whereas formerly they had been placed under the category *ager publicus,* but had nonetheless counted toward a man's financial assessment for position in the census.

The second passage is invoked to support the view that lands with conditions still attached to them were not entered in the census at all: *QUEI AGER LOCUS AEDIFICIUM EI, QUEM IN [ui]ASIEIS UICANISUE EX S(ENATUS) C(ONSULTO) ESSE OPORTET OPORTEBITUE, [ita datus adsignatus relictusue est eritue . . . . . quo magis is ag]ER LOCUS AEDIFICIUM PRIUATUS SIET, QUOUE MAG[is censor, queiquomque erit, eum agrum locum in censum referat . ./. . quoue magis is ager locus aliter, atque u]TEI EST, SIET, EX H. L. N(IHILUM) R(OGATO):* "It is not intended by this law that land, grounds and buildings that have been or shall have been assigned or given or left to a person who by a *senatus consultum* is classed or will be classed as *viasiei* or *vicani,* . . . nor that the censor, whoever he shall be, should record in the census that these lands and grounds . . ." and so on. The mangled state of this passage does not provide enough interpretive leeway to justify the hypothesis of those who appeal to it. It is risky to base generalizations on what is obviously a case of special circumstances that cannot be entirely understood. As a result of the *lex agraria* of 111, many holdings of public land, perhaps including some of those tracts previously distributed by the Gracchan land commission, became the private property of their possessors. The *viasiei* or *vicani* may have been men who cared for the Roman roads in exchange for the usufruct of the public lands they held.[16] This identification, if correct, would mean that the general concession of turning public to private property with no strings attached could not have been made to them since it would have resulted in their ceasing to perform the needed

16. Hardy, *Six Roman Laws,* p. 58, n. 9. For the law of 111 in general, see Johannsen, *Die lex agraria des jahres III v. Chr. Text und Kommentar.*

public service. Their exclusion, however, does not mean that at all times all lands that fell short of absolute ownership were not registered in the census. If the broken lines of the stone tell us anything, it is not that the *ager publicus* of the *viasiei* or *vicani* would go unregistered in the census, but only that it would not be registered in the column headed *"ager privatus"*—(*utei ceteri agri loca aedificia privati, in censum referatur . .*).

Another problem arises if it is supposed that the acquisition of public land would have no effect on a man's standing in the *comitia centuriata*. What Tiberius Gracchus is reported as telling his contemporaries about the military benefits of his *rogatio* if passed into law—that it would generate the manpower the legions needed to maintain and extend empire—must have fallen upon their ears as rank nonsense.[17] For this reason alone the hypothesis must be rejected.

It leads, however, to further complications. An interesting legal device for draft-dodging emerges. A man could remain comfortable by living off the fat of the public land he possessed while avoiding the accumulation, or divesting himself, of private land. Thus he could avoid legionary service abroad, a considerable burden in Rome in these decades. How likely is it that a Roman citizen ever had such an option? Finally, a man's property qualification was recorded, not in *iugera,* but in *asses.*[18] Would not the estimated value of the usufruct of the public land he held be included in that reckoning?

The remaining provisions of Tiberius' proposal (*rogatio*) have to be reconstructed from scattered references in the ancient corpus, since there is no text of them in the extant literary or epigraphical sources. We know that the initial *rogatio* reinforced the clauses of an earlier law that limited the use of public land, while granting new concessions in such use.

The most important and the most generous of the concessions allowed the possessor an additional two hundred and fifty *iugera* of public land for each child (male or female). He would be per-

17. Bourne, "The Gracchan Land Law and the Census," pp. 180–182, esp. n. 10; see n. 14 above. App. *BC* i.11; cf. Plut. *TG* 9.5.
18. Polyb. vi.19.2; Cic. *Rep.* ii.40; Livy i.43.8.

mitted to retain this amount above the previous, statutory five-hundred-*iugera* limit.[19] The rationale, perhaps even the necessity, for this concession can be inferred from an ancient tradition that describes the way the Licinian-Sextian law was customarily violated. The story, ironic and so perhaps apocryphal, relates how C. Licinius Stolo, one of the law's two proposers, was the first man tried and convicted for violating his own law: hoist, as the sources delight in remarking, with his own demagogic petard. He allegedly attempted to skirt the five-hundred-*iugera* limit on the possession of *ager publicus* by emancipating his son and registering a second five hundred *iugera* in his name.[20] The story reveals, as might have been suspected, that placing children *sui iuris* and putting excess amounts of public land in their names was a possible method of accumulating more public land than the law allowed. If Stolo was convicted, it proves that his law had anticipated this obvious loophole; if the story is apocryphal, it must derive its point from the later passage of special legislation closing the loophole Stolo's law had failed to foresee. Whatever the case, the expedient of *emancipatio* cannot have been entirely satisfactory since it deprived the son of all rights of succession. We learn, nevertheless, independent of the Stolo tradition, that transferring illegal holdings of *ager publicus* to one's relatives was a common device for evading the restrictive legislation.[21] Through the child allowance, the *paterfamilias* would be able to retain the title of some land in excess of the previous maximum, rather than have to relinquish it to

19. The two-hundred-fifty-*iugera* child allowance is mentioned only by Appian (*BC* i.9, 11), but there is no cause to doubt his testimony on this detail. Earl (*Tiberius Gracchus,* pp. 15–19) has shown that the concession probably applied to daughters as well as to sons and that there is no good reason for believing that a *paterfamilias* could claim only two such allowances, to a total of one thousand *iugera* possessed in all (following Badian, "From the Gracchi to Sulla," p. 210 with n. 52). See also Badian, *TGBRR,* pp. 702–703. Contra, but unconvincingly, see Molthagen, "Die Durchführung der gracchischen Agrarreform," p. 423, n. 5.

20. Livy vii.16.9 (the year is 357); Dion. Hal. xiv.12; Columella *De Re Rust.* i.3.11; Val. Max viii.6.3; Pliny *NH* xviii.17; Plut. *Cam.* 39.5; Auct. *Vir. Ill.* 20.3–4.

21. Appian, *BC* i.8; cf. Plut. *TG* 8.3.

his children. This would be a remarkable concession. It would legally entitle a wealthy family with, for example, four children, to the usufruct of fifteen hundred *iugera* (almost a thousand acres) of public land. The head of a really large family—one as large as that of Tiberius Gracchus the Elder had all his twelve children survived—could, under this new law, have laid legal claim to the possession of three and a half thousand *iugera* (well over two thousand acres). These figures, moreover, would have represented only the amount of public land a man could possess in addition to lands he owned privately. This new concession would not only relieve some of the violators of the law of the need to use the unhappy device of *emancipatio,* but might also supply an incentive for the procreation of upper-class children.[22] Most important, the new allowance should mean that many of those who had exceeded the legal limit in their accumulation of public land would find little or nothing economically objectionable in this most recent attempt at land reform.

By a second concession, public land that the *possessores* would now hold legally would be given a good title. Even those who expected to lose some land if Tiberius' proposal became law might have felt adequately reimbursed by receiving a clear title to much of what had not been legally theirs before. A third concession awarded some sort of compensation (τιμή) for any excess land reclaimed by the state.[23]

The *rogatio* aimed to ease even further the pain its main provisions would cause, this time by exempting the public land of the *ager Campanus* from reclamation and redistribution.[24] This final concession in effect winked at violators of the law who had confined their activities to land in Campania. Obviously, this provision too would diminish opposition to the bill's passage from senators and their wealthy entrepreneurial clients, and it deserves more attention than it usually receives.

22. For the speech of Q. Caecilius Metellus Macedonicus, censor in 131, to the Senate, urging compulsory marriage in order to produce children, see Livy *Per.* 59; Suet. *Aug.* 89.

23. Plut. *TG* 9.2; App. *BC* i.11.

24. Cic. *Leg. Agr.* i.21, ii.81; cf. Cic. *ad Att.* i.19.4, ii.16.

Rome had acquired northwest Campania at the end of the third century by confiscating the territories of the Capuans, Atellani, Calatini, and Sabatini who had seceded from her during the Hannibalic War.[25] A part of the region, especially the lowlands, would have been suitable and so may have been used for pasturing the livestock of neighboring Lucania in the winter.[26] In 162 the Roman government surveyed some fifty thousand *iugera* of the *ager Campanus'* public land and apportioned it in individual (*viritane*) allotments to small farmers who paid a rent on it and who may have used it for grain cultivation.[27] The Campanian coastline became the favorite site for the luxury villas of the Roman aristocracy, some of which may not have had farms attached.[28] In addition, Campania, as one of the most fertile areas in the peninsula, close to Italy's busiest harbors, provided ideal conditions for the rapid development of the new cash-crop plantations and the export of their produce. Indeed, it forms the background for the discussion in Cato's *De Agri Cultura* of farming the olive and the vine. The *ager publicus* of Campania had therefore become a natural and popular region for entrepreneurs looking for investments. That proportion of it, maybe even forming the major part, not distributed to small farmers for grain cultivation and not belonging to luxury estates, was probably exploited by affluent absentee landlords who cultivated the vine and the olive on the scale and in the manner described by Cato.[29]

In view of such conditions, a *paterfamilias* who might retain, in addition to his private estates, all the *ager publicus* he held in the *ager Campanus,* along with a fixed five-hundred-*iugera* allotment

25. Livy xxvi.16.5–13, 34.1–13.   26. Toynbee, *HL,* II, 228–229.

27. Gran. Lic., p. 9; cf. Livy xli.27.5–13, xlii.1.6, 8.4, 9.7, 19.1–3.

28. See D'Arms, *Romans on the Bay of Naples,* pp. 1–17, esp. pp. 9f.

29. See Yeo, "The Economics of Roman and American Slavery," pp. 445–446, with nn. 60 and 61. On the fertility of the *ager Campanus* see Cic. *Leg. Agr.* ii.76; Strabo v.4.3; Pliny *NH* xviii.110–114; Beloch, *Campanien,* pp. 33–34; Last, "Tiberius Gracchus," pp. 4–5; Frank, *ESAR,* V, 129–135; Toynbee, *HL,* II, 228–229. For the accessibility of good harbors see Polyb. iii.91; Scalais, "Les revenues que les Romains attendaient de l'agriculture," p. 97; Warmington, *The Commerce between the Roman Empire and India,* pp. 4, 265–266.

and two hundred and fifty *iugera* for each of his children, could continue in impressive prosperity and conceivably give up to the reclaiming commissioners little, if any, of the public land he had previously possessed illegally.

The political advantage to be gained from thinning the ranks of the likely opposition cannot be doubted, but these concessions hint at a possible object of the *rogatio* as a whole that cannot be proved, but has important implications if it is correct. Some scholars have believed that the proposal Tiberius Gracchus brought before the *concilium plebis* sought to reclaim productive farmlands for redistribution, and therefore was aimed directly or indirectly at breaking up Italy's flourishing *latifundia*. As previously noted in another context, the *rogatio* has been criticized as a solution for the peninsula's agrarian crisis on the grounds that little advantage was to be gained from taking land away from efficient farmers and returning it to peasants who had already proved themselves incapable, not only of competing successfully, but of surviving in the new economic circumstances of second-century Italy. If, however, the *rogatio* were intended to break up the *latifundia,* why would it simultaneously by special concession exempt that area of the peninsula where plantation farming had probably spread most widely and allow wealthy landowners to retain enough public land to make up several medium-sized plantations such as Cato describes?

The concessions, then, indicate that the proposal did not seek to reclaim public land on which the absentee landlords had their plantations. Its main target must have been acreage currently being used by wealthy ranchers for grazing their enormous herds, but which contemporaries believed, as we shall see, could be converted to arable farmland.[30] The construction of the proposal, and particularly the concessions it makes, certainly point in that direction.

The famous *elogium* discovered at Polla in Lucania strengthens this hypothesis about the law's intent. The inscription, set up a few

30. For the convertibility of pasture lands to farm see Brunt, *IM,* p. 318. White, "Latifundia," p. 75, sees difficulties in such a conversion, but cf. Badian, *TGBRR,* p. 72, n. 102. See Dessau, *ILS,* no. 23.

years after the assassination of Tiberius Gracchus but referring to activities begun in 132, proclaims that its author was "the first to cause grazers to give way to farmers on the public lands" (*primus fecei, ut de agro poplico aratoribus cederent paastores*).[31] The stated intention of the anonymous author, whether he was the praetor for 131 (consul for 128), T. Annius Rufus, or, less probably, the consul for 132, P. Popillius Laenas, is not, in itself, a sure guide to the objectives of the proposal for the agrarian law of 133, but there are reasons to associate the two.[32] Both the *rogatio* and the inscription deal specifically with taking public land away from some people who must have been extremely wealthly in order to bestow it on others who were probably quite poor. The stone's closeness in date to Tiberius' tribunate indicates that at least some among those who sought, or wished to appear to seek, ways of ameliorating the plight of Italy's citizen peasantry believed, right or wrong, that reclaiming arable pasture lands and giving them to the small farmer was a practicable and economically feasible way of returning him to the land. The boast of the stone's author that he was *primus* in implementing such a policy points to, though, of course, it does not demonstrate, a connection with the activities of the Gracchan land commission, the most likely candidate for the implied *secundus*. The individual and the group may have operated with similiar designs and similar methods.

The difficulties apparent in the actual implementation of the *lex Sempronia agraria* lead to the conclusion that the commissioners would have focused primarily on pasture lands. When colonies were founded, the job of distribution was relatively straightforward. The agrarian commissioners simply went to the site to be settled, surveyed it, marked its boundaries, centuriated the area,

---

31. Dessau, *ILS*, no. 23 = Degrassi, *ILLRP*, no. 454.

32. For P. Popillius Laenas see *CIL*, I, 154–155; Degrassi, "Un nuovo miliario calabro della *Via Popillia* e la *Via Annia* del Veneto," pp. 259–265; Hinrichs, "Der römische Strassenbau zur zeit der Gracchen," pp. 162–176; Hinrichs, "Nochmals zur Inschrift von Polla," pp. 251–255. For T. Annius Rufus see the arguments of Wiseman, *"Viae Anniae,"* pp. 21–37; Wiseman, *"Viae Anniae* Again," pp. 82–91. Bracco, "L'Elogium di Polla," pp. 5–38, has suggested T. Annius Luscus, consul in 153.

and then assigned the plots.[33] The Gracchan commissioners should have tried to duplicate this colonial process as far as possible, for the sake of both simplicity and efficiency. To do so would have meant searching for sites on which a single violator, or a group of violators, laid claim to far more land than the *lex Sempronia agraria,* with all its concessions, allowed. Even relatively large *latifundia* of hundreds of acres might not have yielded enough public land to make the surveying done worth the effort. Many wealthy *possessores,* of course, could have had their considerable holdings scattered about on several tracts of *ager publicus,* but in such cases all the tracts would have to be surveyed before very much of any one of them was shown to be held in gross violation of the law. It would be much simpler to concentrate on large ranches of many thousands of arable acres so that the amount of public land held in excess could be ascertained quickly and redistribution be carried out on the spot.

Finally, there remains the most crucial and controversial of the *lex Sempronia agraria*'s possible provisions: was it to benefit Roman citizens alone or Italians as well? [34] The conclusion that in

33. See Salmon, *Roman Colonization under the Republic,* p. 19; Dilke, *The Roman Land Surveyors, An Introduction to the Agrimensores,* pp. 35–36, 51, 63, 105–106, 112.

34. Among those who believe that the Italian allies were included as beneficiaries of Tiberius' land law see: Mommsen, *Röm. Gesch.* II, iii, 86; Greenidge, *A History of Rome, 133–104 B.C.,* p. 115; Meyer, "Untersuchungen zur Geschichte der Gracchan," p. 405; Taeger, *Tiberius Gracchus,* pp. 13–14; Göhler, *Rom und Italien,* pp. 81–83, 145, 158, 161, 174, 203; Shochat, "The Lex Agraria of 133 B.C. and the Italian Allies," pp. 25–45. Among those who believe they were not so included see Beloch, *Der italische Bund unter Roms Hegemonie,* p. 219; Holmes, *The Roman Republic,* I, 15; Kontchalovsky, "Recherches sur l'histoire du mouvement agraire des Gracques," p. 179; Carcopino, *Autour des Gracques,* p. 83; Zancan, *Ager Publicus,* p. 86; Bloch and Carcopino, *Histoire Romaine,* II, 234; Marsh, *A History of the Roman World, 146–30 B.C.,* p. 35; Cardinali, *Studi Graccani,* pp. 169–172; Badian, *FC,* pp. 169–173; Gelzer, "Review of Taeger, *Tiberius Gracchus,*" pp. 298–301; Scullard, *From the Gracchi to Nero,* p. 27; Earl, *Tiberius Gracchus,* pp. 20–23; Nagle, "The Failure of the Roman Political Process in 133 B.C." (1970), pp. 373–379; Badian, *TGBRR,* pp. 701–702; Molthagen, "Die Durchführung der gracchischen Agrarreform," p. 430.

the end only Romans received plots of land is more likely than the conclusion that only they were intended to.[35]

The apparent evidence for the inclusion of non-Roman Italians among the intended beneficiaries of the law occurs in Appian. Several times in his account of the social and economic conditions that led to the legislation of Tiberius Gracchus' tribunate, he says that a central element in the second-century agrarian crisis was the gradual economic and numerical decline of farmers who were poor Italians ('Ιταλιῶται).[36] Appian, moreover, unmistakably believes that the *lex Sempronia agraria* was drafted with an eye to helping these aggrieved allies. Specifically, he writes that "Tiberius Sempronius Gracchus . . . delivered an eloquent speech concerning the Italian people (περὶ τοῦ 'Ιταλικοῦ γένους), lamenting that a people so valiant in war and related in blood to the Romans were declining little by little into pauperism and paucity of numbers without any hope of remedy" [37] (Loeb translation, slightly modified). Any attempt to argue that Italians were excluded from the provisions of the land law of 133 must, therefore, discredit or discount Appian.

Such attempts have been largely unconvincing. We know that Appian was an Alexandrian who wrote his *Histories* in the second century A.D., long after the events he describes in his *Civil Wars*. As a provincial he might naturally evince a special interest in Rome's treatment of her subject peoples. Such an interest could partially account for his inclusion of and great emphasis upon the Italians as the law's beneficiaries, but his particular interest hardly constitutes grounds for rejecting his information.[38] One study has

35. Shochat, "Lex Agraria," pp. 42–44, points out that Appian (i.19) believed that, in the end, the allies did not benefit from the land reform. He explains this disparity by supposing that their exclusion does not illustrate the tribune's intentions but rather the policy of the Senate, which directed the land commission's activities. See App. *BC* i.21.86–88.

36. App. *BC* i.7.   37. App. *BC* i.9.

38. For the view that Asinius Pollio was Appian's source for the period down to and including the Social War, and was therefore responsible for Appian's emphasis on the Italians, see Gabba, *Appiano e la storia delle guerre civili*. Contra, see Cuff, "Prolegomena to a Critical Edition of Appian, B.C. I," pp. 177–188, esp. p. 188.

demonstrated that Appian did not confuse Roman citizens and ᾽Ιταλιῶται and that when he discusses the beneficiaries of Tiberius' law, he refers initially to the Italians. The same study further shows that Appian was not the devoted Italophile that some of his detractors have discerned. Only in the First and Fifth books of his *Civil Wars* does he pay special attention to the Italians, and then quite properly, because of the decisive role he reasonably believes them to have played in bringing about the Civil War.[39] The speech he puts into the mouth of Tiberius Gracchus, therefore, should not be discounted: it could have a firm historical basis. This would mean that the rationale the speech seems to be providing could have been required by a provision in the tribune's *rogatio,* or at least in its original version, giving land to Italians. Such a provision would certainly fit the military purpose of the law, since the Italians constituted a large proportion of Rome's army. Subsequent evidence demonstrating that the Italians did not receive allotments cannot be used as proof that they were never meant to.

The main point against Appian is that Plutarch does not mention Italians anywhere in his account of the land law of 133 or in his description of its beneficiaries. If his work alone survived for the events of this year, none but Roman citizens would appear to have received, or to have been meant to receive, land allotments. Similarly, however, with Plutarch as our sole source we would not know that Italians and not just Romans could legally possess *ager publicus,* and we would have to infer, against the clear implications of other testimony in the biography, that Italian as well as Roman peasants suffered dislocation and depletion because of the changing economic conditions of second-century Italy.[40] The argument from silence on its own ought not to be pushed too hard in the case of Plutarch's omitting to list the Italians as beneficiaries of the law. The patent discrepancy between the accounts of the two major

39. For Appian's correct understanding of the distinction between Romans and Italians, see Cuff, "Prolegomena," p. 181; Shochat, "Lex Agraria," pp. 40–41. Contra, see Kontchalovsky, "Recherches," pp. 162–179. On his emphasis on the Italian allies in *BC* i and v and his reason for it, see Cuff, "Prolegomena," pp. 184–188.

40. Shochat, "Lex Agraria," pp. 25–45, esp. pp. 32–39. Cf. Flor. ii.1.1.

sources for Tiberius' tribunate nevertheless presents a major problem, aggravated by the strong possibility that both authors may
have had the same source for their descriptions of the social and
economic backgrounds to the events of 133.[41] Why, then, did one
writer choose to emphasize the Italians, while the other ignored
them?

Two attempts have been made to solve the problem, using dia-
metrically opposed expedients.[42] One supposes that whenever Appian's source saw the word "Romans" in the original source he
was following, he simply substituted the word "Italians" in his own
text; Appian then copied him.[43] The other claims that Plutarch,
though necessarily aware of the pan-Italic tradition that Appian
faithfully and properly reproduced, deliberately excised it from
his own account of Tiberius' reforms.[44] Neither version produces
a motive for what are taken to be the deliberate changes. The arguments in both cases deserve careful scrutiny.

The substitution theory, advanced by D. Brendan Nagle, holds
that Italians were included as beneficiaries of the land law of 133
for political rather than military or socioeconomic reasons. Since
poor Italian farmers must have made up a considerable proportion
of the total Roman fighting force, a serious military or social reformer might well have viewed their plight—at least as dismal as
that of the poor Roman farmers—with alarm. In Nagle's opinion,
however, the drafters of the *lex Sempronia agraria* were not concerned as much with soldiers and suffering as with voters. Since
Italians did not have the full franchise, they would be unable to
demonstrate their gratitude to their benefactors tangibly by their
behavior in the Roman assemblies. They were, therefore, excluded
from the bill's benefits. Nagle asserts at the same time, however,
that Latins probably were included among the law's beneficiaries

41. Peter, *Die Quellen Plutarchs in den Biographieen der Römer*, pp. 93–
100; Meyer, "Untersuchungen zur Geschichte der Gracchen," p. 397;
Cardinali, *Studi Graccani*, p. 70.
    42. Shochat, "Lex Agraria," and Nagle, "Failure of the Roman Political
Process" (1970) and (1971), respectively.
    43. Nagle, "Failure of the Roman Political Process" (1971), p. 375.
    44. Schochat, "Lex Agraria," pp. 34–39.

because they could cast ballots, if not in the centuriate, at least in the tribal assembly, and that the reformers would have considered them potential clients.[45]

There are drawbacks to this part of Nagle's argument. He neglects the fact that all Latins voted in a single tribe of the *comitia tributa,* to which they were assigned by lot on an ad hoc basis, an arrangement that minimized the political effect of their gratitude.[46] For this reason, and in view of his assumptions about the legislators' motives, the difference in political status between Latins and Italians does not warrant the difference in treatment of the two groups that Nagle hypothesizes.

He then advances two further arguments, based on Appian's text, to support his verdict that that ancient author's testimony for the inclusion of the Italians in the land law is not to be believed.[47] First, at two points (*BC* i.7.27, i.18.74–76) Appian clearly asserts that the allies were allowed by law to occupy the fallow and unassigned portions of the public land: only the centuriated and apportioned sections of it were reserved exclusively for Roman citizens. In another passage, however (*BC* i.35.162), Appian reverses himself completely, according to Nagle, for he speaks of Italians who illegally cultivated undivided sections of the public lands. Nagle resolves this assumed contradiction by suggesting the substitution device.

Appian does indeed say (*BC* i.7.27) that, while some of the public land the Romans acquired by conquest was assigned to colonists, the majority of it, desolated by war and lying fallow, could be used by anyone who was willing to exploit it, provided he pay a toll of the yearly crops. Those who used it for grazing their flocks also had to pay a toll of the animals. Appian makes it quite clear here that he is referring to Italians, for he explains that the Romans followed these procedures "in order to multiply the Italian race, which they considered the most laborious of peoples, so that they might have plenty of allies at home" (App. *BC* i.7.) Again,

45. Nagle, "Failure of the Roman Political Process" (1971), p. 378.
46. Dion. Hal. viii.72.4; Livy xxv.3.16. See also Sherwin-White, *The Roman Citizenship,* pp. 35, 112; Taylor, *RVA,* pp. 70, 79.
47. Nagle, "Failure of the Roman Political Process" (1971), p. 375.

when discussing the activities of the agrarian commission established by the land law of 133, Appian writes (*BC* i.18.74–76) that "the original proclamation authorized anybody to work the undistributed land who wished to do so." This surely refers, as Nagle asserts, to Italians, for he immediately goes on to associate this past Roman policy with the complaints of the Italian allies (οἱ Ἰταλιῶται) to Scipio Aemilianus in 129 that their lands were being interfered with (*BC* i.19.78). Later in his work, in reference to the legislative activities of Livius Drusus the younger in 91, Appian says, "Even the Italians, in whose special interest Drusus was devising these plans, were apprehensive about the law providing for the colonies, because they thought that the Roman public domain which was still undivided and which they were cultivating, some by force and others clandestinely, would at once be taken away from them" (*BC* i.36.162).

As we have seen, Nagle concludes from these three passages that Appian is guilty of a simple contradiction, of claiming that the Italians could legally occupy unassigned public land and in the final passage that they could not. The conclusion is unwarranted, for the third passage cited states only that in 91 some Italians were cultivating public lands illegally, so that they feared detection of their activities and that their illegal acquisitions would be taken from them. To say that some Italians cultivated unassigned public land illegally is hardly to say that it was illegal for Italians to cultivate unassigned public land. Only the latter proposition would produce the contradiction Nagle claims to have found, but Appian never makes such a statement. We know, of course, that by 133 some Romans cultivated public land illegally, but no one would wish to claim on this basis that Romans were not entitled to occupy *ager publicus*.

In fact, the violators of the Roman public domains to whom Appian refers here are almost certainly not poor Italian peasants. Rather, they are the allied counterparts of the Roman large landowners—influential and wealthy Italians, whose crime would probably not have been, as Nagle infers, merely possessing Roman public land. More likely they held too much of it or violated in some other way the existing statutes governing and limiting its use. Certainly the Italian peasant suffered the same social and economic hardships as the Roman. Wealthy allies with capital to invest would have taken advantage of the opportunities for land speculation exploited by Romans in the half-century or so preceding Tiberius' tribunate. In 129, Scipio Aemilianus intervened, on behalf of the Italians, we are told, to curtail the activities of the Gracchan land commission. He was hardly acting at the behest of Italian peasants; more likely, the call came from wealthy allied clients of his whose lands were being threatened.[48] In any case, the land commission, two of whose members soon showed themselves committed to citizenship for the Italians, surely would not choose to attack the Italian poor by reclaiming the meager holdings of *ager publicus* to which they were already legally entitled. Indeed, Scipio's intervention on the Italians' behalf, if successful, probably provided wealthy allied landholders with the shelter they feared would be removed by Drusus' plans to found colonies in 91. The texts Nagle cites indicate that when Appian wrote of Italian holdings of *ager publicus* he had wealthy Italians in mind. He speaks first (*BC* i.7.27) of grazers, men who "kept flocks . . . both of oxen and of small cattle," and in his discussion of Scipio's intervention on the Italians' behalf (*BC* i.18.74–76) he specifically refers to "the injustice done by the rich [Italians]." Finally, in connection with the allies' apprehension about Drusus' activities (*BC* i.35.162), Appian speaks of lands that have been taken by force, therefore taken presumably by men wealthy enough to wield force, rather than poor enough to be its victims. Thus, the contradiction Nagle believes he has discovered in the pages of Appian's *Civil Wars* disappears, and the need for his expedient of reading "Romans" for "Italians" vanishes with it.

Nagle's other argument for not trusting Appian on the inclusion of the Italians depends on the historian's statement (*BC* i.7.30) that the Italians were ruined by poverty, taxes (εἰσφορά), and military service. Nagle identifies the εἰσφορά of this passage with the

48. See Astin, *SA*, p. 238; Molthagen, "Die Durchführung der gracchischen Agrarreform," pp. 429–430.

personal property tax, *tributum,* abolished in 167, that was exacted from Roman citizens; Latins and Italians were never subject to it. He therefore sees this complaint, put into the mouths of Italians by Appian but historically appropriate to Roman mouths alone, as further evidence for the substitution expedient. If the identification of *eisphora* with the *tributum* is correct, is it not odd that Appian should single out a tax defunct for thirty-four years as one of the main causes of the Italians' poverty? In fact, the *eisphora* to which Appian refers might be the *tributa* paid by the Italians, not to the Roman state, but to their own communities, taxes that were still being levied in 133 but go unrecorded in our Roman sources. Even if Nagle is correct and Appian in error, the mistake hardly justifies as sweeping a substitution as Nagle proposes, particularly since an Egyptian provincial writing in the second century might easily lapse into such a mistake.[49]

The second explanation of the discrepancy between the accounts of Appian and Plutarch is that of Yanir Shochat. According to his theory, Plutarch's silence concerning the allies in his biography of Tiberius Gracchus is so unlikely that it can reflect only deliberate omission of the pan-Italic tradition, which Shochat believes was present in at least one of Plutarch's sources.[50] Shochat thinks this omission is betrayed by Plutarch's careful selection from and consequent distortion of the information the source materials provide. Where this happens, Shochat discerns traces of the pan-Italic tradition.

Specifically, he points to the passage in which Plutarch writes (*TG* 8.3) "that soon all Italy was conscious of a dearth of freemen [ἐλευθέρων], and was filled with gangs of foreign slaves by whose aid the rich cultivated their estates, from which they had driven away free citizens [πολίτας]." This sentence, he argues, contains a revealing non sequitur. Plutarch initially contrasts free men and slaves; free men were not only Roman citizens but certainly included Italians as well. The last clause of the sentence, therefore,

---

49. The *tributum* (εἰσφορά) was paid by all inhabitants of the provinces, whether Roman citizens or not, provided their communities had not been granted *ius Italicum.*

50. Shochat, "Lex Agraria," pp. 34–39.

which speaks of Roman citizens only, does not follow logically from the first point and inappropriately narrows what must have been also an Italian group into one exclusively Roman. Shochat maintains that the last words of Plutarch's sentence are superfluous and that they did not appear in the original version from which the rest of the sentence was copied; that version was pan-Italic for it spoke properly of free men, both Romans and Italians, but to it Plutarch appended the phrase about citizens being driven off the lands, in order to be consistent with his earlier description of Tiberius' reforms as directed at Rome rather than at Italy.

He makes a similar historical distortion, Shochat says, in his treatment of Tiberius' famous vote speech. Here he again glosses over the pan-Italic disposition of his source. Shochat assumes that Appian and Plutarch are quoting from the same speech, which both present as intended to obtain the people's approval of the proposed law. Their manner of presentation differs, however. Appian provides the gist of the speech; Plutarch quotes but a single, eloquent sentence from it. Shochat sees in this Plutarch's extreme selectivity, for the contents of the speech Appian provides reveal just how Plutarch omits anything at variance with his account of the intended beneficiaries of the *lex Sempronia agraria*. In addition, the portion of the speech Plutarch quotes is internally inconsistent, further evidence that the biographer knew but glossed over the pan-Italic tradition. Its beginning refers to "those who fought for Italy"—a phrase that has to include Italians—while at its end Plutarch makes these fighters "Romans" (τοσούτων Ῥωμαίων), though we, of course, know that they were not Romans only.

This second theory, attempting to discredit Plutarch rather than Appian, is flawed by a central omission. It does not take into account the fact that Appian presents not one but two speeches by Tiberius on behalf of his land law and that the two have decidedly different slants.[51] The disparity between them affects any conclu-

51. This discrepancy was first pointed out to me by the late C. E. Stevens, sometime Fellow of Magdalen College, Oxford. I owe to him the whole idea that Tiberius may have, at first, included the Italians as beneficiaries but subsequently excluded them for political reasons. Most of the supporting arguments for this interpretation are mine, however, and it should not be supposed that Stevens would have agreed with all or any of them.

sion about Plutarch's testimony and indeed about the whole Italian question.

In the first speech in Appian (at *BC* i.9), delivered at the first assembly, Tiberius speaks specifically of the Italians who desperately needed, and would benefit greatly from, his land law. In the second, however (at *BC* i.11), delivered, according to Appian, just before the first vote on the bill was due, Tiberius is conspicuously silent on the Italian question, making no clear mention of the allies at all. The speech runs as follows:

> When the time for voting came he advanced many other arguments at considerable length and also asked them whether it was not just that the common property be divided in common [τὰ κοινὰ κοινῇ διανέμεσθαι]; whether a citizen [ὁ πολίτης] was not worthy of more consideration at all times than a slave [θεράπων]; whether a man who served in the army [ὁ στρατιώτης] was not more useful than one who did not; and whether one who had a share in the country [ὁ κοινωνός] was not more likely to be devoted to the public interests. He did not dwell long on this comparison [between citizens and slaves] which he considered degrading but proceeded at once to a review of their hopes and fears for the country, saying that they possessed most of their territory by conquest, and that they had hopes of occupying the rest of the habitable world; but now the question of greatest hazard was whether they should gain the rest by having sufficient manpower, or whether, through weakness and jealousy their enemies should take away what they already possessed. After exaggerating the glory and riches on one side and the danger and fear on the other, he admonished the rich to take heed, and said that for the realization of these hopes they ought to bestow this very land as a free gift, if necessary, on men who would rear children, and not, by contending about small things, overlook larger ones. (Loeb translation, slightly modified.)

Not only does this second speech not mention Italians, but Appian, too, makes the linguistic transpositions that Shochat took to invalidate Plutarch's testimony. Specifically, when Appian is presenting Tiberius' view of the deserts of a slave (θεράπων), he contrasts him not with a free man, which term would, of course, have included the Italians, but rather, as Plutarch does, with a citizen. Both authors use the word πολίτης. Moreover, when Appian has

Tiberius speak of the man who fights for Italy (ὁ στρατιώτης), the Italian never enters the picture. Appian puts Tiberius' plea that something be done for such a man in the context of an enumeration of the advantages of treating citizens well; the implied contrast here is, as it was in Plutarch, the slave. Appian's source, at least as regards his version of the vote speech, has a good deal in common with Plutarch's. What is more, to posit distortion of the source by either Appian or Plutarch would involve the unlikely coincidence of both having chosen to distort in the same way—or collusion. The discrepancy to be reconciled, therefore, lies not as much between Plutarch and Appian as between Plutarch's narrative and Appian's second speech, on the one hand, and Appian's first speech, on the other.

Tiberius' curious failure to mention the allies in his second speech as reported by Appian requires special explanation, particularly in light of the emphasis on the Italians in the other speech only two paragraphs earlier. A historical rather than a linguistic hypothesis solves the problem.

The first oration argued on behalf of a provision in the original *rogatio* stipulating that Italians were to be included as beneficiaries. Such a clause could not avoid being controversial—unpopular with the masses of Roman citizens upon whom Tiberius Gracchus would have to call to vote the bill into law. Not only would it leave less land for them, but it might also have offended their long-nourished prejudices against a group they considered inferior to themselves. This first speech would therefore have needed to make a special defense of the provision including the Italians. Apparently, the plea did not succeed as hoped, since his later speech says nothing of the matter. Either the tribune now thought it impolitic even to mention that the bill would benefit Italians as well as Roman citizens, or, more probably, he had by then dropped the provision from his *rogatio* altogether.

The first alternative looks too clumsy politically. Once it was widely known that the *lex Sempronia agraria* would benefit Italians no less than Romans, the opponents of the bill would rush to exploit and attack this unpopular provision. Almost certainly, if the bill still contained the provision when the final speeches were given before the voters in the *concilium plebis,* someone would have attacked it and Tiberius would have had to defend it. Therefore, the silence of the second speech on the Italian question, a speech delivered just before the vote was to be taken, suggests that at that time there was no longer any such provision to attack or to defend. On this view, the apparent confusion in the two main sources reflects confusion in the original events. The differing testimony on whether the allies were included presents no problem if the original proposal explicitly mentioned Italians as intended recipients of the redistributed public land, but was altered to exclude them sometime before the bill passed into law.

This hypothesis, if correct, would constitute just one of the adjustments made by Tiberius Gracchus to make his bill more acceptable. The original drafters of such a crucial reform law would not have failed to calculate the likely effect of its detailed provisions on the fortunes and attitudes of all concerned. Just as the idea of the Italians joining in the benefits of the redistribution would have alienated the citizen masses of Rome, so the prospect of reclamation and distribution of the public lands would certainly have alarmed not only some of the members of the Senate but also some of those private citizens whose wealth could buy them friendship and influence with the makers of public policy. The backers of the *lex Sempronia agraria* could expect formidable opposition. Accordingly, when Tiberius Gracchus brought the proposal before the *concilium plebis,* he was not presenting simply a legal document designed to enforce a law already on the books but fallen into disuse. He had in his hands a highly intelligent product of political calculation designed in part, the concessions make clear, to minimize the number and to conciliate the majority of those who stood to lose by its passage. Its drafters and promoters understood, however, that their attempts to placate could not succeed completely, so they aimed also to isolate their unavoidable opponents. They had more in mind than a demagogic bid for the favor of the majority of poor voters in the *concilium plebis:* the proposal must appeal also to some of the more reasonable men in the Senate, who might support or at least not oppose it, because they held some but not a great deal of *ager publicus* in violation of the new statutes.

The proposal's concessions to landholders in the Senate failed in their purpose. Anonymous members of the body managed to persuade a reluctant Octavius (Plutarch says he "had first tried to hold himself aloof" [52]) to exercise his veto. Tiberius either had to abandon the *rogatio* as Laelius had his bill several years earlier or had to intimidate Octavius into not vetoing. To do the latter necessitated persuading the tribune that a veto would incur such popular wrath as to doom his career. Tiberius, therefore, had to play a different game, in that the proposal drafted with the Senate primarily in mind must be adapted for a different audience.

Plutarch, one of our fullest sources for the provisions devised by the group Tiberius represented, describes not the *lex Sempronia agraria* as finally passed, but the proposal initially drafted in consultation with P. Mucius Scaevola, P. Licinius Crassus, and Ap. Claudius Pulcher. He says explicitly that Gracchus modified this proposal before he had it passed in the *concilium plebis* in such a way that it was "made more pleasing to the multitude." [53] The bill had to be as attractive as possible to the multitude not only to be passed, but also to induce a majority of voters in the *concilium plebis* to dissuade a tribune from vetoing it.

Plutarch gives one change made in the original *rogatio*. He writes that the bill had offered recompense ($\tau\iota\mu\acute{\eta}$) to those who would have to abandon some of their illegal acquisitions, thereby implying that the offer was now withdrawn.[54] A later statement, that Tiberius made the new version "more severe for the wrongdoers since it simply ordered them to vacate the land they held in violation of earlier laws," could also suggest that the compensation provision had been removed.[55] Plutarch's account of a last-minute change in the proposal after Octavius' veto sounds reliable,

52. Plut. *TG* 10.2.

53. Plut. *TG* 10.3. Cf. App. *BC* i.11. Fraccaro, *Studi*, pp. 96–99, dismisses Plutarch here as unreliable, but see Molthagen, "Die Durchführung der gracchischen Agrarreform," p. 424, with n. 10.

54. Plut. *TG* 9.2.   55. Plut. *TG* 10.3.

since it makes no apparent biographical point. The removal of the compensation clause, depending on the nature of the compensation, might not have increased the proposition's appeal to the populace because only the wealthy need have been affected by such a clause. On the other hand, it would have made the proposed law more severe for the wrongdoers.

The question which provisions were excised to make the law appeal more to the people is complicated by Plutarch's failure to explain what form the original compensation took. It could have come in several ways. The most obvious perhaps is cash payment. We should expect that, after it was determined how many *iugera* the large landowner would have to surrender to the agrarian commissioners, the man would have some say in deciding which of his possessions he should relinquish.[56] He would most likely choose, when possible, to give up unimproved acres from pasture lands or from his pleasure estate if he owned one. If he had no alternative to relinquishing land already cultivated or built upon, a provision to pay compensation, such as Plutarch seems to intend, would have conformed with the conciliatory spirit of the original proposal. If these inferences are reasonable—their tentativeness is not disputed—such financial compensation would be a likely candidate for one of the provisions removed after Octavius' veto, the one that made the law more severe against the wrongdoers, since it meant they were simply ordered to vacate the land they held illegally.

Another candidate for removal is the child allowance mentioned by Appian. Eliminating this would make the new proposal more pleasing to the multitude because more land would become available for distribution and it would undoubtedly make things harder on the wrongdoers. In fact, Appian has Tiberius assert during his introduction of the bill, before Octavius' veto, that the undisputed title to five hundred *iugera* of free land and the allowance of two hundred and fifty *iugera* per child are ample compensation ($\tau\iota\mu\acute{\eta}$) for any labor spent on land that would be lost by reclamation.[57] This form of recompense may have made up part of that which Plutarch claims was finally withdrawn.

56. See App. *BC* i.10.39 for protests to the contrary.
57. App. *BC* i.11.47.

Cicero provides the evidence that the public land of the *ager Campanus* was exempted from reclamation. He refers to the exemption in a speech made in 63, an attack on the proposed agrarian legislation of P. Servilius Rullus, saying that neither of the Gracchi had dared to lay hands on the *ager Campanus*.[58] That he was lying, or mistaken, as regards the *lex Sempronia agraria* in its final form has been proved by Gracchan boundary markers found on the *ager Campanus*.[59] These are a more reliable witness than Cicero for exactly what happened, especially since his testimony in the attack on Rullus may be tendentious: he had an obvious ax to grind. Nevertheless, he may not have fabricated his claim out of whole cloth but may instead have followed the tradition about the earlier *rogatio*. The proposed land redistribution could indeed have excluded Campania initially.

One other possible provision of the original proposal remains as a candidate for the revision that would so overwhelm the people with enthusiasm for the bill that the *concilium plebis* would not only vote it into law but depose a tribune to do so. A comparison of the two speeches Appian gives Tiberius has revealed, when considered in conjunction with other circumstances, that the identity of the bill's beneficiaries may have been altered. If it was, Tiberius might have tried to maximize his own popular support by eliminating from the bill the clause the Roman masses in the *concilium plebis* would find most objectionable: that extending its benefits to Italians. Thereby the public land would fall entirely into Roman hands.

The source or sources used by Appian and Plutarch either did not make this change explicit or did not stress it enough to make the two later writers spell it out in their summaries of the law's provisions. Plutarch, as Shochat suggests, may have known of a pan-Italic tradition from one of the speeches attributed to Tiberius which he had before him. If he did, he glossed over its implications in order to keep his narrative clear and consistent. Perhaps as a biographer he found this historical detail a needless complication for the story of his subject's life. Appian, on the other hand, allowed the inconsistency to remain (whether consciously or un-

58. Cic. *Leg. Agr.* ii.81.   59. See Degrassi, *ILLRP*, nos. 467 and 468.

consciously, one cannot know). He found a tradition that emphasized the plight of the allies, and two speeches, one centering on the Italians, the other neglecting them entirely. All found their way into his work.

A passage in Cicero's *Republic* (iii.41, cf. i.31) often provides the basis for the view that only Roman citizens actually received land allotments from the agrarian commissioners. This passage, with Plutarch and Appian, could support the theory just presented. In its mutilated condition the passage seems to say that "Tiberius Gracchus, while he kept faith with his fellow citizens, neglected the rights and treaties of our allies and the Latins" (. . . *Asia Ti. Gracchus, perseveravit in civibus, sociorum nominisque Latini iura neglexit ac foedera.*) The absence of a previous context, as well as the rather obtrusive and bewildering "Asia" with its preceding lacuna, hopelessly obscure the precise allusion here, but the fragment could refer to the tribune's agrarian legislation.[60] If so, it has two possible meanings.

First, Cicero may simply be alluding to the activities of the agrarian commission that caused the Italians to appeal to Scipio Aemilianus in 129.[61] As a result of the appeal, the Senate seems to have assumed direction of the commission's activities, assigning the consuls to supervise it in order to prevent it from interfering with the lands held by the allies. The Senate's justification for such action might have been that the commissioners, by bringing lawsuits against the allies, were infringing on their internal affairs, thereby violating their treaty rights (*iura*).[62] Of course, strictly speaking, Cicero could not fairly or accurately have accused Tiberius here of "neglecting" allied rights; the tribune had been dead since 133. Nevertheless, the enabling legislation bore his name, and the hostile charge against the activities of the land commission could have used the bill's author as culprit.

The second alternative is perhaps simpler and certainly more commonly accepted by scholars: the passage may apply to the specific exclusion of Latins and Italians as recipients of land from

60. Contra, see Shochat, "Lex Agraria," pp. 27–29.
61. App. *BC* i.19. Cf. Sall. *Jug.* 42.1.
62. See, for example, Last, "Tiberius Gracchus," p. 44.

the Gracchan commissioners.[63] This possibility has the virtue of giving point to the fragment's antithesis between citizens with whom Tiberius kept faith (*perseveravit*) and allies whose rights he neglected (*neglexit*). The allies might have wanted to accuse Tiberius of neglecting their rights, although the law and their treaties with Rome provided no basis for the charge, if the *rogatio* initially included them, and if he, the proposing tribune, did eventually sacrifice the promised provision for political reasons. Even though Cicero's sentence cannot on its own confirm decisively that the allies were ultimately excluded from the *lex Sempronia agraria,* it surely encourages such a view.

Another source of information about the law's beneficiaries, in addition to Appian, Plutarch, and Cicero, is the agrarian law passed in 111, twenty-two years after Tiberius' tribunate. Its text has survived, but, unfortunately, like the Cicero fragment, in a mutilated state.[64] Several of the extant passages refer to earlier agrarian legislation and have bearing on the identity of the beneficiaries of the land law of 133. Sections 3 and 15 in particular have been construed as indicating that Romans alone were eligible.[65] Section 3 reads as follows: "Regarding what was the Roman people's public land in Italy during the consulship of P. Mucius and L. Calpurnius [that is, in 133], excluding that land which was prohibited from division by the law or the plebiscite proposed by C. Sempronius Gracchus, son of Tiberius, tribune of the plebs . . . whatever of that land or place a triumvir, according to the law or plebiscite, has granted or assigned to a Roman citizen by lot and which is not in the land or place beyond. . . ." [*quei ager publicus populi Romanei in terra Italia P. Muucio L. Calpurnio cos. fuit, extra eum agrum, quei ager ex lege plebeiue sc(ito), quod C. Sempronius Ti. f. tr. pl. rogauit exceptum cauitumue est nei diuideretur . . . . / . . . . quem agrum locum*] *QUOIEIQUE DE EO AGRO LOCO EX LEGE PLEBEIUE SC(ITO) IIIUIR SORTITO CEIUI ROMANO DEDIT ADISGNAUIT, QUOD NON*

---

63. So, for example, Badian, *FC,* p. 170; Earl, *Tiberius Gracchus,* p. 20.

64. Riccobono, *FIRA,* I, 102–121 = *CIL,* I, 175, 200; = Bruns, *Fontes Iuris Romani Antiqui,* 73.

65. See, for example, Earl, *Tiberius Gracchus,* p. 20; Badian, *FC,* p. 171.

IN EO AGRO LOCO EST, QUOD ULTR[a . . . / . . . .
(and here the text breaks off). Section 15 includes the phrase,
"Regarding the public land of the Roman People in Italy in the
consulship of P. Mucius and L. Calpurnius, possession of which a
triumvir for granting and assigning lands according to the law or
plebiscite by lot to a Roman citizen . . ." *AGER PUBLICUS
POPULI ROMANEI, QUEI IN ITALIA P. MUCIO L. CAL-
PURNIO COS. FUIT, EIUS AGRI IIIUIR A(GREIS) D(AN-
DEIS) A(DSIGNANDEIS) EX LEGE PLEBEIUE SCITO SOR-
TITO QUOI CEIUI ROMA[no agrum dedit adsignauit . . .*
Both passages seem to refer to public land apportioned by lot under C. Gracchus' agrarian law to Roman citizens alone. The allotments being mentioned are not colonial but viritane, so these texts
could indicate that, in accordance with the *lex agraria* of 133, the
Gracchan land commissioners confined their largesse to Roman
citizens.[66] Of course, the law under which such allotments are being granted is not that of Tiberius but of his younger brother;
moreover, Plutarch's simple statement that C. Gracchus "divided
the public land among the poor" (ὁ μὲν ἦν κληρουχικὸς ἀνανέμων τοῖς
πένησι τὴν δημοσίαν) and the equally imprecise reports from other
sources do not permit a confident assessment of the proper relationship between the two agrarian laws of the Gracchi.[67]

Earl has maintained that, since C. Gracchus, known to be a
committed Italophile, excluded the allies as beneficiaries of his law,
as the *lex agraria* of 111 confirms, his elder brother, who evinced
no special regard for them (assuming that Appian's evidence should
be discounted), must have excluded them too.[68] C. Gracchus' reputation as an Italophile depends in part on his having attempted,
albeit in vain, to grant the full franchise to the Latin allies and to
bestow voting rights on the Italians.[69] Had he succeeded, the grant-

66. See Levi, "Intorno alla Legge Agraria del 111 a.C.," pp. 237–240;
Larsen, "*Sortito* and *Sorti* in CIL, I, 200," p. 279.
67. Plut. *CG* 5.1; cf. Cic. *Off.* ii.80; Cic. *Leg. Agr.* ii.10; Livy *Per.* lx;
Vell. ii.6.3; Flor. ii.3.2; App. *BC* i.21; Auct. *Vir. Ill.* 65.3; Oros. v.12.4.
68. Earl, *Tiberius Gracchus*, p. 20.
69. Cic. *Brut.* 99; Cic. *De Orat.* i.38; Vell. ii.6.2; Plut. *CG* 5.1, 9.3, 12.1–2;
Gell. x.3.2, cf. ix.14.16. See also Molthagen, "Die Durchführung der
gracchischen Agrarreform," pp. 448–452.

ing of such rights would presumably have made the new recipients of the franchise eligible for the allotments of land previously awarded by the land commissioners to Roman citizens only. This raises the possibility that C. Gracchus in fact wished to extend the franchise to the allies at least in part to make them eligible for grants of public land being distributed by his commission. If so, the enfranchisement attempt provides independent indication that Gaius sought to award lands to the allies and negates any attempt to see his exclusion of them from his law as evidence of their exclusion from the land law introduced by his elder brother in 133. If Tiberius eventually removed them from his proposed law in order to win popular favor, Gaius' failure to mention them in his plebiscite may reflect a political lesson learned from his elder brother.

After dealing with the Plutarch-Appian confusions, Shochat argues that these passages of the *lex agraria* of 111 imply only that some public land, which was awarded by lot, went exclusively to Roman citizens.[70] This assumption does not rule out the possibility that other portions of the public lands were distributed by other means and that for such lands Italians were eligible. Because the inscription is damaged it is unclear whether any such lands were given to Italians, but section 5 of the law refers to the triumvirs distributing *ager publicus* throughout Italy without casting lots. Regrettably, the lacunae in the inscription prevent definite conclusions about the activity being described, for there is no information on whether the distributions were carried out *ex lege plebeiue scito*. Sections 6 and 7 of the law also deal with the distribution of public land, but again the damage to the text hides the identity of the beneficiaries.

Shochat has, however, pointed to Section 29 of the law and its clear assertion that a *lex plebisue scitum* did not discriminate against the Italian allies. What a Roman citizen may do with public land, it says, may be done "in a like manner by a Latin or other non-citizen, from the consulship of M. Livius and L. Calpurnius [that is, in 112] in accordance with a law or plebiscite or special

70. Shochat, *"Lex Agraria,"* p. 30.

treaty. . . ." *ceiui*] *ROMANO FACERE LICEBIT, ITEM LA-
TINO PEREGRINOQUE, QUIBUS M. LIUIO L. CALPURNIO*
[*cos. in eis agris id facere* . . . . *ex lege pleb*]*EIUE
SC(ITO) EXUE FOEDERE LICUIT.* Shochat infers that, far
from being generally discriminated against, the Italian allies, according to the terms of a plebiscite, may even have been granted
certain rights concerning the public lands that were not granted to
citizens.

Of course, as Shochat himself freely admits, the phrase *"ex lege
plebeiue scito"* may not always refer to the land law of C. Gracchus,
nor can the provisions of the *lex Sempronia agraria* of 133 be certainly distinguished from those of Gaius' law, if indeed they can
even be assumed to provide the basis for it. The surviving portions
of the *lex agraria* of 111 do not, therefore, decide the question of
whether the Italians were finally included as beneficiaries of Tiberius' land law of 133. The other evidence must suffice for a judgment: Cicero's statement in his *Republic* that Tiberius Gracchus
neglected the rights of the allies; Plutarch's utter silence on the inclusion of the Italians as beneficiaries of the law; Tiberius Gracchus' failure to mention non-Romans in Appian's version of the
second and final speech on behalf of the land law; Appian's belief
that the Italians did not finally benefit from the law.[71] Finally, the
Scholia Bobiensia, commenting on Cicero's oration *Pro Sestio*
(103), say explicitly that Tiberius' agrarian law divided the public
land among the Roman plebs.[72] The weight of this evidence, and
the haziness of what is adduced to contradict it, points to the conclusion, albeit cautious and tentative, that in the end Italians did
not receive the Gracchan land grants.

The possibility remains, however, that in the beginning the bill
had a different shape, a possibility suggested by Appian's references to the Italians and by a further consideration. If Tiberius and
his sponsors were primarily concerned with the military implications of the crisis the Roman state faced on the eve of Gracchus'

71. Cic. *Rep.* iii.41, cf. i.31; App. *BC* i.11, cf. 21.
72. Schol. Bob. 135 Stangl: "Agrariam Tiberius . . . ferebat: . . . ut
ager publicus Romanae plebi divideretur, quae lex ei magnam conflavit
invidiam."

tribunate—and how could they not have been?—surely they would have paid serious attention to the plight of their military allies, especially those impoverished Italian peasants who formed the largest contingent in Rome's total fighting force.[73] The Senate had, in fact, taken up this problem earlier in the century. Italian soldiers received plots of land and donatives upon their military discharge, as did their Roman counterparts, and, on two separate occasions, in the years 187 and 177 (the latter instance occurring during the first consulship of the father of the Gracchi), the Senate showed itself willing to respond to the difficulties caused the Latins by military recruitment.[74] Those difficulties must have increased sharply in the succeeding decades, as they did for Romans, so that the reformers of 133 could hardly have been indifferent to them.

The men who drafted the initial version of the *lex Sempronia agraria* created a moderate and conciliatory piece of legislation.[75]

73. See about, pp. 75–76.

74. In 187 the question of the exercise of the *ius migrandi* by the Latins was brought before the Senate (Livy xxxix.3.4–6). In 177 the Latins complained again that large numbers of their citizens had migrated to Rome and had thereby been enrolled in the Roman census (Livy xli.8.6–12). They said that if this practice were allowed to continue, towns and farms would be deserted and they would be unable, because of the resulting dearth of manpower, to furnish Rome with soldiers. The previous methods the Roman authorities had instituted to control this sort of emigration had been either evaded through legal chicanery or simply ignored. The Latins asked the Senate to direct these migrants to return to their towns, to close the legal loopholes that were permitting Latins to emigrate (presumably to avoid their local drafts), and finally to declare invalid grants of Roman citizenship that had been obtained this way. The Senate granted all these requests. See Badian, *FC*, p. 150, with n. 4.

75. The simple question sometimes asked, whether the law was conservative or radical, is not answerable. It was conservative to the extent that it may have sought to mend the old social fabric of the Republic and maintain its dominions by preserving Rome's ability to wage war. On the other hand, insofar as the law intended to achieve these goals by redistributing the properties of the wealthy to the poor, the well-informed Roman mind must have linked it with the revolutionary tradition of the Hellenistic East (see below, pp. 179–180). But that the Romans themselves debated the law's merits in these terms is unlikely. If, for example, as many scholars

The analysis of it undertaken in this chapter has emphasized the numerous special concessions that were probably made to the propertied classes: the child allowances; the compensation to be paid when improved lands were reclaimed; the clear title to lands that would be retained; the exemption of the *ager Campanus.* The law may not have intended or resulted in large-scale destruction of efficient farms belonging to the richer landowners of Italy. Rather, the evidence suggests that the law's devisers hoped, for the most part, to reclaim arable pasture lands to distribute them to the poor.

The *rogatio* was skillfully designed to deal with the central problem facing the Roman state in 133—the displacement, impoverishment, and numerical decrease of the peninsula's peasantry. That contemporary crisis had several manifestations—simple human suffering, of course; the creation of a disgruntled rural proletariat increasingly dissatisfied with the diminishing *beneficia* for which they gave, as clients, their *officium;* the depletion of the reservoir of men willing and able to serve in the Roman legions and in their auxiliaries; perhaps even a limited but disturbing migration by some of the rural poor to the country towns and to Rome. All these symptoms, whether social, economic, political, military, or demographic, resulted from the peasantry's displacement. Was it not reasonable to believe that all could be treated by the application of a single remedy? Whatever their ultimate motives, the drafters of the land law of 133 intended to return the peasantry to the land and to keep them and their heirs on it permanently by making the lands granted inalienable.[76] If Rome's problem admitted a

---

seem to believe (among others, Zancan, *Ager Publicus,* p. 48; Tibiletti, "Il possesso dell' *ager publicus"* [1949], p. 39; Boren, *The Gracchi,* p. 44), the law was a conservative measure, what label are we to attach to its earliest opponents? Surely, to say that they objected to the tribune's manner rather than to the substance of his proposal is insufficient. Octavius' veto preceded Tiberius' unorthodox tactics: it was certainly not a response to them. The deposition of Octavius could have been avoided only at the cost of postponing or abandoning the proposal.

76. Like its supporters, all drafters of the bill may not have had identical motives. My argument is, however, that the inclusion of the inalienability

legislative solution, one more intelligent than the *lex Sempronia agraria* is difficult to envisage. It promised, over the long run, to ameliorate and perhaps even to eliminate the dilemma.[77]

No one can tell how the Republic's history might have differed had the law's implementation not been thwarted in the end. The difficulties over land and army stood at the center of the process of revolution and dissolution.[78] Appian's final judgment, too, that "this law of Gracchus' was a most excellent and useful one, if only it could have been carried out" must give food for thought.[79] Symptoms of the sickness that was to kill the Republic had begun to appear well before the tribunate of Tiberius Sempronius Gracchus, but if events in 133 and after had gone otherwise, this crucial year might have seen their development effectively arrested, rather than temporarily inhibited.

---

clause implies that someone involved in the law's creation was concerned more with solving a problem than with amassing support.

77. So Frederiksen, "The Contribution of Archaeology to the Agrarian Problem in the Gracchan Period," pp. 349–356. Contra see Gabba, "Motivazioni economiche nell'opposizione alla legge agraria di Tib. Sempronio Gracco," pp. 129–138; cf. Gabba, "Studi su Dionigi D'Alicarnasso," pp. 29–41.

78. Brunt, "The Army and the Land in the Roman Revolution," pp. 69–86.

79. App. *BC* i.27.123.

6 The Presentation of the *Lex Sempronia Agraria* and the Deposition of Octavius

Quin ipsum Ti. Gracchum non solum neglectus, sed etiam sublatus intercessor evertit, quid enim illum aliud perculit, nisi quod potestatem intercedenti collegae abrogavit?
—Cicero, *De Legibus* iii.24

When Tiberius Gracchus and his nine colleagues assumed their offices on December 10, 134, observers could not have foreseen how his term would close, but many must have anticipated trouble. The notable politicians who had taken part in the drafting of the agrarian law, and others who intended to back it, must have openly supported the candidacy of the tribune whom they had chosen to bring the controversial *rogatio* before the *concilium plebis*.

Anyone who looked closely would have found Tiberius Sempronius Gracchus a troubling figure. An ambitious politician who had distinguished family connections and a formidable inherited *clientela,* he now represented an array of high-level political figures. The Mancinus affair may have tainted his name among those of his own class, but it enabled him to present himself for election as tribune of the People as a long-suffering savior of the lives of thousands of ordinary Romans who had served reluctantly in Spain. His popularity would have been enhanced by his willingness to be a public advocate of land reform. While he was by no means unassailable, Tiberius Gracchus was a contender to be feared, the more so since he must have nursed considerable resentment.

The supporters of land reform would have tried to secure the election of as many favorably disposed tribunes as possible. Had they been able, they would undoubtedly have locked out any potential obstructionist by filling all ten positions with their own men.

M. Octavius' presence in the college and his subsequent actions suggest, of course, that they failed.

The group's active political opponents and the rest of the habitually cautious politicians in the Senate may not have known about the plan to promote a controversial piece of agrarian legislation before the formal declarations of candidacy for office (*professiones*). They may, however, have learned of it soon afterward from Tiberius' early campaign speeches (*contiones*). Their strategy then probably consisted in uniting behind a single, reliable candidate in order to concentrate their strength and ensure that at least one of their adherents would be in a position to block passage of the legislation, for one alone was needed.[1]

We know the names of only two of the other tribunes elected, both distinguished for their opposition to Tiberius. One, P. Satureius, reportedly struck the first blow against his colleague in the assault that ended Gracchus' life.[2] The other, a certain Rubrius, presided over the tribunician elections for 132 and appears to have obstructed Gracchus' re-election. As a result, presumably at a moment when the Gracchans were temporarily ascendant, Rubrius lost his position to Q. Mucius, who had replaced the deposed Octavius and was reputedly a client ($\pi\epsilon\lambda\acute{a}\tau\eta s$) of Tiberius.[3]

Satureius' enthusiastic role in the murder of Tiberius may suggest enmity preceding their tribuneship, or simply the desire to escape an anonymity that would otherwise have been complete. Except for Octavius, however, the evidence for the hostility to Tiberius of the tribunician college follows the deposition and his generally unorthodox behavior after the law was vetoed. By the end of his tribunate, the whole college appears to have ranged itself with the Senate in firm opposition both to the man and to

1. Jones, *"De Tribunis Plebis Reficiendis,"* p. 37.

2. Plut. *TG* 19.6. One L. Rufus laid proud claim to striking the second blow.

3. The name of the successor to Octavius, the man who now replaced Rubrius, is given by Plutarch as Mucius (*TG* 13.2, 18.1); by Appian as Mummius (*BC* i.12, 14); by Orosius as Minucius (v.8.3). For appropriately inconclusive speculation on the man's identity, see Earl, "M. Octavius, trib. pleb. 133 B.C., and His Successor," pp. 666–669.

his bid for re-election.[4] Individual attitudes may, of course, have been different when the tribunes first took office. Appian informs us that after Octavius' second veto they fell to wrangling with each other.[5] Perhaps at this early stage Tiberius did not stand alone in his dispute with oppositionist colleagues, but had support from other tribunes motivated by conviction or personal affiliation. Then again, some members of the college may have been neutral.

Although the land reform bill of 133 originated with some prominent senators, it did not finally come before the Roman People with the blessing of the Senate as a body (*ex auctoritate senatus*). Quite the opposite. Tiberius Gracchus, acting in his official capacity as a tribune of the People, brought the *rogatio* directly to the *concilium plebis,* ignoring the Senate's traditional prerogative of granting the bill its formal imprimatur. Even if we did not know of Octavius' subsequent veto, the choice of this course in itself would indicate that the bill's backers considered the Senate's refusal to endorse the scheme a foregone conclusion. Sidestepping the Senate with a direct appeal to the *concilium plebis* flouted customary procedure, but was neither unprecedented nor revolutionary.[6] Had he so wished, Tiberius could have appealed to the examples set by various others not too long before, examples that increased in frequency during the 140s and 130s.

No actual proof exists that earlier *rogationes* were put to the People without prior debate in the Senate. Some proposals, however, must have been presented to the *concilium plebis* without senatorial approval, and this is what really matters.[7] For instance, the Senate can hardly have granted official approval to the proposal of C. Licinius Crassus, tribune in 145, to fill vacancies in the priestly colleges by popular election instead of by cooptation. Nor would they have given their blessing to C. Curiatius' public recommendation in 138 that the consuls propose to the Senate that grain be purchased by the state.[8] Although neither of these proposals be-

---

4. App. *BC* i.15.65–66; Plut. *TG* 16.2.   5. App. *BC* i.12.50.
6. Badian, *TGBRR,* pp. 694–695.   7. *Ibid.*
8. For C. Licinius Crassus' proposal see Cic. *Amic.* 96; cf. Varro *De Agr. Cult.* i.2.9; Plut. *CG* 5.3. Not until 104 did the tribune Cn. Domitius Ahenobarbus get a law passed that allowed the tribal assembly to elect the

came law, the three *rogationes* introducing secret balloting for, respectively, the election of magistrates, appeal trials before the people, and legislation, were passed in the 130s, and they could not have been brought to the People with the Senate's corporate endorsement. The laws in question clearly ran counter to the interests of the senatorial order, which as a whole cannot have responded favorably to them.

The sort of legislative approach just described was a sign of the particular social and economic changes occurring during the period. To be sure, senatorial aristocrats would not have been entirely unaccustomed to making concessions to or capitalizing on popular sentiment. The near-crisis conditions of these decades, however, produced such occasions more frequently and began to transform the nature of Roman politics. The altering economic, social, demographic, and military situation eventually affected the realities of political power in Italy.

As we have seen, the dislocation of the peasantry strained the bonds of *clientela,* in some cases perhaps to the breaking point.[9] As the extremity of their need induced more and more rural voters to take an independent line on elections or legislation, the temptation grew for certain members of the ruling oligarchy to court these voters so as to advance their own careers or their causes. By promising a piece of legislation attractive to the disaffected rural poor, a candidate might win his office and later climb higher up the ladder of a political career (*cursus honorum*) than his political assets would otherwise have allowed. What is particularly noticeable and at the same time potentially revolutionary about the decade of the 130s is that more often and on issues of increasing importance, major political figures and coalitions appear to have been willing to contemplate such tactics.

The new attitude would later have a dramatic effect on the power structure of the Roman state. Meanwhile, because direct

---

members of the four major priestly colleges. See Szemler, *The Priests of the Roman Republic,* p. 30. For C. Curiatius' recommendation to the consuls see Val. Max. iii.7.3.

9. See above, pp. 98–101.

popular appeal was becoming more common and because it had
often proved effective, the inducement to resort to it at moments
of political deadlock within the Senate grew. Not only selfishly
ambitious demagogues, but some statesmen concerned about issues
of vital interest to the country might choose the popular path to
their ends.

Both kinds of motive could have underlain the legislation being
introduced and sometimes passed in this period. C. Licinius
Crassus' proposal in 145 indicates that some among the ruling
oligarchy sought to open wider the doors to religious office and
public prestige now that conditions increasingly allowed. Crassus,
of course, did not succeed, but the tribunes who proposed the
three secret ballot laws (*leges tabellariae*) did. Their legislation
must have institutionalized such populist procedures and carried
them into areas where oligarchic authority had previously reigned
unperturbed. From this point on, that authority was to be questioned and challenged.

Against such a background, Tiberius' direct appeal to the People
must have appeared as the latest in a line of unhappy precedents
for the oligarchy. To present a land distribution bill directly to the
concilium plebis, without the Senate's imprimatur, was to place it
squarely in a growing political tradition that was seen as threatening
—and did indeed threaten—the interests of the oligarchy. For that
reason alone, the bill must have worried many of the members of
that class, even though it had been drafted by a respected and
powerful coalition of senators. When discussing the bill with their
peers, such men would have known that they must justify its im-
plicit challenge to the established order by emphasizing the remedy
it offered not only for the military aspects of Italy's growing
agrarian crisis, but also for the disruptive political effects of that
crisis. After all, if the crisis could be countered, its political effects
might be reversed. In addition, the displaced peasantry to whom
the bill directed its appeal would be settled on plots of public
land several days' journey from Rome. This would limit the opportunities for appeal to the People against the Senate's authority.
The bill's supporters could therefore use the paradoxical argument
that this was the law to end all such laws, for its passage would

strike a death blow at the menacing trend toward popular legislation.

The response, nevertheless, cannot have been enthusiastic. The bill's fate was too uncertain—not only might it fail to pass, but its implementation could be blocked. How could the dangerous precedent of resorting to populist means to manipulate domestic policy be justified under present conditions? To exploit the conditions one was trying to ameliorate and to invoke the precedent one would like to abandon was surely dangerous politics. The People must not fall into the mistake of thinking they had the right to arbitrate a dispute between opposing senatorial coalitions. Let no one risk making fact what had until then been merely an awkward and dangerous constitutional theory—the sovereignty of the Roman People.

A group within the Senate, some spurred by personal ambition, some by a farsighted conviction that land reform was in the long-term interests of the Roman state, decided to support the bill. In view of the negative response to be expected from the rest of the Senate, they countenanced a direct appeal to the *Populus Romanus*. Only a conviction that the Senate's official approval was unattainable could have reconciled them to such a course. Certainly a number of large landowners among the senators bitterly opposed land reform, as would have been revealed by the recent experience of the practical and prudent Laelius. Some senators obviously believed there was a chance for passage but the obstacles to success would be formidable. The bill's contents as well as the manner of its presentation would decide its fate, and supporters could not feel confident. The law's drafters had done what they could to tempt and to soothe all but the most implacable opposition, but even artful politicians would be severely tested as they attempted to guide the *rogatio* through the political channels into law. Unfortunately, Tiberius Gracchus, as we shall see, was not especially artful.

He probably did not delay very long before bringing the proposal to the People. Plutarch gives the impression that the tribune took up the task immediately upon assuming office.[10] Since the year of

10. Plut. *TG* 8.4: ὁ Τιβέριος δὲ δήμαρχος ἀποδειχθεὶς εὐθὺς ἐπ' αὐτὴν ὥρμησε τὴν πρᾶξιν.

the tribunate began on December 10 (that of the consuls and most other magistrates began on the first day of the year), Tiberius probably brought the bill to the *concilium plebis* around the middle of the winter. It has been suggested, albeit cautiously, that Appian's first assembly, when the issue was formally introduced, took place on January 31, one of the nineteen days in that month on which a public assembly could be legally convened (*dies comitialis*).[11] The month seems a reasonable enough estimate, the day less so, given the lack of precision of the sources' accounts and the vagaries to which the Roman calendar might have been subject.

Thus, on a midwinter day in 133, in an atmosphere that must have been tense with anticipation, the young tribune, "an illustrious man, eager for glory," [12] mounted the rostra to introduce the *rogatio* drafted under the auspices of distinguished senators. In his first speech to the assembled masses, Tiberius defended the bill with an appeal to interests of state. Appian, our source for this public meeting (*contio*), writes: "He inveighed against the multitude of slaves as useless in war and never faithful to their masters, and adduced the recent calamity brought upon the masters by their slaves in Sicily where the demands of agriculture greatly increased the number of the latter; recalling also the war against them by the Romans, which was neither easy nor short, but long-protracted and full of vicissitudes and dangers." [13] No doubt he said more, but few minds were likely to have been changed that day by Tiberius' oratory. He was either preaching to the converted or sermonizing to the incorrigibly profane.

At least one of the law's provisions required a special defense. I have argued in an earlier chapter that the original draft of the *lex Sempronia agraria,* the one Tiberius was presenting in this

11. Geer, "Notes on the Land Law of Tiberius Gracchus," pp. 30–32.

12. App. i.9: ἀνὴρ ἐπιφανὴς καὶ λαμπρὸς ἐς φιλοτιμίαν.

13. App. *BC* i.9. See above, pp. 72–73. See also Geer, "Plutarch and Appian on Tiberius Gracchus," pp. 105–106, replying to the arguments of Carcopino (*Autour des Gracques,* pp. 9–23). Geer shows how an apparent contradiction, which Carcopino claims is real, disappears when we understand that Appian describes the first meeting of the assembly, Plutarch the second, though the latter's account presupposes, without explicitly mentioning, the earlier meeting.

contio, proposed to distribute reclaimed public land not only to Roman citizens, but to Latins and Italians as well. A conscientious reformer—not necessarily Tiberius Gracchus— fearing the military ramifications of the displacement of Italy's peasantry, would have pressed for their inclusion as beneficiaries. While the Roman oligarchy might generally be expected to remain indifferent to the allies' plight, in this case it would have shown more concern because the allies were having difficulty in meeting their draft quotas. Indeed, in 187 and again in 177, at the request of the Latin magistrates, the Senate had restricted the allies' right to emigrate to Roman territory (*ius migrandi*).[14] Since some of the allies had been allowed to remain as renters on their territory when it was conquered and annexed by Rome, moreover, the *lex Sempronia agraria* might have proposed to go one step further by allowing them to live, as renters, on reclaimed public lands.

Finally, the speech Appian attributes to Tiberius contains an explicit and appropriate defense for a clause including the Italians as beneficiaries: "[Tiberius] delivered an eloquent discourse . . . concerning the Italian race, lamenting that a people so valiant in war, and related in blood to the Romans, were declining little by little into pauperism and paucity of numbers without any hope of remedy." [15] Needless to say, whatever enthusiasm Tiberius' speech aroused for a bill that would give Romans plots of public land, these words would have received a cool reception from his voting audience. Poverty-stricken Roman small holders would not leave their work and trek to the city to hear about the valor of the allied peasantry and the social injustices they had endured; nor would they come to vote into law a bill dealing with the pressing needs of others. They might, of course, vote for a *rogatio* that included Latins and Italians as recipients of public land if that were the only way to obtain land themselves. The drafters of the bill—or at least those among them who had urged the inclusion of the allies— must have relied on such reasoning. Yet this clause would not have been popular and it might have provided grounds for an attack on the bill that would find favor with the Roman voters. Tiberius

14. See above, pp. 75–76, 156–157 with n. 74; Livy xxxix.3.4–6, xli.8.6–12.
15. App. *BC* i.9.

should have played down the provision or avoided mentioning it altogether. At any rate, the reception accorded this part of his speech must have discouraged him. As we shall see, he excised the provision before the *concilium plebis* met to vote on the bill, in order to make the land reform as a whole "more pleasing to the multitude." [16]

The meeting may have followed the day after the speech or as much as two weeks later. Without an exact date for the *contio,* that of the next comitial day on the Roman calendar cannot be reliably estimated. His audience, however, was vast—far larger than normal—and primed for the occasion. Supporters had labored hard to get out the independent rural vote so that the assembly on the Capitoline was packed with the indigent from the country who would be the law's principal beneficiaries. The opposition, of course, also had mobilized its loyal clients to come and vote against the land reform proposal. Appian describes the great numbers of country people who became involved, "colonists, or inhabitants of the free towns, or persons otherwise interested in the land and who were under like apprehensions, [and who] flocked in and sided with their respective partisans." [17] (Loeb translation, slightly modified). Diodorus, a less reliable source but certainly not tendentious in this passage, substantiates Appian's testimony and gives a more graphic view of the city at the time: "The crowds poured into Rome from the country like rivers into the all-receptive sea, buoyed up with the hope of effecting their own salvation, since the law was their leader and ally, and their champion a man subject neither to favor nor to fear—a man, moreover, who for the sake

16. Plut. *TG* 10.3. Mommsen (*Röm. Staats.* III, 371) argues that a measure could not be legally changed once it had been promulgated, so that Gracchus must have promulgated a new law and allowed the full legal interval before presenting it to the assembly for a vote. I am inclined to agree with Geer ("Plutarch and Appian on Tiberius Gracchus," p. 107, n. 4) that Mommsen has not established the existence of the rule forbidding alterations in a law after promulgation, at least at the time of the Gracchi. As Mommsen himself admits, there were frequent exceptions to the rule if it did exist, as well as to the whole requirement for a *trinum nundinum* between promulgation and presentation to the assembly for action.

17. App. *BC* i.10. For supporters already in the city, see p. 89.

of restoring the land to the people was determined to endure any toil or danger to his last breath. [The opposition] was not a group just recently assembled and drawn from many tribes, but comprised the most politically alert and the well-to-do segments of the populace. Since, then, the strength on both sides was evenly balanced, and the scales tipped now this way, now that, the two parties, being assembled many thousand strong, clashed violently, and in the public assemblies there appeared billowing forms and patterns like waves of the sea." [18]

Appian recounts how, in the interim, the opposing sides "exasperated each other and kindled considerable disturbances as they eagerly awaited the vote on the new law," while Plutarch tells of people who "posted writings on porticoes, house walls and monuments calling upon Tiberius to recover the public land for the poor." [19] The behavior of the thousands of rural visitors must have had an enormous impact on the city and on the atmosphere in the *concilium plebis*.

When the *concilium plebis* convened Tiberius again spoke, defending his altered proposal and emphasizing, among other things, that only citizens would enjoy its benefits. [20] On this occasion he rose to heights of eloquence. "The wild beasts that roam Italy have every one of them a cave or lair to lurk in; but the men who fight and die for Italy enjoy the common air and light but nothing else; houseless and homeless they wander about with their wives and children. It is with lying lips that their commanders exhort the soldiers in their battles to defend sepulchres and shrines from the enemy; for not a man of them has an hereditary altar, not one of all these many Romans ['Ρωμαίων] an ancestral tomb, but they

18. Diod. xxxiv/xxxv.6.

19. App. *BC* i.10.42; Plut. *TG* 8.7. Plutarch claims that these writings were said to have helped inspire Tiberius to confront the land question in the first place, but they probably were not addressed to Tiberius personally before he actually announced his intention to propose the law. Therefore, if one of the ultimate sources of Plutarch did see such writings, they more likely belong to this period than to some unspecified time before Tiberius' tribunate.

20. Plut. *TG* 10.3. For the other changes in the law, see above, pp. 149–152.

fight and die to support others in wealth and luxury, and though they are styled masters of the world, they have not a single clod of earth that is their own." [21] Furthermore, he said, to divide the public lands among the citizenry was just. Was not a citizen (ὁ πολίτης) at all times more valuable than a slave; a man who served in the legions more useful than one who did not; someone with a stake in the country more likely to be devoted to the public interest than someone without one? The Romans, of course, possessed their vast territory by conquest and even entertained hopes of similarily occupying the rest of the habitable world. Yet they now ran the risk, not only of failing to realize their imperial ambitions, but of losing what they already possessed through a shortage of free men available for legionary service. To avert this danger the wealthy ought to bestow the land as a free gift upon families who would rear children.[22]

When Tiberius finished his speech he ordered the clerk to read the *rogatio* to the assembly before the vote on it. Since the vote could surely go only one way, the opposition, understandably, was unwilling to try the issue. Octavius reluctantly interposed his veto under pressure from the wealthy and implacable opponents of land reform.[23] Tiberius then adjourned the assembly until the next comitial day, though the length of that interval cannot be fixed.

Tiberius undoubtedly used what time he had to put pressure on his colleague to withdraw the veto. Apparently the two tribunes debated daily in public. Plutarch assures us that both the young men observed a dignified decorum throughout the proceedings by refraining from personal attacks on each other. His description of the debates, however, belies his assertion. Tiberius offered to compensate Octavius from his own private funds for the public land the vetoer would lose as a prominent offender.[24] The remark surely was intended to show Octavius in the worst possible light. When

21. Plut. *TG* 9.4–5.

22. App. *BC* i.11. See also the famous speech delivered by the censor, Q. Caecilius Metellus Macedonicus, to the assembled people urging that everyone be compelled to marry in order to produce children (Livy, *Per.* lix; cf. Suet. *Aug.* lxxxix; Gell. i.6.1; Berger, "A Note on Gellius," pp. 302–303).

23. Plut. *TG* 10.1–3; cf. App. *BC* i.12.   24. Plut. *TG* 10.4–5.

slander failed to produce the agreement Tiberius sought, he turned his attention to the men behind the obstructing tribune. He declared that he would veto all subsequent public business, and he sealed the state treasury (*aerarium*) until a vote should be allowed on his agrarian law, that is, until Octavius should withdraw his veto.[25]

Although Tiberius' actions were unusual and extreme, they were not entirely unprecedented. In 184 a group of tribunes had threatened to veto all subsequent public business in the Senate if one of the rival tribunes vetoed an impending resolution to bring the veteran armies back from Spain. Later, in 148, a tribune threatened to veto the consular elections if Scipio, who was below the legal age, was not granted a dispensation and allowed to run for the office.[26] In both instances the threats to obstruct sufficed; they did not have to be carried out. Therefore Tiberius' behavior might have been anticipated by those who were well versed in the history of tribunician machinations and understood the highly controversial nature of the issue that faced the state. Above all, it would not have surprised those who knew the character of this most ambitious young man and what a second public failure would mean for his political future. Yet to be prepared is hardly to approve. The mere existence of infrequent and unfortunate prece-

25. Plut. *TG* 10.6. There has been considerable controversy, both legal and historical, over whether Gracchus had the power to, and actually did, halt public business as Plutarch claims. Carcopino (*Autour des Gracques,* pp. 16–17) argues unconvincingly against the authenticity of Plutarch's report. Most scholars who have written on the subject accept the Plutarchian version in spite of Appian's silence (see, among others, Mommsen, *Röm. Staats.* I³, 263–264, II³, 290–301, III, 1048, 1063–1064; Fraccaro, *Studi,* p. 100; Münzer, *RE,* IIA, 1416; Geer, "Plutarch and Appian on Tiberius Gracchus," p. 107; Last, "Tiberius Gracchus," p. 25). Niccolini (*I Fasti dei Tribuni della Plebe,* pp. 111–112) thinks that a tribune did not have the legal power to declare a *iustitium* (from *iuris stitium = ius sistere*) but accepts Plutarch's report as a description of a de facto halt in all public business, resulting from the exercise of the tribunician veto. Cf. Thomsen, "Erliess Tiberius Gracchus ein Iustitium?" pp. 60–61; Gelzer, "Review of Carcopino, *Autour des Gracques,*" pp. 649–650; Astin, *SA,* p. 204.

26. Both episodes are cited by Astin, *SA,* p. 204. For the event in 184 see Livy xxxix.38.9; for 148 see App. *Lib.* 112; cf. Cic. *Phil.* xi.17; Vell. i.12.3.

dents did not automatically make their repetition acceptable to the
majority of Roman senators as they watched Tiberius and Octavius
bring the state closer to deadlock. Moreover, Tiberius did not
merely copy the maneuvers of 184 and 148; he expanded and
improved upon them. A bemused oligarchy must have wondered
how and where it would all end.

The story goes that, during this interval between assembly meetings, Tiberius took to carrying a conspicuously concealed short
sword in response to rumors of an improbable assassination plot
by the propertied. When the *concilium plebis* finally did recon-
vene, he appeared with a bodyguard to intimidate Octavius.[27] Both
actions, if they really occurred, were probably melodramatic and
not altogether dignified responses to any violence that might have
already occurred—perhaps brawls between the mob of desperate
small holders and the faithful clients of their opponents.[28] Certainly
land reform was a matter of life and death for Tiberius' peasant
supporters. Octavius' vetoes on behalf of the vested interests of the
state's wealthiest segment must have infuriated the indigent. Tensions in the city would have continued to mount, tempers to
flare. Tiberius' behavior did nothing to cool things down: quite
naturally, for that would hardly have helped the passage of his
bill. In the end, however, it proved not to be in his own long-term
interests to be responsible for driving the state closer to open
violence.

On the day of the next assembly, Tiberius began marshaling his
supporters for what promised to be the decisive confrontation.
Plutarch claims that the wealthy opponents of land reform arranged
to have the voting urns (αἱ ὑδρίαι) stolen, thereby throwing the
preparations into disarray.[29] One may readily believe that there
was great confusion on this day, but not that it was caused by the

27. Plut. *TG* 10.7; App. *BC* i.12.49.
28. Astin (*SA*, p. 347) rejects as propaganda after the event the suggestion of both our main sources that "the Gracchans threatened or
contemplated the use of force." Given the circumstances of these days the
possibility of violence cannot have escaped anyone. Surely it figured in
Octavius' failure to veto the deposition proceedings.
29. Plut. *TG* 11.1.

theft the biographer reports. "Askers" (*rogatores*), not ballot counters, would reckon the outcome of the vote on the bill.[30] The law that instituted the ballot for legislative voting was introduced by Gracchus' friend, C. Papirius Carbo, but not until 131.[31] Whatever the precise nature of the disturbance designed to forestall the meeting, inconvenience Tiberius' rural followers, and prevent the vote from finally being taken, the rustic supporters of land reform were earnest enough, numerous enough, and very probably undisciplined enough to force the issue if it came to a test of strength. In the end, the *concilium plebis* met, and Octavius once again had to use his veto to prevent the *rogatio* from becoming law.[32] To avert the explosion that must have seemed imminent, two distinguished senior senators (probably M'. Manilius, consul for 149, and one of the four Fulvii who had held the consulship since 149) intervened and persuaded Tiberius to submit the issue to senatorial arbitration.[33]

Tiberius could hardly have refused this request from former consuls without setting himself outside the pale of the established order. In any case, he probably had a sincere desire to avoid the collision toward which his course and Octavius' were leading. Given the locus of political power at that period, it was surely in his own interests to escape having to put his dispute with Octavius in the hands of the People by asking them to depose his colleague, provided that he could, at the same time, get his bill voted into law. Appian claims that Tiberius positively welcomed the idea that the Senate intervene.[34] The author may, of course, have been following a pro-Gracchan tradition stressing the tribune's modera-

30. See Taylor, *RVA*, pp. 34–35.

31. Or possibly in 130. See Cic. *Leg.* iii.35; Cic. *Amic.* 41; Cic. *De Orat.* ii.170; Broughton, *MRR*, I, 502.

32. Plutarch (*TG* 11.1–2) does not mention Octavius' veto but simply has the two consulars beg Tiberius to seek senatorial arbitration when the party of the rich fails to avert the assembly's meeting. Appian (*BC* i.12.50), more reasonably, has Tiberius agree to bring the matter before the Senate as a result of Octavius' veto.

33. See Chap. 4, n. 21, for the senators' names and see above, n. 31, for references.

34. App. *BC* i.12.50; cf. Plut. *TG* 11.2.

tion and willingness to negotiate. Yet the report of Tiberius' eager-
ness may be accurate, for there is good reason to believe that the
champion of land reform thought the Senate would apply its considerable pressure, not to himself, but to his vetoing colleague.

Octavius' persistence in his veto might have been more unprecedented and constitutionally outrageous than Tiberius' tactics.[35]
Never before had the official elected specifically to protect the
People's interests blocked legislation demonstrably favored by an
overwhelming majority of the populace. Octavius' stand was a betrayal of his trust as a tribune of the People. What is more, all
recent instances of analogous political deadlock had ended with
withdrawal of the tribunician veto. Tiberius might have expected
to make some concession, to give certain private assurances, but
with precedent and the People behind him, he could now hope,
as Appian implies, that his formidable backers within the Senate
would guide or goad the body into tipping the balance in his
favor.

The meeting of the Senate did not go as Tiberius had hoped.
Unfortunately, we have no significant information on what actually
transpired, no precise reason for the Senate's inability or unwillingness to arbitrate the dispute. Appian says only that when
Tiberius arrived he was upbraided by the rich (ὑπὸ τῶν πλουσίων)
and that he had few supporters there.[36] Plutarch corroborates but
hardly improves upon Appian by writing that "the Senate in this
session accomplished nothing because of the prevailing influence
of the wealthy (διὰ τοὺς πλουσίους)." [37] These reports are not very
illuminating. Even Appian's remark that Tiberius did not have
many senatorial supporters does not allow us to conclude con-
fidently that most senators were actively opposed. These sentences
tell us only that some wealthy senatorial landowners—they need
not have been many—placed their own economic interests above
the long-term interests of class and state. These were the men
behind Octavius, men willing to disregard the spirit of their ancestral constitution, to violate the very procedures that allowed

35. Badian, *TGBRR*, pp. 697–701, 706–707.   36. App. *BC* i.12.51.
37. Plut. *TG* 11.2.

them to retain their positions as governors. Their names and number remain unknown.

The problem presented to the senators at this special session inspired by the two former consuls was whether to take steps to ameliorate the conditions of Italy's displaced peasantry. They had compelling reasons to do so. In public Tiberius had professed a concern for national interest, not just for the alleviation of human suffering. The purposes of his proposal as he announced them were not easily dismissed: to enforce the existing law; to perserve and extend empire; to modify the dangerous effects of an expanding rural slave population; and to assert the right of the common people to share the common property.

Privately the proponents of land reform could stress the problem's political side effects and the class interests involved. A complex system of patronage had long ruled Rome. Now, the argument would run, a coalition of disgruntled citizens and opportunistic oligarchs threatened to pull down the fragile structure. The governing class could not afford to turn a blind eye to this unhappy political fact of life; by remedying troubled social conditions, it must deprive the unscrupulous of proliferating opportunities to use the People for private ends. To all this the bill's supporters could add that Tiberius Gracchus had the legal right and the constitutional means to deal with the plight of the peasantry. The *concilium plebis* was designed to operate as a safety valve for popular pressure, but it could not do so as long as its proper functioning was blocked, scandalously and dangerously, by misuse of the tribunician *intercessio*.

What arguments, then, could the opposition set against these, that would allow men to do with virtuous conviction what they wished to do by inclination? Many, perhaps most, members of the Senate, along with some of their wealthiest and most valuable clients, would lose land if Tiberius' bill became law. While undeniably legal, such action could not be just. The poor would reap the benefits of lands tilled and improved by the propertied. The land commission would reclaim and hand over to the poor flourishing vineyards, estates improved and built upon with the dowries of their owners' wives, properties mortgaged as security for loans, even plots in which were buried the remains of their ancestors.[38]

Such dire predictions were obvious scare tactics, rhetorical as well as inevitable. The opponents of land reform in 133 were not the first, nor would they be the last, to try to discredit an uncongenial legislative proposal by seizing upon the ways in which it might be abused when implemented. In fact, the fears thus aroused had little foundation. The violators would probably have some say in the decision about which of their illegally held public lands they should surrender for redistribution. Arable pasture lands hitherto uncultivated and unimproved would be the most likely candidates for reclamation, though, of course, the proposal may not have guaranteed this explicitly.[39] The charges Appian records do make clear by the extravagance of their emotional appeal to what lengths the bill's opponents were driven to find grounds for righteous complaint. They testify to the acuity and moderation of its terms.

Our sources' sources do not seem to have had access to the words spoken at this session of the Senate, and Plutarch and Appian barely mention the motives acknowledged by Tiberius' opponents or the arguments they advanced against the bill. Certainly the opposition's intransigence stemmed partly from self-interest, partly from fear of the *gratia* Tiberius and the other agrarian commissioners would receive, but such explanations oversimplify what must have been a more subtle and more complex situation. The Roman aristocrat's basic prejudices and conservative view of the human condition must also have stood between Tiberius' proposal and its passage into law. Those involved in the debate could have taken such shared assumptions so much for granted that they never thought to articulate them, but this is hardly likely.

In a society with an imperial foreign policy as successful as that of Rome, the brutal canons that guided political action abroad inevitably had serious repercussions on the standards of acceptable behavior at home. The ruling class, at this stage of its social and intellectual development, would have acknowledged the right of the strong to take what they would and the necessity for the weak to suffer it. The survival of the fittest for them was a perfectly proper

38. App. *BC* i.10.38–40.   39. See above, pp. 135–137.

rule of political life. Ancillary to such a view, of course, comes the belief that striving and achievement improve a man's character, while disinterested generosity corrodes his spirit and dignity.

An agrarian society, which measured a man's quality partly by the amount of land he owned, would be instinctively reluctant to make a gift of that vital social commodity, as Tiberius Gracchus' *rogatio* proposed to do. Polybius, for example, the contemporary Greek historian of the Roman imperial experience and the confidant of Scipio Aemilianus, expresses this attitude in a famous and revealing passage. He describes how, in 232, "the Romans divided among their citizens the territory in Gaul known as Picenum, from which they had ejected the Senones when they conquered them," and he comments ruefully, "C. Flaminius was the originator of this popular policy which we must pronounce to have been, one may say, the first step in the demoralization of the populace." [40] As a rule, it would not be safe to infer the opinions of the Roman oligarchy from those of Polybius, a Greek. Yet independent evidence shows that they shared an identical view of the *lex agraria* of 232.

We know that C. Flaminius, as tribune, had had to ram his bill through the *concilium plebis* against stiff senatorial resistance, and that his success and the Senate's defeat were extraordinary enough to have left a permanent mark on the Roman historical tradition.[41] Polybius never says why he thinks this particular distribution of land had a demoralizing effect on the populace, but Cicero, also less than enthusiastic over Flaminius' achievement, provides the key. He says that the land settlements of Gracchus' spiritual predecessor were not given out to colonies of settlers but rather to in-

40. Polyb. ii.21.7–8.

41. Cato, frag. 43 Peter = Varro *De Agr. Cult.* i.2.7; Cic. *Sen.* 11; Cic. *Invent.* ii.52; Cic. *Acad. pr.* ii.13; Cic. *Brut.* 57; Cic. *Leg.* iii.20; Livy xxi.63.2; Val. Max. v.4.5. Walbank (*COP,* I, 193, following Gelzer, "Römische Politik bei Fabius Pictor," p. 150, reprinted in *Kl. Schr.* III, 51–92) believes that Polybius' hostility toward Flaminius is a reflection of that of the tribune's senatorial opponents, transmitted through Fabius Pictor. He rightly doubts Meyer's view ("Untersuchungen zur Geschichte der Gracchen," p. 374) that Polybius inserted this passage after the events of 133. Indeed, there is no real need for Meyer's hypothesis.

dividuals (that is, they were viritane allotments),[42] which indicates that they were not communities established primarily to furnish an organized defense of the area. Their purpose, Polybius might naturally conclude, was more social and economic than military.[43] This distinction is important for it means that men were not getting the land in exchange for services due. Nor were they getting it for services rendered, as was sometimes the case in the next century when former legionaries received plots of land as donatives or bonuses on their discharge.[44] Polybius' choice of words is revealing; he calls Flaminius' popular policy (ταύτην τὴν δημαγωγίαν) "demoralizing" (τῆς ἐπὶ τὸ χεῖρον τοῦ δήμου διαστροφῆς), implying that what aroused his disapproval, and very probably that of the Roman oligarchy as well, was that state land was being given away free. The same objection could have been leveled against the Gracchan land law one hundred years later, with the essential difference that in the earlier case the land formed part of newly conquered territories, whereas the Gracchan proposal affected land already possessed by individual Romans.[45] Needless to say, de facto possession would intensify the possessors' opposition to giving away land.

More sinister charges were directed not only against Tiberius'

42. Cic. *Sen.* 11; Cic. *Brut.* 57. See also Cato, frag. 43 Peter.

43. Strictly speaking, Flaminius' viritane assignments were not the first of their kind. They had been anticipated in the fourth century at Veii and in the *ager Falernus.* See Salmon's *Roman Colonization under the Republic,* (pp. 13–15) for the difference between colonial and viritane settlements and for the military ineffectiveness of the latter (pp. 88–91). For the military motive behind the establishment of colonies see also his earlier article, "Roman Colonization from the Second Punic War to the Gracchi," pp. 47–67; cf. McDonald, "The History of Rome and Italy in the Second Century B.C.," p. 128.

44. See above, p. 81, with n. 34.

45. Appian (*BC* i.11.46) reports that the *lex Sempronia agraria* allowed the large landowners to gain good title to the *ager publicus* they legally retained without having to pay a rent on it. At the same time Plutarch (*CG* 9.2–3) implies that the impoverished recipients of reclaimed *ager publicus* paid rent on the plots assigned to them; his implication has been pronounced paradoxical and possibly inaccurate. Yet the provisions may be historical, attempts to forestall the sort of objections discussed in the text and reflecting Roman prejudices rather than our own.

agrarian proposal but at his character and motives. Early in the year, certainly before his deposition of Octavius had become an issue, Tiberius' enemies claimed that he was "introducing a land redistribution in order to confuse the body politic and stir up a general revolution." [46] This accusation might not have surfaced for the first time at this meeting of the Senate, but the bill's enemies could hardly forego repeating it then. However standard and unfair the charge may seem now, it must have had considerable impact on second-century Roman oligarchs who were devoted to the entrenched order and to the ancient social system that inextricably entwined prestige and political power with possession of land.

Later the accusations that a desire for revolution and tyranny ultimately lay behind Tiberius' proposal undoubtedly gained plausibility from his actions as the troubles of 133 continued to spiral toward their bloody conclusion. At this earlier stage, though, the charge would have derived its effectiveness from the association that could easily and plausibly have been made between the whole-sale land redistribution envisaged in Tiberius' proposal and aspects of the revolutionary tradition of the Greek East where redistribution of land and the abolition of all debts formed the basis of the appeal of demagogic leaders seeking to foment rebellion against an entrenched oligarchy. Polybius provides an example of the association his Roman peers might have made, for he specifically connects land redistribution with revolution and the establishment of tyranny. He writes, for example, of the Lacedaemonian, Cheilon, who was the legitimate heir to the Spartan throne and deeply resented having lost the kingship to Lycurgus, the ephors' choice. Polybius comments that "he resolved [in 219] to bring about a revolution. Thinking that if he followed in Cleomenes' footsteps and held out to the multitude the hope of allotments and redivision of the land, he would soon have the masses behind him, he set out to work on his design." [47] Again, Polybius calls a certain Mol-

---

46. Plut. *TG* 9.3. See Boren, "Tiberius Gracchus: The Opposition View," pp. 358–369, who overemphasizes the effect of Polybius' theories and underestimates that of the recent history of the Greek world and Polybius' account of it.

47. Polyb. iv.81.2–3.

pagoras at Cius in 202 "a demagogue greedy for power [who] by
flattering the populace, by inciting the rabble against the men of
means, . . . and banishing some whose property he confiscated
and distributed among the people, soon attained by these means
to supreme power." [48]

All senators who either had direct contacts with the Greek world
or knew something about its history should have come across this
association between land distribution and revolution. The Greek
experience must have influenced their perceptions of the origin and
nature of tyranny. Tiberius' opponents certainly could have used
the parallels they and their colleagues would have seen to discredit
the ambitious elder son of Cornelia. To a great extent the man's
subsequent actions would determine how effectively his enemies
could tar him with the revolutionary brush and convince the un-
decided that this extraordinary young tribune sought to bring the
politics of the agora to the Capitoline.

At any rate, the arguments, the interests, the power, perhaps
even the persistence, of the opponents of land reform combined to
frustrate those in the Senate who sought arbitration. Octavius, as
far as we can tell, was subjected to no senatorial pressures to withdraw his veto, and his sponsors were not persuaded to call him off.
Tiberius had to return to the Capitoline with the situation essentially unchanged by his visit to the Senate House. Thus the destiny
of the state lay in the hands of two young and relatively inexperienced tribunes, left by Rome's elder statesmen to their own devices
in their battle over the constitutional dispute their actions were
creating.

Tiberius now had only two real options open to him. He could
withdraw, surrender before the obstinacy of his colleague, and allow the issue to be shelved for the time being. Perhaps, in another
year, with all potential obstructionists locked out of the college at
the elections, some other tribune would be able to steer a similar
agrarian bill through the *concilium plebis*. On the other hand, to
have come all this way only to retreat ignominiously, to suffer a

48. Polyb. xv.21. See Fuks, "Patterns and Types of Social-Economic
Revolution in Greece from the Fourth to the Second Century B.C.," pp. 51–
81.

second public defeat and humiliation, must have seemed quite unthinkable to the grandson of the great Scipio Africanus. Alternatively, Tiberius could fight on, confident that in the *concilium
plebis,* at least, he would not fight alone. This course, however,
would entail frightening Octavius into withdrawing his veto, an
end to be achieved only by a threat to remove him from office.
Such action would be dangerous, for if Octavius called his bluff,
Tiberius would have to make good his threat, which would provoke
a dismaying constitutional crisis, responsibility for which would
fall squarely upon Tiberius' shoulders.

The expedient was drastic, and the idea must have daunted even
a man as determined as Tiberius Gracchus. Whatever constitutional
arguments he might eventually muster in defense of his action, the
fact would remain that he had induced the People to thwart the
will of a substantial segment of the Senate on the most crucial issue
of the day. Many would believe that, were the process of deposition now completed, it might be repeated often, and the oligarchy
would lose an important instrument of social control.

Tiberius characteristically chose the path of greatest resistance.
He launched a frontal attack on the vested interests and constitutional prerogatives of his class. This probably was not the first
time that he conceived the deposition idea, though clearly the
Senate's failure to arbitrate induced him to take the fateful decision to begin proceedings against Octavius.[49]

When Tiberius returned to the plebeian assembly, he announced
that on the following comitial day he intended to take a vote on
the resolution that an official of the People who acted against its
interests could not remain in office.[50] Tiberius' original plan, however, may have been more devious and more moderate sounding
than the one he finally executed. Plutarch says that initially he proposed to break the deadlock by putting his own deposition, and
not Octavius', to a vote of the People. If they should determine
that he did not represent their true wishes and was responsible for
the constitutional crisis that had brought public business to a grind-
ing halt, he would immediately step down and retire to private

49. Plut. *TG* 11.2; App. *BC* i.12.51.   50. App. *BC* i.12.51.

life.[51] The report in the fragment of Diodorus Siculus (Posidonius) confirms, though it muddles, this story.[52] The expedient was, of course, simple but powerful propaganda, since such a vote, if allowed, would enormously strengthen Tiberius' constitutional position. It would unequivocally document the sentiments of the voting populace and indict Octavius' thwarting of their will. Octavius, however, immediately let it be known that he would not be swayed by the vote and had no intention of honoring the implications of its outcome: a vote of confidence for Tiberius would not induce him to withdraw his veto. The acknowledgment was surely a token victory, since it finally revealed Octavius, incontrovertibly, as the agent of vested interests who flaunted the popular will. The public debates thus reached their conclusion. The propaganda contest was over. Tiberius had won, yet it availed him nothing. His *rogatio* was no closer to becoming a *lex*.

This fact, and possibly the time element, combined to convince him that he must threaten to depose Octavius and, if necessary, carry out the threat. He must have hoped that, if he did so, he would be able to defend his action by reference to the popular will and the spirit of the Roman constitution. If this was his reckoning, however, he failed to gauge correctly the strength of the undertow of class interest.

When the *concilium plebis* reconvened, Octavius stood firm, as he had promised, so that Tiberius had no real option but to make good his public threat. Since the tribunician right of *intercessio* entitled Octavius to prevent the vote on Gracchus' agrarian proposal, why did he not obstruct the vote on the deposition proposal in the same way? [53] The depth of feeling, the outright fury, exhibited

51. Plut. *TG* 11.2–4. Contra, see Meyer, "Untersuchungen zur Geschichte der Gracchen," p. 394.

52. Diod. xxxiv/xxxv.5.7. He claims that, before introducing the vote on deposition, Gracchus proposed a plebiscite that would take the form of a simultaneous motion. If some unspecified proposals were voted to be legal, both he and Octavius would retire into private life. If the vote went the other way and they were judged unconstitutional, both would continue in office.

53. Fraccaro, *Studi,* p. 112, n. 2.

by Tiberius' many rural supporters in the *concilium plebis* may explain why the other tribunes did not intervene on Octavius' behalf. It does not explain Octavius' failure to intercede and save himself. He cannot have been intimidated, since his actions had already ensured him the undying enmity of Tiberius' beneficiaries. That he did not veto the deposition proceedings must mean that he could not.[54]

On the one hand, Octavius may not have vetoed because the action to oust him took the same form as a tribunician election which, there is good reason to believe, a tribune had no legal right to obstruct.[55] On the other hand, the proceedings may have been legislative, in which case the spirit of the law would have forbidden an officeholder to interfere with a vote on his own deposition.[56] The latter is more likely. Plutarch specifically uses the word νόμος (law) for the action, while Diodorus speaks of a ψήφισμα, that is, a decree of the popular assembly. Although Appian does not mention a law, he, like Plutarch, describes a process in which the tribes declare themselves successively.[57] This method was appropriate only in legislative and judicial assemblies. Simultaneous voting characterized elections.

The first of the thirty-five tribes cast its vote to end Octavius' magistracy. Gracchus immediately halted the voting in order to allow and coax his colleague to withdraw his veto now that he could see the way things were going.[58] Octavius, however, was not alarmed enough to retract, and Gracchus responded by taking the verdicts of the next sixteen tribes. All of them declared for deposition, and with seventeen votes for Octavius' ouster, Tiberius needed only one more from the remaining eighteen. The margin of victory within the seventeen tribes that had already declared was broad enough to make it all but certain that the next vote would complete

54. Pace Fraccaro, *Studi*, p. 112, n. 2, who believes that Octavius voluntarily withheld his veto so as not to acknowledge the proceedings' validity in any way.

55. Geer, "Plutarch and Appian on Tiberius Gracchus," p. 109.

56. Mommsen, *Röm. Staats.* I³, 287, n. 1.

57. App. *BC* i.12.51–54; Plut. *TG* 12.1; Diod. xxxiv/xxxv.7.1.

58. App. *BC* i.12.52.

the process.[59] At this dramatic moment Gracchus interrupted the proceedings once again with his final, theatrical appeal to Octavius.

This appeal was, in the main, both blunt and patently self-serving. Octavius, his cause clearly lost, was reminded, for the last time, that he was obstructing a proposal that would greatly ameliorate Italy's pressing problems. In opposing it he was indeed betraying the People who earnestly desired the bill's passage and whose interests he had a sacred obligation to protect. Then, suddenly, deserting persuasion for pathos, Tiberius begged Octavius not to force him to execute the deposition and to spare him the obloquy that would inevitably accompany such an action.[60] That Tiberius would not be spared was, of course, now one of Octavius' few consolations.

Plutarch's lively account of this scene portrays an Octavius who was deeply affected by Gracchus' entreaties in these final moments as he wavered between persisting and relenting. He must certainly have been anguished at the possibility of his own imminent political demise, wondering whether even his senatorial backers could save his career in face of the undying enmity of the populace. According to Plutarch, the pressures of the "men of substance" were too much for their pawn to resist; he allowed them to push him over the ledge into deposition and political limbo. This picture is too uncharitable. Octavius, ever tenacious, deserves credit for intense courage as he stood his ground and preserved his dignity to the bitter end by curtly bidding Tiberius to do as he liked.[61] The eighteenth tribe cast its vote as its predecessors had done, and Octavius became a private citizen. One tradition reports that, bereft of his tribunician sacrosanctity, Octavius was rescued only with great difficulty from the angry mob that immediately set upon him. It is a more probable tale than that which depicts him slinking inconspicuosly from the Capitoline to quiet anonymity.[62]

How did the Roman oligarchy view these dramatic develop-

59. App. *BC* i.12.53.   60. App. *BC* i.12.52–54; Plut. *TG* 12.2.
61. Plut. *TG* 12.3.
62. Plutarch (*TG* 12.5) gives the more plausible account. The other is preserved by Appian (*BC* i.12.54).

ments? Did Tiberius' deposition of Octavius finally unite the Senate against him? Was Tiberius' action a decisive step toward his assassination later in the year? Cicero thought so: "It was the fact that Tiberius Gracchus not only disregarded another tribune's veto, but even deprived him of his powers, that caused his own downfall. For what else overthrew him but his act of expelling his colleague from office when he exercised the right of veto against him." [63]

How revolutionary was Tiberius' action? The deposition might not have been the bolt from the blue it is sometimes taken to be. Despite the exceptionally scanty evidence for these years, traces exist of several attempts to circumvent a tribunician veto. These might have provided partial precedents for Tiberius' behavior. In 151, for example, the tribunes imprisoned the consuls. The tribunes must have exercised their veto, either against the levy as a whole or, more probably, against the drafting of certain individuals, and the consuls tried to carry on in spite of it. The incident forms part of a trend, for the consul Caepio ignored Asellus' veto on his departure from Rome in 140, and in 138 the consuls were imprisoned, which again implies their disregard of a veto. Finally, in the next year, the tribune Briso was persuaded or forced to withdraw his veto of the *lex Cassia*. While Tiberius' deposition of Octavius was unprecedented, it can be seen as a radical extension of a clear, historical trend.[64]

Octavius' persistence in his veto was a flagrant and unprecedented breach of constitutional custom. The tribune's right of *intercessio* was not meant to prevent the Roman People from deciding issues that vitally affected their interests. On the contrary, the

63. Cic. *Leg.* iii.24. See also Cic. *Mil.* 72; Cic. *Brut.* 95; Livy *Per.* lviii; Flor. ii.2.5; Auct. *Vir. Ill.* 64.4.

64. See Astin, *SA*, pp. 42–45, 173–174, 186–187. For the imprisonment of the consuls in 151 see Livy *Per.* xlviii; App. *Iber.* 49. For Asellus' veto in 140, see Livy *Oxy. Per.* liv. For the imprisonment of the consuls in 138, see Cic. *Leg.* iii.20; Livy *Per.* lv; Livy *Oxy. Per.* lv; Frontin. *Str.* iv.120. For Briso and the *lex Cassia* see Cic. *Brut.* 97, 106; Cic. *Leg.* iii.35–37; Cic. *Sest.* 103; Cic. *Amic.* 41. See also Taylor, "Forerunners of the Gracchi," pp. 19–27; Bleicken, *Das Volkstribunat der klassischen Republik,* pp. 102–105.

constitutional precedents offered by the sources suggest that the veto served in such instances merely as a delaying tactic to prevent controversial legislation from becoming law until senatorial supporters and opponents hammered out a compromise measure.[65]

As he searched for a means to resolve the constitutional impasse, Tiberius found his task complicated by the lack of a precedent for dealing with Octavius' behavior. He had to set precedent himself. For guidance in such a case, the statesman had to search the constitutional principles that underlay *mos maiorum*—that, at any rate, was the theory.[66] Tiberius may have assiduously searched constitutional principles, yet it was obvious that Octavius was the fly in the ointment, that without him all things were possible, and that he would have to go. As a practical politician Tiberius sought, not constitutional guidance, but arguments to justify the obvious decision: deposition.

Some of the arguments with which Tiberius defended the deposition survive in a passage of Plutarch that is almost certainly authentic.[67] The biographer says he has taken them from a speech presented later in the year to the People, who had become unhappy with Tiberius' (and presumably their own) action against Octavius. He has selected these arguments because they illustrate the man's "subtlety and persuasiveness"; they must also have constituted the heart of his defense. Though Plutarch's version of the speech rambles, there are three main points, as follows.[68]

First, although a tribune receives *sacrosanctitas* from the People, this cannot confer immunity to all criminal prosecution. We do not normally expect our popularly elected officials to violate the laws, but when they do there must be a way to deal with them. A tribune may not, in virtue of his inviolability, demolish the Capitol or set fire to the naval arsenal with impunity. Consuls who violate the laws and the expressed spirit of the constitution can be, indeed have been, imprisoned for their actions. Tribunes, like consuls, are the People's elected officials and must be liable to similar sanctions. At least in principle, it must be possible to deprive a

65. See Badian, *TGBRR*, p. 706.   66. See *ibid.*, pp. 709–711.
67. See *ibid.*, p. 708, for the speech's authenticity.
68. Plut. *TG* 15; cf. App. *BC* i.12.51.

tribune of his office and so of his inviolability, if only to deal with him in cases such as these.

Second, the tribune possesses *sacrosanctitas* as a result of being consecrated in the name of the Roman People, but consecration is neither absolute nor irrevocable. A king is consecrated to the gods, but we expelled Tarquin from the city for his misdeeds. In fact, if we reflect on the issue for a moment, we find that no Roman institution is so holy or so venerable as to have inalienable power. Even a vestal virgin can be buried alive when she breaks her sacred vows. The important point is that her sin against the gods to whom she is consecrated deprives her of immunity.

Finally, then, the resolution that we passed to break the deadlock was both obvious and appropriate. We have seen how it must be possible in principle to deprive a tribune of his powers. We have also seen how such a punishment is especially fitting when the officeholder betrays that from which he derives his immunity. A tribune receives *sacrosanctitas* from the Roman People to enable him to protect their interests. If he betrays this trust, acts against the interests or wishes of the People, prevents them from exercising their right to vote on matters vitally affecting them, he is no lawful tribune. Accordingly, he forfeits the privilege of sacrosanctity and deserves to be deposed.

Was there consensus in 133 that the function of a tribune was to implement the wishes of the Roman People? If there was, Tiberius' constitutional arguments must have been irrefutable and should have won the day for him, not only in the assembly, where Plutarch says they were presented, but in the Senate as well. A passage in the sixth book of Polybius' *Histories* (a book almost certainly completed by 150) implies that such a consensus existed.[69] In his famous digression on the Roman constitution the historian states that "the tribunes are always obliged to act as the People decree and to pay every attention to their wishes." If Poly-

---

69. Polyb. vi.16.5: ὀφείλουσι δ'ἀεὶ ποιεῖν οἱ δήμαρχοι τὸ δοκοῦν τῷ δήμῳ καὶ μάλιστα στοχάζεσθαι τῆς τούτου βουλήσεως. For the date of composition of book vi, see Walbank, *Polybius*, p. 20 with notes; cf. Brink and Walbank, "The Construction of the Sixth Book of Polybius," pp. 100–101; Walbank, *COP*, I, 636.

bius is reporting the view of the tribune's role that was widely accepted in the middle of the second century, Octavius was a patent villain from a constitutional point of view, while Tiberius Gracchus acted in accord with the best traditions of *mos maiorum*. The vetoer's unconstitutional behavior should have induced fair-minded senators to regard the deposition, if not with enthusiasm, at least with gloomy resignation.

Is Polybius' statement a sound indication of oligarchic consensus? The ancient tradition aside from Polybius clearly disapproves of Tiberius' deposition of Octavius.[70] The illogicality of such disapproval in light of Polybius' version of the tribunes' duty has led to attempts to explain away the latter with the suggestion that Polybius inserted his sentence about the tribunate after, and in light of, the events of 133. His prejudices, however, make it unlikely that he would have done any such thing.[71] He strongly disapproved of democracy and from private observation feared that Rome's mixed constitution might become dominated by its democratic element. Moreover, he was a close friend of Scipio Aemilianus, who had proclaimed in public that his brother-in-law was justly killed.[72] What motive, then, could Polybius have had for inserting into his work a conception of the tribunate that was alien to his own political precepts and strengthened Tiberius' constitutional position? The question seems unanswerable.

There is another question, however: why did Tiberius feel it incumbent on him to argue in such detail the case for a tribune's duties being first to the People? If such was the accepted view, why did he have to urge it? Perhaps the proper function of a tribune might have been open to varying interpretations, only one of which is presented by Polybius. Plutarch's particular interest in the subtlety of Tiberius' arguments suggests that the views the tribune

70. For the sources' disapproval of Tiberius' action see Cic. *Mil.* 72; Cic. *Leg.* iii.10.24; Cic. *Brut.,* 95; Dio frag. 83; Dio xlvi.49.2; Livy *Per.* lviii; Vell. ii.2.3; Flor. ii.2.5; Auct. *Vir. Ill.* 64.4.

71. Badian, *TGBRR,* p. 709.

72. Cic. *De Orat.* ii.106; Cic. *Mil.* 8; Livy *Per.* lix; Diod. xxxiv/xxxv.7.3 = Poseid. frag. 110 f. FGrH; Val. Max. vi.2.3; Vell. ii.4.4; Plut. *TG* 21.7; Plut. *Apophth. Scip.* 22–23; Auct. *Vir. Ill.* 58.8.

expressed, and the assumptions underlying those views, were neither standard nor generally accepted.

In any case, a statement in Polybius' constitutional digression does not provide the most reliable basis for a picture of what contemporaries expected from the tribunate. As an account of the actual workings of Roman government institutions, the digression is most unsatisfactory. Its omissions make it enigmatic, and it is distortingly theoretical. Indeed, Polybius does not seem to have understood how Roman government really worked.[73] Yet he was to act as political adviser to Scipio Aemilianus. How could he so totally misunderstand the workings of the system through which he would have to guide his prominent pupil?

Polybius states that he has undertaken his work in order to comprehend Rome's greatness and her imperial successes and that as a necessary preliminary he must comprehend the workings of her constitution. He ought therefore to have concentrated particularly on learning the realities of the Roman system. If his analysis of Roman government was to help his Greek audience to understand the people with whom they were increasingly having to deal, surely Polybius had to present the reality, not merely the theory, of the power structure in Rome. What he does, though, is to deny the truth: he attacks those Greek rulers who believe that a senatorial oligarchy governs Rome and asserts, simplifying and idealizing, that the Roman system was a perfectly balanced blend of monarchy, aristocracy, and democracy.[74]

This paradoxical naiveté cannot be believed. Polybius may not have idealized his statement about the tribunate on Tiberius Gracchus' behalf, but a Greek hostage of his political sympathies could have had more personal and compelling reasons for presenting his Greek audience with less than the whole truth about the political position of Rome's ruling oligarchy. Besides masking with direct statements the realities of the oligarchy's power, he ignores the system of patronage and clientship and the way it combined with Rome's open voting procedures to curtail the common citizen's ability to vote freely. That system made the ordinary Roman vul-

73. Walbank, *COP*, I, 692; Walbank, *Polybius*, pp. 155–156.
74. Polyb. vi.13.8–9.

nerable to the crudest economic intimidation, yet it nowhere figures in Polybius' explanation of the Senate's controls on the behavior of the populace.

His introduction to the constitutional digression in the sixth book informs the reader that what follows will be imperfect owing to the omission of certain details. Such omissions, Polybius says, will be obvious to anyone who really understands how Roman government works, and, he adds, the reader should not suppose that they betoken ignorance on the author's part: they are deliberate.[75] This warning could be accepted at face value, as a cautious scholar's disclaimer. On the other hand, it could be a clever man's surreptitious indication to the sophisticated or knowledgeable reader that what follows should be taken with a large pinch of salt. The digression ends with Polybius' assertion that he intends to describe the branches of government "as they were and, with a few modifications, still are." [76] The interesting phrase, "with a few modifications," casts further doubt on any attempt to use Polybius' description of the Roman constitution as evidence for current practice, as opposed to traditional theory.

Other ancient sources offer quite a different view of the tribunate's function at this stage in the Republic's history. Although the office was created to protect plebeian rights from infringement by a patrician ruling class, the tribune's role underwent a gradual change as plebeian influence grew. A plebeian nobility developed, and in 287 the *lex Hortensia* gave proposals passed in the *concilium plebis* the force of laws binding patrician and plebeian alike. Changing conditions in the period between the Hannibalic War and the tribunate of Tiberius Gracchus caused the tribunes to exercise their authority in new ways. From protectors of plebeian rights they turned into promoters of senatorial policies. In Livy's words, the tribunes became *mancipia nobilium,* servants of the nobles, and acted as instruments for social control rather than

75. Polyb. vi.11.8: ἐὰν δὲ πᾶν τὸ λεγόμενον ἀληθὲς ᾖ, συγχωρεῖν διότι κἀκεῖνα παρασιωπᾶται κατὰ κρίσιν, οὐ κατ'ἄγνοιαν.

76. Polyb. vi.11.13: ὧν δ'ἕκαστον εἶδος μερῶν τῆς πολιτείας ἐπεκράτει, καὶ τότε καὶ νῦν ἔτι πλὴν ὀλίγων τινῶν ταῦτ' ἐστίν.

checks on senatorial policy.[77] This happened in large part because the threatening events of the Second Punic War had united the state under the Senate's authoritative and, more important, successful leadership. The Senate then capitalized on its resultant prestige to enhance and consolidate its power. In the process, the People's tribunes came under the Senate's control and became life members of that body. Since legislation passed by the *concilium plebis* had become binding on the entire community, senators could and did use a tribune to introduce their proposals before the People. Tribunes thus became the politically ambitious agents of distinguished noble senators, and sometimes, on behalf of their patrons, they might promote policies that were uncongenial to the majority of senators. This practice goes back at least to the Scipios, who excelled at putting through legislation to increase their power and to further their policies at the expense of opponents within the Senate. In all such cases, however, the behavior of the proposing tribunes was, quite obviously, no more revolutionary than that of the eminent figures who employed their services.[78]

During this same period, as another facet of the same phenomenon, the tribune's right of veto became a tool of senatorial politics. The right of *intercessio* had been created to protect a plebeian citizen from the magisterial *imperium* of the members of the patrician ruling class. It was part of and supported the tribunes' *ius auxilii*. Now, however, its use had to be cleared with the Senate, or at least with some group of leading senators. Thus, the veto gradually developed into an important means of preventing ordinary magistrates from initiating proceedings objectionable to some or all of the senators.

This history of tribunician subservience to the Senate would have furnished Octavius with at least one hundred and fifty years' worth of precedents for his veto of the land law. Yet Tiberius Gracchus' deposition of his colleague because of the way he had used his veto obviously defied not the ancient spirit, but the con-

77. Livy x.37.11.
78. See Bleicken, *Das Volkstribunat der klassischen Republik,* esp. pp. 150–153.

temporary application of the Roman constitution. Which view of the tribunate is correct?

The conflict between Polybius' and Livy's descriptions of the role of the tribunate betokens a duality that had developed in the actual function of the office by 133. Hence a desperate Tiberius Gracchus could find in the duality grounds for a constitutional case against Octavius' persistent veto and, thereby, justification for his own response of deposition. The tension between ancient theory and recent practice existed precisely because the tribunes did not shed their old image as defenders of plebeian rights while they were gradually acquiring their new role as *mancipia nobilium.* If the tribunes were to perform effectively as conduits for senatorial legislation, rather than merely to duplicate through their vetoes means of social control already available, they had to maintain their popular aspect.

These officials owed their position ultimately to the voters of the *concilium plebis* whose electoral behavior was not wholly determined by their patrons' instructions. Tribunes' campaign oratory should therefore have played to some degree to the people whose votes the candidates courted. More concretely, in their capacity as presiders over the assembly, they would presumably choose to bring before it legislation that appealed in some measure to the class of people predominant in the body.

The two decades immediately preceding Tiberius Gracchus' tribunate saw a dramatic increase in such tribunician activity. A study of Gracchan forerunners notes, "This year of tribunicial intransigence (151) follows a period of fifteen years (166–52) in which, with Livy's history gone, except for the inadequate *Periochae,* there is only one dubious record of tribunicial activity in the scattered sources. In contrast, in the next eighteen years before the tribunate of Tiberius Gracchus, years of equally scattered sources for events in Rome, there are no less than twenty-three recorded episodes of the tribunate. It seems clear that there was a revival of initiative and independence of the tribunes." [79] The increase in activity does not, in fact, imply increased independence. If the initia-

---

79. Taylor, "Forerunners of the Gracchi," p. 22.

tive shown by Tiberius Gracchus represented in some sense the culmination of a trend set by these active forerunners, as the study argues, it is well to remember that at the beginning he probably did not act independently, though he may have found himself doing so later.[80]

The renascence of tribunician activity was not independent of the established oligarchy, but rather a symptom of the Senate's response to the changing political conditions described earlier.[81] As the bonds of *clientela* loosened, the voters of the *concilium plebis* exercised greater freedom, providing new scope for the ambitions of Roman politicians, who could bypass the Senate and consuls by appealing directly, through the tribunes, to an increasingly discontented citizenry.

Every instance of tribunician activity in the eighteen years before Tiberius Gracchus' tenure of the office could be explained by this process. The famous incident of 151 in which the consuls were imprisoned by tribunes in a confrontation over the military draft provides an example.

Appian and Livy's epitomator are our sources for the event. Appian reports that in the course of the levy, "many complained that they had been treated unjustly by the consuls [L. Licinius Lucullus and A. Postumius Albinus] in the enrollment, and some had been chosen for easier service." [82] The epitomator defends the consuls' actions, claiming that they were "conducting the levy strictly and exempting no one as a favor." [83] Whatever the truth of the allegations reported by Appian and denied by Livy's epitomator, it is very difficult to imagine young tribunes, ambitious for further honors, jailing the consuls entirely on their own initiative. Without powerful senatorial backing, such action would almost certainly have destroyed the tribunes' political futures by alienating every senator who placed class solidarity above ancient constitutional theory.

The full story probably ran as follows. Once the levy had begun, certain inductees with powerful patrons objected to the treatment they were receiving, and appealed for assistance to their benefac-

80. See above, p.119.   81. See about, pp. 97–101.
82. App. *Iber.* 49.   83. Livy *Per.* xlviii.

tors, who then approached their men in the tribunician college. The present position and political future of such men would have depended on the senior senators who now required their services. So the tribunes used their veto, either against the levying of certain individuals or against the levy as a whole. In response, the consuls took the virtually unprecedented step of attempting to carry on despite the veto, technically violating the sacrosanctity of the tribunes. The tribunes therefore imprisoned them.[84]

Did the oligarchy allow this because it was the tribunes' constitutional duty to protect plebeian rights and interests, or because the consuls had challenged a Roman noble's prerogative, established by custom, to manipulate tribunician vetoes on his own behalf? While there is no definitive answer to the question, surely the senators would have responded far more strongly to a precedent-setting blow at their own power of *intercessio* by proxy than to an attack on the tribunes' ancient constitutional function. They would not want to lose their ability to avert proceedings that were harming their interests, or damaging their reputations, or undermining their authority, but must preserve that ability even at the cost of allowing or encouraging junior plebeian magistrates to imprison consuls.

The ingrained conservatism of Roman society would have made this course of action the natural one. The Latin expression meaning "revolution" is *res novae* (literally "new things"), and a basic principle underlying the constitution gave the advantage in any dispute to the side that meant to preserve the existing state of affairs. The power to block innovation was written into the structure of government. Hence, the will of the consul opposed to the innovating activity of his peer, whatever it might be, always prevailed. This, of course, is the principle of collegiality.

This same principle had recently been extended to (or possibly reasserted for) magistrates besides the one who happened to be presiding. A clause of the Aelian and Fufian legislation granted to them a right of obstruction similar to the tribunician *intercessio*. Called *obnuntiatio*, it allowed a magistrate, not necessarily a tri-

84. Astin, *SA*, p. 43; cf. Bleicken, *Das Volkstribunat der klassischen Republik*, pp. 102–105.

bune or the one chairing an assembly, to announce that he was searching the sky for an adverse omen or that he had actually seen one.[85] Since such an omen might invalidate any action taken in the assembly, *obnuntiatio* provided yet another means whereby an influential senator might prevent a change in the status quo, and it was accessible to any senator who, in a given year, chanced to lack a vetoer among the ten tribunes. This power grew even more vital as some members of the oligarchy increasingly turned to the People to push through their partisan programs against the wishes of their peers.

The ancient tradition allowed only one acceptable way of circumventing an obstructing tribune, and it was not by abrogating his magistracy. The classic, if not entirely specific, formulation of the appropriate strategy is attributed to another Ap. Claudius who lived centuries earlier.[86] Stated simply, the idea was to set one veto against another. According to the rules publicly accepted by the oligarchy, a tribune could be intimidated into withdrawing his veto through what amounted to a vote of no confidence by a substantial number of the other members of the college. The public obloquy to which a display of their united, or near united, opposition would subject him was a legitimate weapon. They could apply further pressure by threatening to use their vetoes against any subsequent action he or his backers might propose. If a show of opposing tribunes could not be mustered, the veto of one man would have to suffice.[87] The resultant deadlock would encourage backroom negotiations that might pry the vetoing adversaries apart. If they would not come to a gentleman's agreement, practical men of affairs could intervene to effect a compromise—men who understood the need to avoid paralysis of the government machinery to which they owed their power and positions.

Specifically ruled out of order, however, was recourse to any demagogic expedient that might destroy the tribunician veto as an effective oligarchic method of social control. Politicians would

85. See Taylor, "Forerunners of the Gracchi," pp. 22–23.

86. Dion. Hal. ix.1.3f.; Livy ii.44.1; cf. Dion. Hal. ix.5.1; Livy iv.48.1–11 and 15, iv.49.6, x.37.9–12.

87. Livy ii.44.1.

occasionally warn the People that in their own interests they must not allow their behavior to cause destruction of the veto, as that would deprive the tribune of his ultimate recourse in defense of their rights. Of course, the prediction contained a grain of truth, but the Senate was obviously serving its own interests as it handed out this bit of propaganda to the citizenry. This same argument was used to great effect against Tiberius Gracchus, if Plutarch can be trusted.[88] Livy recounts an episode that illustrates the strategy and that, though it apparently took place in 393, may reflect in some of its details practices current when Livy was writing. This fact increases, rather than lessens, its relevance to attitudes in 133.[89]

In 395, two plebeian tribunes working on the Senate's behalf prevented with their vetoes the passage of a very popular law. Two years later they stood trial for their action, and the Senate's influence did not protect them from the wrath of the populace: they were sentenced to pay a fine of ten thousand *asses*. Thus, Livy comments, a most unfortunate precedent (*pessimum exemplum*) was set. In the wake of the decision, Camillus denounced the People for their depravity in turning against their own representatives! They had failed to understand that by their wicked judgment on these tribunes they had destroyed the veto and thereby nullified tribunician power.[90] Undoubtedly the People in 133 were publicly accused of a similar lack of intelligent self-interest.

Tiberius' deposition of Octavius consequently carried with it sinister implications for the Roman ruling class. It demonstrated that a popular vote could negate an oligarch's ability to use the'

88. Plut. *TG* 14.5–6: "Annius said [to Tiberius]: 'If you wish to insult me and degrade me, and I invoke the aid of one of your colleagues in office, and he mounts the rostra to speak in my defense, and you fly into a passion, will you deprive that colleague of his office?' At this question, we are told, Tiberius was so disconcerted that, although he was of all men most ready in speech and most vehement in courage, he held his peace." Cf. Plut. *TG* xv.1. See Badian, *TGBRR*, p. 715 with n. 137.

89. Livy v.29.6f. For the anachronistic details see Ogilvie, *COL*, pp. 691–692, with references.

90. Livy v.29.8–9.

veto in protection of his interests. Popular politics thereby received a substantial boost at the expense of established procedures. This very traditionalist governing class must have regarded Tiberius' action with the utmost apprehension.

7 The Assassination

> He was maddened by the delays which human perversity interposed to so urgent and glorious a duty. . . . He went too far; his only safety lay in going further.
>
> —John Buchan, *Oliver Cromwell*

In 137, before the Mancinus affair, Tiberius Gracchus was a young man on the threshold of his career, marked for political success by every advantage of birth and patronage; in the spring of 133, he had become a renegade, standing almost alone among his own class, relying for his support and his future upon the most indigent of Rome's citizens. Through the months to come he would discover the price to be paid for crossing the limits set by established political procedure. Each time he broke the rules, he further tempted his opponents to do the same in their search for a means of dealing with the threat he presented.

At first, after deposing Octavius, he had his way. His proposal became the *lex Sempronia agraria* immediately after Octavius stepped (or was pulled) down and his replacement took office. Then, in the customary manner, the People elected three men to the agrarian commission and entrusted them with the task of resettling the peasantry. These men, by virtue of the *imperium* they received, would survey and parcel out the public lands at their discretion but in the name of the Roman People.[1] Those elected were Tiberius Gracchus himself, his father-in-law Ap. Claudius, and Tiberius' younger brother, the twenty-year-old Gaius. The last was

---

1. For the customary procedure and the granting of the *imperium* see Salmon, *Roman Colonization under the Republic*, p. 19 with notes. Plutarch (*TG* 13.1–3), Cicero (*Leg. Agr.* ii.31), Valerius Maximus (vii.2.6), and Appian (*BC* i.13) all indicate that the commissioners were elected. Livy (*Per.* lviii) and Velleius Paterculus (ii.2.3) suggest they were appointed.

not even in Rome at the time, for he was serving in Spain under Scipio Aemilianus in the expedition against Numantia.

Appian produces a justification for this extraordinary trio, which must have looked more like a family cabal than a legitimate agrarian commission. He writes that the People elected these men because "they still feared that the law might fail of execution unless Gracchus should take the lead with his whole family." [2] No doubt such fears were real, and they were exploited. The candidates willingly stood for office, of course, making their enthusiasm apparent to an already favorably disposed electorate. Plutarch supplements Appian's explanation, attributing the People's choice to the unopposed backstage machinations of Tiberius Gracchus.[3] The decision that the tribune should run for the commission, along with his brother and his father-in-law, is odd and requires more explanation than Appian provides. Far less controversy would have arisen if reliable men such as Crassus, Flaccus, and Carbo (all of whom did eventually serve as agrarian commissioners) had become the first appointees. Clearly, Tiberius saw advantages to filling the positions himself, with close family.

The most obvious of these was that the proposer of colonial legislation, that is, legislation settling citizens on state lands, customarily received credit for his exertions: the law's beneficiaries were expected to prove their gratitude by becoming his clients. The acquisition of such clients, settled in a single colony on the periphery of the *ager Romanus,* with any political influence they might have thereby safely neutralized, would probably not provoke strong opposition on the part of jealous *nobiles.* This method of augmenting *clientelae* may nevertheless have worried the establishment: the desire to close it off could have played a part in halting citizen colonization during the second century.[4]

The settlements that the *lex Sempronia agraria* provided for were not colonial but viritane. The beneficiaries would not be gathered together in isolated groups, but spread individually throughout the peninsula.[5] The difference is crucial. As a result of this law, the

---

2. App. *BC* i.13.56.   3. Plut. *TG* 13.2.
4. See Salmon, *Roman Colonization,* pp. 113–114.
5. Nagle, ("The Failure of the Roman Political Process in 133 B.C."

members of its commission would gain vast numbers of devoted clients. Since land in public possession was not assigned to a tribe, presumably these clients would still be registered and voting in the thirty-five tribes from which they had originally come. At the same time, as residents on the public lands where they had been relocated, they were freed from most of the economic pressures their previous patrons had exerted. The commissioners would decide how close to Rome and to the polls these men would be settled. The proposer of the *lex Sempronia agraria* would therefore strengthen his political influence in the *concilium plebis* to an unprecedented extent.

Is it then surprising that Tiberius Gracchus should have secured the places on the commission for himself and those who shared his interests? To make the commission entirely the preserve of a particular family, however, to make it, in effect, a Claudian junta, was to go far beyond anything ever sanctioned before. Two tribunician laws, the *lex Licinia* and the *lex Aebutia,* specifically prohibited a law's proposer, or any member of his family, whether related by blood or by marriage, from sitting on a commission or assuming any legal power created by his law.[6] Unfortunately, neither of these laws can be dated precisely. We know only that they were passed sometime before 63, when Cicero mentions them in his attack on Rullus' agrarian proposal. If they were passed in the first half of the second century, Tiberius' action in organizing his commission violated them, but this hardly seems likely. First, had the laws been effective then, they would have provided grounds for an immediate challenge to the commission, especially since C. Gracchus continued to be a member. Second, Tiberius does not at this point seem to have been ready to disregard the law so blatantly. He still preferred to invoke constitutional theory or some

---

[1970], p. 385) asserts that Tiberius' supporters came from the areas where we know settlements subsequently were placed by the land commission. There seems to be no reason to accept this identification.

6. Cic. *Leg. Agr.* ii.8.21: "Licinia est lex et altera Aebutia, quae non modo eum, qui tulerit de aliqua curatione ac potestate, sed etiam collegas eius, cognatos, adfines excipit, ne eis ea potestas curatiove mandetur." Cf. Cic. *Domo* 51.

precedent on behalf of his actions. This time, he could refer to one case, at least, of a colonial land bill whose proposing tribune had served on the land commission it established.[7]

Surely, then, Mommsen is correct in believing that the two tribunician laws were passed in reaction to Tiberius' hand-picked commission (and conceivably even to analogous behavior by his brother), to close a dangerous loophole Tiberius had opened.[8] The specific categories of violators cited by Cicero fit so exactly the identity of the three actual commissioners that the laws must have followed the election, not vice versa. So the proposer himself covers Tiberius Gracchus, any kinsmen (*cognatos*) covers C. Gracchus, and any relatives by marriage (*adfines*) covers Ap. Claudius.

These three fortunate *patroni* would as commissioners have control over a great bloc of new votes. No wonder, then, that the prospect struck fear into the hearts of the rest of the oligarchy, who had just witnessed a demonstration of the political power the peasantry could wield when sufficiently aroused to make the journey from the fields to the city. No Roman aristocrat would fail to realize that this law, enforced by these commissioners, could occasion a radical shift in voting patterns and thus in the balance of power. He would fear more than just the loss of some public land whose usufruct he had previously enjoyed. He was about to lose also some of his former clients—tenants, sharecroppers, full- or part-time employees—in short, all the landless citizens who would no longer need the diminished *beneficia* their patron had conferred. Tiberius Gracchus, his brother, and his father-in-law would inherit these clients and would leave them in no doubt about the identity of their benefactors. The names of the commissioners would appear on every boundary marker delineating the newly allotted farms.[9] This transfer of power to the three men, and to a *concilium*

7. Salmon, *Roman Colonization,* p. 104 with notes. For the tribune see Livy xxxiv.53.1–2, xxxv.9.7.

8. Mommsen, *Röm. Staats.* I³, 501, esp. n. 2. Contra see, for example, Last, "Tiberius Gracchus," p. 30. See also Broughton, *MRR,* II, 468 and 470. Gaius seems to have been his own road maker (Plut. *CG* 7) as Tiberius intended to be his own land commissioner.

9. For the commission's boundary markers that have survived see *CIL* I², nos. 639–645 = Degrassi, *ILLRP,* nos. 467–475.

plebis dominated by them, would be the effect of the land reform scheme of 133 that would most appall the great majority of the established order. They would surely set themselves to thwart it.

The rigging of the land commission, following hard on the heels of the deposition of Octavius, must have made Tiberius, the author of both, an even more conspicuous and controversial figure than before. It would have intensified the feelings both of those who loved and of those who hated him. The *nobiles* may have understood that, in proposing a bill for land reform, Tiberius was the agent—albeit not exactly a colorless one—for more senior senators. The deposition of Octavius, however, was most likely his own initiative (as Octavius' intransigence was his). The sources do not say whether his backers in the Senate approved this action, but the lack of information suggests that at least they kept their names out of it. In the eyes of all senators, the responsibility for Octavius' removal would have rested squarely on Tiberius', not his sponsors', shoulders. Most of the Senate must have united against him and made him the prime target of their resentment—giving him another reason to place both himself and his brother on the agrarian commission, even though he had a more statesman-like, less offensively partisan, alternative. Faced with a Senate solidly opposed to him and determined to block the normal avenues of political advancement, Tiberius may have believed that his only chance of avoiding political extinction was to claim credit for, and keep himself in the forefront of, the movement to distribute land. The commissioner's *imperium,* moreover, might furnish a partial shelter from any legal prosecution arising from the deposition. If this interpretation of his motives is correct, Tiberius need not have decided on the commission's composition when he first introduced the land bill. Rather, he may have taken the step only after assessing the consequences of deposing Octavius.

The suggested earlier argument in favor of the *lex Sempronia agraria,* that it would curb popular politics by returning a disgruntled peasantry to the soil, would now have been totally discredited. By removing Octavius from office Tiberius had, in effect, removed an obstacle from the path of the popular politician. In making the land commission so partisan, he made it crystal clear for whose purpose the path was being prepared.

After the deposition assembly, enthusiastic crowds of rustics escorted the victorious tribune, now a popular hero, back to his home, and, elated by their successes, returned to the fields. Inevitably, the notables, who had lost the battle, did not share the jubilation of the People. They remained in the city to consider their next move to thwart the expropriation of the public land they held and the resultant increase in their adversaries' *clientelae*. Apparently they remained in the city also to plot how they might deal with this irresponsibly ambitious upstart when he tried to renew his ascent of the *cursus honorum*. Assassination surely did not figure in their plans at this stage, but the report that powerful men of state were enraged and feared Tiberius' growing power is not difficult to believe.[10]

When Tiberius approached the Senate to request the commissioner's tent, customarily provided at public expense, they refused it. Instead they allotted him an insulting pittance for his operating expenses, no doubt intending to increase the smart of the rebuke and to impede application of the law.[11] The public purse normally bore the expense of surveying public land and assigning the allotments, and the Senate alone controlled its strings. Can Tiberius really have believed that the Senate would docilely appropriate the monies to finance implementation of the law? To have presumed that they would, would betoken an ingenuousness extraordinary in any Roman politician, but he may, of course, have hoped the Senate would carry out its duty. For him to have such an expectation would not be totally inconsistent with our picture of the man who had seen himself as the hero of the Spanish fiasco.

10. Plut. *TG* 13.2; App. *BC* i.13.57. Cicero's famous remark (*Amic.* 37), "Tiberium quidem Gracchum rem publicam vexantem a Q. Tuberone aequalibusque amicis derelictum videbamus" (cf. *Leg.* iii.10.24), probably pertains to the events we are now describing. I suspect the desertions occurred immediately after the deposition (contra, see Astin, *SA*, pp. 349–350; Badian, *TGBRR*, p. 711) though certainly no later than the revelation of the commission's membership.

11. Plut. *TG* 13.2–3.

Plutarch names Scipio Nasica as the originator of the Senate's rebuffs, and there is no good reason to doubt the report. He also reproduces the contemporary allegation that Nasica led the opposition because he held particularly large amounts of public land and that greed inspired his hatred of Tiberius Gracchus.[12] The same stock charge had, of course, been leveled against Octavius earlier and was faithfully recorded by Plutarch.[13] Naturally, Nasica may have resented the idea of surrendering land to a duly financed agrarian commission, but a conservative Roman oligarch had, by now, plenty of other legitimate reasons to fear, and so to hate, Tiberius Gracchus. If Nasica had not proposed locking the *aerarium* against Tiberius, another similarly disposed oligarch would probably have done so.

How, then, had Tiberius planned to get around this financial impasse? Even if he did not foresee it, how could he have dealt with it had a sudden windfall not solved his problem? The land law itself probably did not contain any explicit provision funding the commission's activities. Such a clause would have encroached upon the Senate's traditional economic prerogatives by surrendering the key of the *aerarium* to the People, which would have affronted all members of the body and been poor politics when the bill's drafters were still working to conciliate as many senators as possible.[14]

One possible alternative was private funding. Unfortunately, the cost of the necessary land survey cannot be estimated with any accuracy.[15] In dealing with the more usual colonial settlements, the

12. Plut. *TG* 13.3.   13. Plut. *TG* 10.5.   14. See above, p. 170.

15. Cicero, in his attack on Rullus' agrarian proposal of 63 (*Leg. Agr.* ii.32), says that that bill "provides them [sc. the agrarian commissioners] with appraisers (*apparitores*), clerks (*scribae*), secretaries (*librarii*), criers (*praecones*), and architects (*architecti*) and in addition with mules, tents, provisions, furniture: he [the commissioner] draws money for their expenses from the treasury and supplements them with more from the allies; two hundred surveyors (*finitores*) from the equestrian order, and twenty attendants (*stipatores corporis*) for each are appointed as the servants and henchmen of their power." This passage, as Badian has pointed out (*TGBRR*, p. 713, n. 130), tells us nothing about the scale on which the *lex Sempronia agraria* operated. It is useful, however, in that it presents a

agrarian commissioners journeyed to the site with a full complement of legally trained surveyors, surveyed the land and marked
the boundaries, centuriated the area, and assigned the plots. For
this purpose the Senate normally granted the commissioners a
three-year *imperium*.[16] The surveyors were probably paid by the
day until the job was done.[17] The nature of the *lex Sempronia
agraria* made the process more complicated and far more expensive. It did not provide for a single, fixed colonial site. Before
centuriation and allocation could begin, areas of public land would
have to be located and surveyed and deeds examined in order to
determine who claimed to possess them and how much of the land
in any particular tract the claimant actually possessed. Next the
commission would have to discover whether a particular possessor
held more land than the law permitted him on this site. If so, it
could be reclaimed for future redistribution. In instances where
possessores' holdings of public land were scattered about, the officials might have to survey several sites in this manner before they
could prove an individual was breaking the law, and so before any
land became available for reallocation. This formidable project,
therefore, promised to drag on for years and, in fact, it did. The
expense would probably be more than private resources could
stand. To accomplish the task, the state would have to pay, assuming there was money enough in the treasury.[18]

There was only one way for Tiberius to ensure that the treasury
would pay. He must go to the People again and do what his law
itself had tactfully avoided doing. The *concilium plebis* would have
to turn the key in the *aerarium*'s lock. He would have to initiate
another plebiscite and thereby infringe on the Senate's exclusive
and heretofore unquestioned right to regulate the state's financial
affairs.

---

picture of the sorts of skilled experts and the materials present in the en-
tourage of a Roman land commission.

16. See Salmon, *Roman Colonization,* p. 19. See also, Dilke, *The
Roman Land Surveyors, An Introduction to the Agrimensores,* pp. 35–36,
51, 63, 105–106, 112.

17. Plut. *TG* 13.3.

18. See Boren, "Numismatic Light on the Gracchan Crisis," pp. 140–141,
for the view that the *aerarium* was in bad straits at this time.

The Senate's refusal to appropriate the funds to implement the *lex Sempronia agraria* predictably enraged the People, who had passed it. Then a curious event intervened, significant enough to find its way into one of our sources and possibly connected, if true, to what followed.[19] An unnamed and presumably unimportant client of Tiberius apparently died unexpectedly. The rumor flew around that the enemies of land reform had poisoned him as an act of intimidation. In ostentatious response, great crowds of Tiberius' supporters flocked to the funeral, carried the dead man's bier, and attended the ceremonies. When the body had been readied for cremation, two attempts to ignite it failed. This was seen as further confirmation that the man had been poisoned, and it further enraged the People.

If Tiberius did not actually stage this scene, he certainly exploited it for all it was worth. He intimated that this murder was but a threatening prelude to his own. He began to appear in the Forum in mourning and begged the People to care for his wife and children in the event that he, too, should fall victim to an assassin's hand. What was the purpose of such behavior?

It does not seem likely that, at this point, some enraged oligarch would contemplate, or even threaten, assassination. To be sure, Tiberius had been playing the demagogue, and his enemies might have characterized him as an aspiring tyrant since he had provided some grounds for the charge, but he had not yet appropriated any public money or, more important, announced his intention of standing for a consecutive tribunate. His enemies in the Senate could afford to be patient. For all anyone now knew, Tiberius would shed his tribunician sacrosanctity in a matter of months and could be dealt with then. There was no need for assassination.

Political destruction, however, was an entirely different matter, and by now the message must have filtered through to Tiberius that an alarming number of senators intended this for him. There is no proof, of course, but such a prospect may have inspired the public histrionics that followed the death of his anonymous friend. They could betoken a preliminary effort to stir up popular senti-

19. See Plut. *TG* 13.4–5 for the story.

ment against his opponents in preparation for another controversial plebiscite, this time to deprive the Senate of exclusive control of the treasury. At any rate, his next wild escalation of the conflict hardly seems an appropriate response from a man who genuinely feared for his life.

At this point, an envoy from Pergamum, Eudemus, arrived in Rome with the news that King Attalus Philometer had died and bequeathed his kingdom to the Roman people.[20] Eudemus stayed at the house of Cornelia as a *hospes,* for Attalus had been a foreign client of Tiberius Gracchus' father.[21] The connection had arisen from the elder Gracchus' embassy to Pergamum in 165, when he had brought a favorable report back to Rome, and as a result of this *beneficium* had become the Roman patron of the Pergamene monarch.[22]

The son had apparently inherited his father's foreign client and so learned early of Attalus' legacy from his guest.[23] He modified his latest plan in light of the news. No longer would he simply introduce a proposal to appropriate funds from the *aerarium*. Instead he proposed, Plutarch says, to use part of the bequest to supply the recipients of land with money to buy stock and equipment for their farms.[24] Plutarch does not say that the bill also provided for the commission's operating expenses, though this seems the natural conclusion. Livy, on the other hand, claims that Tiberius' new bill proposed to give Pergamene money to those who were eligible for land allotments and had been encouraged by Gracchus to expect them, but were bound to be disappointed since there was not enough land to go around.[25] Though Plutarch's report sounds intrinsically more plausible, the two versions are not, of course, incompatible; both may conceivably be accurate.[26]

Finally, Tiberius announced that he intended to bring before the *concilium plebis* the question of some Attalid cities that the

20. Plut. *TG* 14.1.

21. See Badian, *FC,* p. 174; Badian, *TGBRR,* pp. 712–713.

22. See above, p. 39.   23. See n. 21 above.

24. Plut. *TG* 14.1.   25. Livy, *Per.* lviii.

26. Astin, *SA,* pp. 350–351, accepts Plutarch's version; Earl, *Tiberius Gracchus,* p. 94–95, Livy's.

king had freed in his will.[27] The assembly, not the Senate, would decide their fate. Thus, while Tiberius avoided the charge of beggaring the treasury, at a single stroke he challenged the Senate's right not only to manage the state's financial affairs, but to direct its foreign policy as well.

What drove Tiberius to threaten to take over the Attalid inheritance in this revolutionary, high-handed manner? Was his behavior a miscalculation, a senseless overreaction that at last set the Senate irrevocably against him?[28] Such a view might be acceptable had Tiberius intended to appropriate only enough money from the inheritance to cover the operational expenses of his land commission. That would suggest that he had merely sought a solution to another dilemma, as the shortsighted intransigence of the Senate forced him to choose between abandoning his reform or once again infringing on a precious senatorial prerogative. This is not, however, what actually happened.

First, Tiberius proposed to give farm stock and equipment to his land recipients, using money that would otherwise have found its way into the state treasury to finance personal largesse. Second, if Livy is right, he may even have promised to give away some of the Attalid money to citizens who would not receive farms because of the anticipated shortage of land available for redistribution. Finally, he ordained that a delicate bit of foreign policy should be decided by, and therefore presumably in the interests of, the People. None of this had anything to do with the smooth functioning of the land commission.

Such measures surely do not look like misjudgments, and even Tiberius could not have failed to predict the fury they would arouse among the oligarchy. The only answer is that these actions were premeditated demagoguery. Tiberius must have known what an

27. Plut. *TG* 14.2. See also Badian, *TGBRR,* pp. 713–714, on the Attalid cities.

28. Badian, *TGBRR,* pp. 713–714, believes that the agrarian law itself, the deposition of Octavius, and the composition of the land commission were disliked but not actually feared by the oligarchy. Tiberius' handling of the Attalid will was the real turning point, for it was the unconstitutional action of an aspiring tyrant and cast these earlier deeds in a far more sinister light.

overwhelming majority of senators would think and what they would now try to do to his political future. He knew, but he no longer cared because, by this time, he understood that his deposition of Octavius had alienated the Senate beyond redemption. He had nothing more to fear from the Senate as a body even if he pursued a patently demagogic policy. And in demagoguery lay his only hope of keeping his political career alive.

Octavius' veto had transformed this overambitious advocate of land reform into someone much more sinister—a radical demagogue. Had Tiberius submitted to the veto, he would have confirmed the impression created by his role in the Mancinus affair. That episode had made him appear to be a man who could neither keep his word nor effect his will. As such, he could have no individual standing in the Roman political arena. Such insignificance, for a man of his distinguished lineage and high ambition, was not to be borne. Rather than sink without trace through a second defeat, Tiberius removed his colleague from office, thereby imprisoning himself in the role of popular politician, totally dependent for his political survival upon the very conditions which some had probably hoped his law might ameliorate.

The threatened appropriation of the Pergamene funds revealed to the Senate the unparalleled, and quite possibly the unexpected, lengths to which Tiberius was prepared to go. The episode was an important watershed in his relations with them, for it marks the appearance of a number of established senators from varied political backgrounds who now, for the first time, opposed Tiberius Gracchus in public. At the same time it marks what is, in the long run, far more important: a change in the strategy of the opposition. Henceforth senatorial attacks on the land law ceased. Their target became exclusively the man. Proposal and proposer became separated as Tiberius' enemies realized the overriding importance of defeating this renegade. To do so, they must destroy his power at its source, discredit Tiberius Gracchus in the eyes of the People, and to the People the oligarchy soon turned.

The campaign began in the Senate.[29] Q. Pompeius, consul for

29. Plut. *TG* 14.2–6.

141, onetime associate but now open enemy of Scipio Aemilianus, made the inevitable and in the circumstances plausible charge that Tiberius was aiming at a tyranny (*regnum*).[30] Pompeius lived close to the Gracchi and claimed to have actually seen Eudemus, the Pergamene envoy, present Tiberius with a king's diadem and a purple robe; apparently this ambassador from the East was convinced that it was only a matter of time before the tribune became Rome's monarch.

Next, Q. Metellus, consul for 143, another opponent of Scipio though no friend of Pompeius, in a pointed comparison, upbraided Tiberius with failing to live up to the standards set by his distinguished father.[31] The elder Gracchus' proud sobriety was such that whenever, during his notoriously severe censorship, he returned home after dining out, the Roman citizens who lived on his way extinguished their lights for fear he might think they were indulging themselves immoderately with parties and drinking bouts. The son, however, was so much the unabashed demagogue that his way home at night was lit by the dregs of the populace, with whom he caroused.

Finally, the acerbic T. Annius Luscus, consular of twenty years' standing, challenged Tiberius in the Senate to a judicial wager (ὁρισμός, in Latin *sponsio*) concerning his deposition of Octavius.[32] The formal procedure required that Tiberius answer immediately the question Annius would ask. "Did you not, Tiberius, brand with infamy a colleague who was sacrosanct by law?" We are told that Tiberius reacted to the Senate's hearty applause by calling the People together. He then ordered Annius to be brought before them with the intention of denouncing him publicly. Annius, however, produced a different argument for this audience. He put a tried and true rhetorical question to his young antagonist: "If I appeal to a tribune against an injury that you have inflicted on me, and he

30. On Pompeius' relations with Scipio, see Astin, *SA,* pp. 24, 89–90, 94, 121–123, 175, 257, 311–312.

31. See also Cic. *Brut.* 81. On Metellus' relations with Scipio see Astin, *SA,* pp. 24, 75, 85, 89–90, 94, 100, 123, 231, 244, 311–315. On his relations with Pompeius see Astin, *SA,* pp. 94, 129, 181 with n. 2.

32. Plut. *TG* 14.4; Livy *Per.* lviii; see Badian, *TGBRR,* p. 715 with n. 137.

grants me his aid [*auxilium*], will you then depose him?" [33] This point apparently had the intended effect on the crowd. Tiberius was disconcerted since he perceived that not only the Senate but the populace as well were displeased with him for deposing Octavius.

As a result, Tiberius felt constrained to defend his action in the lengthy speech on a tribune's *sacrosanctitas* discussed earlier.[34] Plutarch went out of his way to say that what he had reproduced was not the whole of Tiberius' argument. He chose to preserve those portions of it that illustrated the tribune's subtlety and persuasiveness. Perhaps, then, he omitted a simple point Tiberius should have added if Annius' rhetorical question truly took him aback. Strictly speaking, he had not deposed Octavius—the tribal assembly had done it. He had only proposed the action, which the assembly could have rejected. How dangerous to the People, therefore, was the precedent that had just been set? If another tribune exercising the *auxilium* were to be removed from office, another analogous vote by the People would be required to bring it about. Presumably, this would happen only in another case of the *auxilium* being used against what the People judged to be their interests.[35]

How would the Roman citizenry have received such counterarguments? It might be a mistake to suppose that "the People" now shared a single reaction. Naturally, self-interest would have inclined the supporters of the bill and the deposers of Octavius to believe their champion's rhetoric. Yet Annius' blast had made some uneasy, and apparently Tiberius' extended rejoinder did not entirely allay their disquiet.

By now friend and foe alike must have found Tiberius Gracchus a daunting figure. His ruthlessness would have lent credence to the allegations made by Pompeius and Metellus that he aspired to a demagogic tyranny. Many may have rejoiced at having so fearless a leader. "Their champion [was] a man subject neither to favor

33. I have used Badian's rendering (*TGBRR*, p. 715 with n. 137), of the question.

34. See above, pp. 186–187.

35. Badian, *TGBRR,* p. 715 with n. 137, thinks Annius' question was unanswerable. I agree with him if he means that there were no completely satisfactory answers.

nor to fear—a man, moreover, who for the sake of restoring the land to the people was determined to endure any toil or danger, to his last breath." [36] A man like that might nevertheless have inspired more awe and fascination than confidence. Most important, although his supporters may have been desperate, they were not yet revolutionaries. Indeed, the whole situation was not revolutionary. None of Tiberius' rural supporters sought either to transform or to destroy the Roman system of government. None of them even perceived that his actions might have this effect. The populace would have been concerned only with the immediate effects of whatever Tiberius was doing. They could turn a blind eye to the sinister long-term implications of his alienation of the Senate's right to determine financial and foreign policy. The ordinary Roman probably paid little attention to these matters, for they did not really touch his life. Any faint stirrings of conscience about the upheaval such measures were causing would quickly surrender to the enticing prospect of land allotments.

The only issue on which the Senate could realistically hope to attack Tiberius to any effect was the deposition. Here alone was he vulnerable in the eyes of his own constituency. The People had been willing to violate the sacrosanctity of a tribune who was thwarting them by vetoing a particularly choice piece of legislation. Annius, however, had pointed out to them the full implications of their action. The fall of Octavius carried with it the inviolability of the tribune's *auxilium*. Tribunes either had sacrosanctity or they did not, Tiberius' arguments notwithstanding. The attribute does not admit of degree or allow exception. The People, quite properly, set great store by the *auxilium*. It combined with *sacrosanctitas* to guarantee that a tribune could aid a citizen in distress without hindrance. It was a right with which even Sulla hesitated to interfere.[37]

Thus, Annius and the Senate probably succeeded in impairing the confidence of some of the citizenry in their new leader. Tiberius did not lose most, or even many, of his supporters now, but a

36. Diod. xxxiv/xxxv.6.1.

37. The point is made by Badian. See *TGBRR*, p. 716 with n. 138, for references.

shadow had touched the zealous tribune, and some of his followers may even have begun to feel compromised by the excesses of their leader. Should other senators promise to implement the law, Tiberius' supporters might accept their land and desert their benefactor.

Summer had come, and the tribunician elections were again approaching. When the call came for the candidates' *professiones,* Tiberius declared his intention to seek re-election to the office, an enterprise of dubious legality. It was to prove a fateful decision.

His reasons for taking the step do not emerge clearly from the sources. Plutarch, whose account here is obviously sympathetic to Tiberius, is not much help. He claims that the tribune required prodding from his friends to run again. They succeeded in convincing him that a second term was necessary to ensure his personal safety.[38] Appian is no more informative, though he is less partisan, and reports that Tiberius himself fretted over the evil fate he believed was about to befall him.[39] Whether prompted by outsiders or not, Gracchus resolved now, with flagrant hypocrisy, to seek refuge in the very tribunician sacrosanctity of which he had deprived his colleague.

Tiberius surely expected that his powerful and ever more numerous enemies would do their utmost to block his path if he later ran for higher office before the timocratic centuriate assembly (*comitia centuriata*). Were he now, suddenly, to begin playing by the rules once more and relinquish his tribunate in the customary manner, there was an excellent chance that he would never hold political office again, for he would never be able to placate the enmity he had aroused. To see that he rose no higher in the *cursus honorum* and never attained the praetorship or consulship would probably present little difficulty. His future activities as an agrarian commissioner might be popular enough with the landless masses and the poor generally to maintain his influence in the *concilium plebis.* An aspiring Roman politician, however, could rise only so high by pursuing that path. As an obstacle to the demagogue the Roman political genius had created the *comitia centuriata,* a legis-

38. Plut. *TG* 16.1.   39. App. *BC* i.14.58.

lative and electoral assembly in which the vote was weighted in favor of the propertied classes. This assembly elected the praetors and consuls and before it Tiberius, thanks to his persistent assaults on vested interests, would not find the warm reception he had grown used to in the tribal assembly.

Tiberius' political career might well end when he departed from office, even if he survived the ordeal that almost certainly awaited him in the courts. We know that some members of the Senate were preparing to bring judicial proceedings against him as soon as he shed his protective office. Annius' challenge to a judicial wager implied that Tiberius had been guilty of treason (*perduellio*) for deposing Octavius. This reproach may have prefigured, or actually represented, a first attempt at a trial for treason.[40] The attack would, of course, be renewed when Tiberius became a private citizen again. The penalty for *perduellio* was exile, and the chances for conviction were probably quite high, since the case would be tried before a *iudicium populi* which, despite its title, was likely to be under the sway of the oligarchs. The secret ballot, which had been introduced in 137, did not apply to trials for *perduellio*, so that Tiberius' senatorial enemies would exert the great influence on the jurors' final verdict to which their wealth and station entitled them.[41] Tiberius had indeed something to fear.

Given these prospects and the instincts of the man as indicated by his past performance, it ought not to come as a great shock that Tiberius resolved to seek re-election. This decision, however, ultimately cost him his life. It made him an even more threatening figure. The oligarchy might wonder how, indeed if, this unscrupulous tribune, a traitor to his class, could be stopped. If Tiberius now sought to retain his tribunician sacrosanctity in order to remain immune to criminal prosecution, would he feel any more secure as his second term of office drew to an end? Would he not go on to demand yet a third, fourth, fifth, and sixth protective term

40. For general threats against Tiberius see App. *BC* i.13.57. For the episode with T. Annius Luscus see Livy *Per.* lviii; Plut. *TG* 14.4–6. See also Fraccaro, *Studi*, p. 144, and Gruen, *RPCC*, pp. 55–56.

41. See Jones, *The Criminal Courts of the Roman Republic and Principate,* chap. 1, esp. pp. 3–4, 11–13.

of office? He would, of course, have to promote popular legislation to ensure this interminable skein of tribunates, legislation that
would be increasingly inimical to the oligarchy. The Senate nevertheless made one more effort to defeat him using traditional constitutional means.

As the day for the elections approached, Tiberius' wealthy enemies made a concerted effort to keep him out of office. Appian
tells us how they earnestly promoted the candidacies of those who
were most opposed to him. Tiberius responded by summoning his
rural supporters to attend the election. They failed to respond to
the call, Appian says, because they were occupied with the harvest.[42] Plutarch has less to say, but confirms their absence. He explains how later Tiberius' allies understood they were losing the
election because all the People were not present.[43]

Why should Tiberius' would-be beneficiaries have chosen to
desert him now? A conflict between the harvest and the elections
can have been only part of the reason. After all, these were men
whose very hope for survival had rested with Tiberius. Only
months before they had withstood fearlessly the threats their
patroni must have unleashed. They had deposed a tribune, passed
the controversial agrarian law, and provided the votes necessary
to appropriate the Attalid inheritance. Can Italy's indigent have
allowed the call of the harvest to deafen their ears to the call
of their benefactor if his survival were necessary for theirs? They
must have been convinced that it was not. Tiberius' enemies must
have hit upon the most obvious and the only really effective strategy for preventing his re-election—they must have given their
word publicly as men of honor that the agrarian law would be implemented,[44] demanding in return a free hand to deal with its proposer. That we never hear Tiberius claim that only his re-election
would ensure implementation of his law strengthens the view that
the Senate had guaranteed it.[45]

There is a tradition, reasonable in this context, that in order to

42. App. *BC* i.14.58–59.   43. Plut. *TG* 16.2.

44. See Earl, *Tiberius Gracchus,* pp. 114–117; cf. Earl "Tiberius
Gracchus' Last Assembly," pp. 103–104; Badian, *TGBRR,* pp. 719–720.

45. Badian, *TGBRR,* pp. 719–720.

promote his re-election, Tiberius now announced a plan to introduce a series of popular laws. Appian, as on much else, has nothing
to say on the subject. Dio Cassius speaks vaguely of "certain laws
for the benefit of those serving in the army" and says that Tiberius
was going to transfer the courts from the Senate to the Knights. He
also reproduces the highly improbable accusation that all three
agrarian commissioners were attempting to win political office for
132. Supposedly, both Gracchi intended to run for tribunates while
Ap. Claudius sought another consulship.[46] Plutarch provides the
most complete account of the proposals. He lists three: a reduc-
tion in the duration of military service; a grant of the right to appeal the verdicts of judges (*ius provocationis*); and appointment
of men from the equestrian order as additional judges (presumably
on the new extortion court, set up in 149 to try cases of provincial
maladministration), their number to equal that of the existing
judges, who were all senators.[47]

These proposals have been said to duplicate suspiciously some
of C. Gracchus' laws, suggesting that the sources mistakenly attributed to the elder brother what properly belonged to the younger.[48]
Of course, such a mistake could have happened, but in the context
of the dilemma that Tiberius was facing, such a legislative program
was a natural and probably a necessary device to extend his term
in office. It is possible, too, that Tiberius promised these bills for
obvious political reasons and that Gaius passed similar legislation a
decade later because he was inspired by his brother's example to
seek the same kind of support.

In any case, the proposals are not identical to Gaius' laws but
merely resemble them. This makes the sort of blunder envisaged
less plausible. Though C. Gracchus did pass some military laws, a
bill for shorter terms of service was not among them. Evidence
indicates that someone else passed such a law, conceivably be-

46. For the tradition see Vell. ii.2; Plut. *TG* 16.1; Dio frag. lxxxiii.7;
Ampelius 26.1. See Dio for the offices allegedly sought by the three agrarian
commissioners.
47. Plut. *TG* 16.1.
48. See, for example, Carcopino, *Autour des Gracques,* pp. 41–45.

tween the brothers' tribunates.[49] Tiberius' proposal to shorten
military eligibility appears designed to accomplish two things and
thereby to attract the votes of the two groups who would gain by
it. First, the law might have provided protection for some of the
beneficiaries of the *lex Sempronia agraria* who had lost their original land through serving in the legions. They would not have to
stand by and see their new farms fail for the same reason if their
past service records proved they had already fulfilled their obligation under the new law. Second, the proposal would have been a
boon to rural voters who had yet to benefit from the legislation
of Tiberius' first tribunate. These were the peasant proprietors who
still had land but were in danger of losing it because of the problems created by military service. They had served and survived,
but feared being recalled since they were now especially prized for
their experience in the field. If Tiberius' enemies had attempted to
induce the beneficiaries of the *lex Sempronia agraria* to desert its
proposer by guaranteeing implementation of the law, his promise
of shorter terms of military service makes good political sense.

Unfortunately, Plutarch's brief remark about Tiberius' plan to
grant or possibly in some way to strengthen the *ius provocationis*
gives too few specifics to indicate against what judges the right of
appeal is being asserted. Since, as we have seen, judicial proceedings hung over Tiberius' head like Damocles' sword, self-interest
may have prompted some tampering with the *ius provocationis*
now. Another possibility is that "the courts and judges referred to
by Plutarch and Dio can only be those set up by the *lex Calpurnia*
to try provincial governors *de rebus repetundis* and before which
it seems unlikely any of the mob would have to appear." Such a
grant of appeal, the theory goes, "would safeguard Ap. Claudius
and his faction if their enemies, the majority of senators, attempted
to use the court for vengeance." [50] This hypothesis shows why the

49. Smith, *Service in the Post-Marian Roman Army*, pp. 8–9. For Gaius'
military law see Diod. xxxiv/xxxv.25.1; cf. Ascon. 68C.

50. Earl, *Tiberius Gracchus*, p. 114, though he is skeptical about the
proposal's authenticity. In two articles, however, Taylor accepts the validity
of the entire legislative tradition: "Was Tiberius Gracchus' Last Assembly

Claudian faction might wish to see Tiberius' bill passed, but does not explain, as it must if it is to command agreement, what attraction such a proposal would have for any significant part of the voting populace. C. Gracchus did propose a law providing that any magistrate who banished a citizen without a trial and thereby violated that citizen's *ius provocationis* would be liable to public prosecution. Our inability to say precisely what Tiberius' proposal on the right of appeal was all about makes it impossible for us to determine his intention in advancing it. This lack of an explanation renders more plausible the theory that Plutarch has, indeed, confused the actions of the two Gracchi, but it does not establish the confusion as fact. At any rate, Tiberius' measure, if authentic, presumably represented a demagogic attempt to find favor with the populace in some way.

Finally, Plutarch accuses Tiberius of acting vindictively in proposing to add to the exclusively senatorial judiciary on the extortion court an equal number of equestrian judges. Anger and contentiousness, Plutarch says, rather than a sense of justice or a concern for the public good, drove the tribune to attack the Senate's power. The scheme does not duplicate the judicial proposal, never legislated, which Plutarch attributes to Gaius. The younger brother's resolution reportedly sought to double the number of senators by adding three hundred equestrians to the body and then selecting the judges from the entire six hundred.[51] If Tiberius did

---

Electoral or Legislative?" pp. 51–69; "Appian and Plutarch on Tiberius Gracchus' Last Assembly," pp. 238–250.

51. For Gaius' doubling of the number of senators see Plut. *CG* 5.2–3; cf. Livy *Per.* lx who puts the number of new equestrians being adlected into the Senate at six hundred. For the law by which Gaius turned the extortion court over to the equestrian order see Cic. *Verr.* i.38; Cic. *Leg.* iii.20; Diod. xxxiv/xxxv.27, 37.9; Vell. ii.6.3 and 32.3; Pliny *NH* xxxiii.34; Tac. *Ann.* xii.60; Flor. ii.5.3. Taylor ("Was Tiberius Gracchus' Last Assembly Electoral or Legislative?" p. 55, n.7) has suggested that the speech of Scipio Aemilianus *contra legem iudiciariam Ti. Gracchi* (Macrob. *Sat.* iii.14.6 = Malcovati, *ORF,* 3d ed., p. 133) was not, as is commonly assumed, an attack on the removal of the judicial powers of the land commissioners (App. *BC* i.19), but rather on this law of Tiberius' on equestrian jurors in the courts. See Pliny *NH* xxxiii.34 for the attitude toward the jury reform of

indeed propose the measure Plutarch describes, his aim was probably to conciliate those wealthy members of the equestrian order who, as might have been expected even without Livy's evidence, had turned against him on account of the *lex Sempronia agraria*.[52] He would have hoped that these men, in order to get a foot inside a door previously closed to their order and gain some control over the courts, would throw the votes they manipulated in the *concilium plebis* behind his candidacy.

The day set for the elections brought the inevitable commotion over Tiberius' consecutive candidacy. Chaos reigned in the assembly as the mutual recriminations of the conflicting groups destroyed any pretence to orderly procedure.[53] Our sources reflect the confusion.

According to Appian, after the first two tribes had already declared for Tiberius, "the rich" intervened, afraid that they were about to lose their battle to keep their enemy from a second tribunate.[54] The opposition complained to the officer presiding over the elections, the tribune Rubrius, that iteration of the tribunate was not proper, though whether they claimed it violated custom (*mos*) or the law (*lex*) is not clear. Presumably they told Rubrius that he ought not to have admitted Gracchus' candidature in the first place. At any rate he became confused and, proving unable to cope with the controversy, agreed to turn the meeting's presidency

---

both Gracchi, and also Tacitus *Ann.* xii.60, who writes: *"cum Semproniis rogationibus equester ordo in possessione iudiciorum locaretur."* Gruen has rightly objected to Taylor's suggestion, however. He points out that Scipio was in Spain in 133 and could not have spoken against a bill of Tiberius' and that Macrobius' phrase *lex iudiciaria* implies a law, not a mere proposal that failed to pass (*RPCC*, p. 58).

52. Livy *Per.* lviii: "Tib. Sempronius Gracchus tribunus plebis cum legem agrariam ferret adversus voluntatem senatus et equestris ordinis."

53. "No one will ever know exactly what happened on the Capitol that day" (Astin, *SA*, p. 224, cited by Badian, *TGBRR*, p. 725). As anyone knows who has ever tried to draw together a logical, consistent account of a riot from various different witnesses, reports of such events are particularly apt to become confused and tendentious. What follows here is, therefore, only a tentative reconstruction.

54. App. *BC* i.14.58–62.

over to Mucius, Octavius' replacement and a known underling of Tiberius.[55] This development caused the other members of the tribunician college, most if not all of whom were hostile to Gracchus and his candidacy, to protest vigorously the appointment of Mucius. They demanded that Rubrius' replacement be selected, as Rubrius himself had been, by lot. This procedural point proved harder to gainsay than the issue of iteration had been; when the Gracchans saw that they were getting the worst of the dispute, they decided to wreck the elections rather than risk having one of the tribunes disallow Tiberius' candidacy. They shut down the assembly altogether.[56]

The elections had to be postponed until the next comitial (perhaps the very next) day while Tiberius labored feverishly to increase the number of his supporters. His enemies must have worked equally hard for the opposite goal. Tiberius even turned to the urban plebs, but whether he courted the votes of those of them registered in rural tribes, or, anticipating violence, sought the physical protection they might provide, can only be guessed.[57] The alternatives are not, of course, mutually exclusive. Tiberius certainly claimed that he was in bodily danger and pronounced publicly that he suspected his enemies might try to kill him while he slept.[58] He stationed great numbers of his supporters around his house to spend their nights on guard against the anticipated foul play. His public suspicion may, of course, have been yet another instance of the theatrics to which he had resorted before, designed to dramatize the precariousness of his position and emphasize the great risk he was taking on behalf of the poor. By this time, however, Tiberius Gracchus may have realized the real physical danger involved in the course he had been pursuing and, most especially, in his latest challenge to the system that upheld the power of his own class.

The night before the elections, a great throng of clients and sup-

55. On the name of the tribune who replaced Octavius, see above, Chap. 6, n. 3.

56. Plut. *TG* 16.3; Oros. v.9.1–4.

57. App. *BC* i.14.59. Cf. Plut. *TG* 16.3.

58. Plut. *TG* 16.3; cf. App. *BC* i.14.62.

porters escorted Tiberius back to his house to bolster their champion's sinking spirits and to encourage him for the ordeal he would face on the morrow.[59] Before daybreak he assembled his partisans and advised them of the signal he would make if the meeting turned violent and he required their physical assistance.

The last day of Tiberius' life began, according to our sources, with the usual highly colored ill omens.[60] At dawn a man brought to Tiberius' house the birds from which the auspices were to be taken. He threw their food before them, but, with a single exception, the creatures refused to emerge from their box, much less take their feed, despite the keeper's strenuous efforts to shake them out. The one bird that finally put in an appearance failed to offer much encouragement. He stretched a wing, raised a leg, and then beat a hasty retreat to his box and his waiting colleagues, without touching his food. Bad as these auspices were, Tiberius became further depressed when he associated them with an earlier omen: a pair of snakes had taken up residence in one of his favorite helmets, where they hatched their eggs. He decided, nevertheless, to go to the Capitol as soon as he learned that the People had assembled and awaited his arrival. He had gone no further than his doorway, however, when he stubbed his big toe on the threshold. The blow was so severe that the nail was broken and quantities of blood gushed out from his sandal. Only slightly taken aback by this, he went on his way, but after a short distance ravens were seen fighting on the roof of a house to his left, and though many people were gathered in the immediate vicinity, the roof tile dislodged by one of the battling birds fell at Tiberius' foot. This gave pause even to the boldest of his company, but the committed Blossius of Cumae was at hand to urge his champion on. He used a very Roman—and not at all a Stoic—argument, pointing out the shame and disgrace that would accrue if the son of Tiberius Gracchus, the grandson of Scipio Africanus, should refuse to respond to the citizenry's summons for fear of a raven. (Such contempt for omens is in itself odd for a Stoic.)

59. App. *BC* i.15.63–64; Semp. Asellio frag. 6 Peter = Gell. ii.13.
60. For the omens see Val. Max. i.4.3; Plut. *TG* 17.1–5; Auct. *Vir. Ill.* 64.8; Obsequ. 27a.

When Tiberius ascended the Capitoline, his men had already occupied its central section.[61] The highly partisan crowd greeted their champion with an enthusiastic shout, and then his supporters quickly surrounded Tiberius so that they would be in a position to protect him should the meeting grow violent. When the assembly finally came to order, Mucius presided. It is unlikely that the eight opposing tribunes had suddenly changed their minds about the propriety of choosing the presiding officer by lot; unlikely, as well, that the lot fell to Tiberius' only known ally in the college. The occupation of the Capitoline and the presidency of Mucius both point to the main reason for the Gracchans' anticipation of violence—they were planning to dispense with constitutional niceties. With the opposition locked out, Mucius would preside over an assembly packed with *Gracchani,* thereby ensuring Tiberius' reelection.

Indeed, no sooner had the voting begun than a disturbance broke out on the outskirts of the mob as Tiberius' opponents tried to make their way into the center of the assembly to cast their votes.[62] The struggle that followed prevented the election from taking place, but the Gracchan strategy was now revealed to all who had eyes. The Senate soon received reports of it as they met at the Temple of Fides to debate an appropriate response to the morning's events. Then Fulvius Flaccus, Tiberius' most trusted and loyal ally, appeared on the edge of the assembly.[63] The great din drowned out his voice, and Tiberius had to signal his supporters to make way so that Flaccus could reach him with the news of what had just transpired in the Senate's meeting.

Nasica, the pontifex maximus, had addressed the assembled senators and demanded that the consul come to the aid of the state by eliminating the tyrant. Nasica seems to have been urging, perhaps had actually procured, what amounted to a declaration of a state of emergency (*senatus consultum ultimum*), but the consul, P. Mucius Scaevola, who would have to implement the Senate's decree, demurred. He boldly refused to resort to violence and stated that he would put no citizen to death without a trial. "How-

61. App. *BC* i.15.64; Plut. *TG* 17.5; Oros. v.9.1–3.
62. Plut. *TG* 18.1.   63. Plut. *TG* 18.1–2.

ever," he continued, with a clear allusion to the unorthodox tactics now being employed, "if the People, under persuasion or compulsion from Tiberius, should vote anything that is unlawful, I will not regard the vote as binding." [64] Nasica was infuriated by the consul's response. He sprang to his feet and exclaimed, "Since the consul betrays the State, those of you who wish to come to the aid of the laws, follow me." He then wound the border of the toga around his head in imitation, some have thought, of the sacrificial dress known as the *cinctus Gabinus* and, followed by a great number of other senators with their togas similarly draped, set off for the Capitoline.[65] With them, of course, went crowds of their clients, who carried staves and clubs brought from their homes.[66]

Gracchus' partisans were prepared to do battle with the band of armed clients. They had not, however, anticipated the appearance of the *nobiles* themselves on this violent scene. When Nasica and the senators reached the Capitol, Tiberius' ruffians, overawed by the collective dignity of the august throng, simply yielded before them.[67] This would not have happened in the next century. Though the senators' attendants and Tiberius' supporters fought each other with clubs and staves, the anti-Gracchan senators appeared at the fray without arms. At this time, day-to-day politics in the Forum had not yet deteriorated to the point where the methods employed

64. Val. Max. iii.2.17; Plut. *TG* 19.2–3; cf. Cic. *Domo.* 91; App. *BC* i.16.68. See Plaumann, "Das sogenannte *Senatus Consultum Ultimum,* die Quasidiktatur der späteren römischen Republik," pp. 359–360. Contra, see Pürkel, *Untersuchungen zum spätrepublikanischen Notstandrecht: Senatusconsultum und hostis-Erklärung,* pp. 10–14. The latter suggests persuasively that no *senatus consultum ultimum* was passed in 133 (the first instance is generally thought to have occurred in the period of Gaius Gracchus) but less persuasively that Nasica was not advocating one. See also Rödl, *Das Senatus Consultum Ultimum und der Tod der Gracchen,* pp. 105–148, esp. p. 170.

65. Cic. *Tusc. Disp.* iv.51; Val. Max. iii.2.17; Vell. ii.3.1–4; Plut. *TG* 19.3–4; App. *BC* i.16.67–68 (see Gabba, *Appiani, Bellorum Civilium Liber Primus, ad loc.*); Auct. *Vir. Ill.* 64.8. On the possible significance of the *cinctus Gabinus* see Badian, *TGBRR,* pp. 725–726 with notes; Badian, "Three Fragments," pp. 3–5.

66. Plut. *TG* 19.5; Vell. ii.3.2; *"intacta perniciosis consiliis plebs."*

67. App. *BC* i.16.69; Plut. *TG* 19.4.

by Caesar's assassins in 44 should seem appropriate to the participants of 133. How many senators would a knife-wielding Nasica have drawn with him from the Temple of Fides to the Capitoline? The senators' lack of weapons suggests that they did not, at least as a group, come with the intention of murdering Tiberius,[68] but cannot count as proof that none among them was bent on assassination.

Murder was, of course, a drastic way for Tiberius' enemies to deal with him, but it was not irrational.[69] During these final months they had consistently portrayed him as an aspiring tyrant.[70] He had indeed given them cause. Now he was attempting to ride roughshod over the constitutional principle of annuality, using force on the Capitoline to secure a second term of dubious legality. If allowed to succeed he could, at the very least, become a permanently disruptive fixture on the tribunician college, and so dominate the Roman political scene. His behavior must have confirmed every suspicion about his ultimate intentions, giving him even more the image of the aspiring *rex*. All but his supporters must have feared that, even if he and those he led could somehow be driven from the Capitoline today, tomorrow would see their return with some new subterfuge designed to capture a consecutive tribunate. What threat could the Roman aristocracy use to intimidate this shameless renegade who thought nothing of violating the most sacred conventions of his class? How else but by killing him could they stop a man who would stop at nothing? Anyone who had come to believe that Tiberius was trying to establish a *regnum* would have little difficulty in convincing himself of the propriety of, even the necessity

68. So Astin, *SA*, p. 221.

69. Contra see Astin (*SA*, pp. 220–221) who writes: "But in reality to have set out to kill citizens without trial would have been, to say the least, a grave risk, both personal and political, and furthermore quite unnecessary; their central interest was to prevent Tiberius being re-elected tribune, and to that end they needed to break up the assembly which they believed was being conducted in an illegal manner." By saying that the action was not an irrational one, I do not mean to imply that there were not irrational elements in the manner of execution. On this, see Badian, *TGBRR*, pp. 725–726.

70. Sall. *Jug.* 31.7; Cic. *Phil.* 8.13; Cic. *Brut.* 212; Cic. *Amic.* 41; Diod. xxxiv/xxxv.33.6; Plut. *TG* 14.2–3, 19.2; Auct. *Vir. Ill.* 64.8.

for, tyrannicide now. That action, at least, was sanctioned by *mos*.

Amid the violence of the general riot on the Capitoline such logic would hardly have found a place, and no doubt the frenzied, hate-filled atmosphere had more to do with turning the company of senators into a murdering mob. Caught up in the hysteria of the moment, they seized the legs of the benches that had been broken in the fray and made directly for Tiberius Gracchus. First they attacked those members of his bodyguard who had not yielded before them. As Tiberius himself tried to escape, someone caught hold of his toga, which he was forced to abandon. Clad only in his tunic, he fled from the senators, but as he ran, in the confusion of the riot, he stumbled and fell over the bodies of those who had fallen before him. When he tried to scramble to his feet, the tribune P. Satureius struck him on the head with a bench leg. A certain L. Rufus delivered the second of the series of blows that would kill him. When the riot ended, not only Tiberius, but two or three hundred of his followers had lost their lives.[71]

Although Tiberius' assassination was probably unpremeditated, his murderers were not contrite. Despite a request that they allow Tiberius' body to be buried at night, they threw the corpse into the Tiber along with all the others.[72] Thereafter a senatorial tribunal supervised the banishment or execution without trial of a number of Gracchus' followers, among them his teacher, Diophanes.[73] On learning of what had happened, far off in Numantia, Scipio Aemilianus, Tiberius' brother-in-law, responded with a quotation from Homer (*Odyssey* i.47): "So perish also all others who do such things." [74] The sentiment on Scipio's lips must also have been in the hearts of the great majority of those who controlled politics at Rome.

71. Psuedo-Cic. *Rhet. Her.* iv.68; Vell. ii.3.1–4; App. *BC* i.16.69–17.72; Plut. *TG* 19.1–6; Oros. v.9.1–3. Orosius says only two hundred of Gracchus' partisans were slain.

72. Val. Max. iv.7.1, vi.3.la; Vell. ii.6.7; App. *BC* i.16.70; Plut. *TG* 20.2; Auct. *Vir. Ill.* 64.8; Oros. v.9.1–3.

73. Cic. *Amic.* 37; Val. Max. iv.7.1; Vell. ii.7.4; Plut. *TG* 20.3–4.

74. "ὡς ἀπόλοιτο καὶ ἄλλος ὅτις τοιαῦτά γε ῥέξοι." Quoted by Plut. *TG* 21.4 and Diod. xxxiv/xxxv.7.3 = Poseid. frag. 110f. FGrH.

Epilogue

αἰὲν ἀριστεύειν καὶ ὑπείροχον ἔμμεναι ἄλλων, μηδὲ γένος πατέρων
ἀισχυνέμεν.

—Homer, The Iliad vi.208–209

The ancients themselves noted that with these murders blood
was spilled in civil strife in Rome for the first time since the expulsion of the Tarquins. A hundred years would pass before it
ceased to flow. The death of Tiberius Gracchus gave grim warning
of a new intensity in the city's political struggles. Above all, the
taboo inhibiting assassination had been violated, and the action
would inevitably prove easier to repeat than it had been to initiate.
This was the legacy of the tribunate of Tiberius Sempronius Gracchus, which ushered in an era of growing anarchy. Calm would
return only after the destruction of Republican government. The
violence endemic in Roman society during the hundred years between the Gracchi and Augustus, together with the corrosive social
problems underlying attempts at land reform, give the age its revolutionary character.

Historians, ancient and modern, have naturally interpreted the
events of Tiberius' tribunate and the motives of the man in light
of what came after, seeing his assassination as initiating the revolutionary process that culminated in dictatorship. The contemporaries who witnessed the deed, however, did not have the advantage of any such perspective. Some may have shuddered at the implications of the murder of a People's tribune by Roman senators,
but most must have perceived his death chiefly as the climax of the
tensions—social, economic, political, and personal—that preceded
it. Previous events and present circumstances, rather than future
trends, would have dominated the conversation when men, whatever their sympathies, discussed and speculated upon what had
happened. This book has approached the developments of 133
from the perspective of the time.

Many scholars have seen the man who generated these developments as the epitome of the sincere reformer. What he sought to reform depended upon what the most pressing need of the period was taken to be. Only recently has the reading of Tiberius Gracchus' intentions and motives changed, as a result of a shift in emphasis from social and economic conditions to the workings of Roman politics. With issues yielding to alliances as the subject for study, his persistence, previously taken as an indication of his selfless commitment to the cause of land reform, has become a mark of his dedication to the interests of his "faction." While the factional theory has illuminated a vital aspect of the Roman decision-making process, its more enthusiastic proponents have gone too far. They often neglect, or merely pay lip service to, anything that might have disrupted the predictable interplay of the old *amicitiae*. To admit, for example, the development of a crisis in social conditions in the Italian countryside would entail recognition of its inevitable effect on the way the oligarchy conducted politics. Unwillingness to accept the idea that the faction did not dominate politics to the extent expected, and that its position was weakening, has produced an unconvincing attack on the reliability of those ancient sources who most unambiguously report the rural crisis. The peninsula's social fabric must remain essentially intact for the old rules of purely partisan politics to prevail unchanged and unchallenged. The desire to maintain that they did so prevail leads, more generally, to a tendency to exaggerate continuity. Since continuity can almost always be traced in history, it has proved relatively easy to find evidence to support the view that the political system functioned more or less as it had previously, a view not as much false as incomplete, in that it refuses to take account of coexisting evidence for change.[1]

The ancient testimony reveals unmistakably that the procedures by which the oligarchy had long governed were being modified. According to a schema still gaining adherents, the consequence of

1. Gruen presents such a view in *The Last Generation of the Roman Republic*. Since the work deals with the first century, a consideration of its thesis here would seem intrusive. Readers may wish, however, to consult my review, "The Accidental Revolution," *Arion*, 4 (1977).

the deteriorating living conditions among the rural peasantry was a vast migration of the dispossessed to Rome, but this picture hardly does justice to what was a far more complex reality. It fails to take account of the strain that the rural crisis placed on the traditional rules of politics, as some men sought to accommodate and capitalize on the new socioeconomic facts of life, while others tried to minimize or nullify their political effects.

The changes were both rapid and profound. Sometime near the middle of the second century a ban was placed on legislative activity during the period when the peasantry was in the city for the elections. The next decade saw a proposal to fill vacancies on the priestly colleges by popular election instead of by collegial cooptation. Three laws passed in the 130s replaced the traditional voice vote with the secret ballot. In 133 the principle of collegiality was contravened as a vote of the People removed a sacrosanct tribune from office for attempting to veto a land law designed to benefit the poor. The proposer of that law, another sacrosanct tribune, who had exploited the power of the populace as it had never been exploited before, was murdered by his fellow *nobiles* when he sought to transgress the principle of annuality.

Surely, if there are watersheds in history, the tribunate of Tiberius Gracchus counts among them. Governing elites do not desert the established procedures that are serving them well. Nor do they, without good reason, suddenly seize opportunities that have always existed. The changing world of Italy at this time provided the inspiration to bend old rules and substitute new ones. Tiberius Gracchus in 133 showed himself willing to engage in the process with a vengeance.

His actions in the year leading up to his death certainly represented an extraordinary journey beyond the pale of accepted behavior as it was set down for his class. Understanding what he conceived of himself as doing, and what his motives were, does not, however, require the postulate that he converted to some radically new world view. By birth, by training, and indeed, to begin with, by inclination, Tiberius Gracchus was a traditional aristocrat, heir to the onerous legacy of his father's success and raised by a fiercely ambitious woman who in the eyes of many exemplified Roman motherhood. When his father died, he lost not only the political influence but the reassuring advice of that pragmatic politician. It is not entirely surprising, then, that this young man of thirty grievously lacked the foresight as well as the judgment that marks the true statesman. Things might have developed differently had the elder Tiberius Gracchus survived to place a steadying hand on his son's shoulder at moments of decision. Surely he would have pointed out that the all-or-nothing gamble involved, first in proposing, then in fighting for a bill dealing with the most controversial issue of the day, was a perilous undertaking for the "hero" of the Spanish fiasco.

The proposal of 133 to redistribute the public lands was a carefully calculated document, drafted by the finest legal minds of the day, and also by some who were among the most astute politically. In its original form it was conciliatory, designed to minimize the number of those who opposed it, perhaps even to isolate them. The drafters appear to have avoided deliberately the reclamation of cultivated farm lands, preferring instead to distribute arable pastures to the displaced poor. The thoughtfulness and thoroughness of the proposal indicates that its authors took seriously its social and military purpose, that they meant the law to work. They included a clause prohibiting alienation of the redistributed land to ensure that recipients could profit only from the usufruct of their allotment and not from its sale price. The same clause, of course, would guarantee further that the poor would not lose their land again. The original proposal, with its concern for the military as well as the social consequences of the dwindling of the peasantry, may have sought to give parcels of land to Italians as well as Romans.

For all its wisdom, practical and judicial, such a bill would require a shrewd, flexible proposer in order to pass. His political standing would have to be secure enough, as Laelius' had been earlier, to allow him to absorb a defeat and withdraw with dignity, if that became the prudent course. He must also possess the political judgment to enable him to recognize that the moment for retreat had arrived. Given Tiberius' weak position, he should never have chosen for the project that would redeem him, the one in which he had to succeed because it was his last chance, an enterprise with such a high risk of failure.

Whatever Tiberius' intentions and motives may have been, whether he was deeply committed to the cause of land reform or not, he could not afford, and so was totally unwilling to accept, defeat and a second public humiliation. Therefore, this hitherto typical product of a traditional Roman aristocratic upbringing responded to the opposition of his own class, expressed in Octavius' threatened veto, by turning to the People. To intimidate his fellow tribune, he increased the bill's appeal to the common citizen by increasing the amount of land available for distribution to the indigent: he removed the concessions to the wealthy and also may have eliminated the Italians as beneficiaries. When these measures proved ineffective, Tiberius, regarding submission to the established order as dooming his career, deposed Octavius. The step was irretrievable, and each subsequent action seemed determined by its predecessor, committing Tiberius ineluctably to populist politics. In fighting to overcome the obstacles the opponents of land reform placed in his path, he attacked first one and then another of the oligarchy's cherished prerogatives, political and financial, thereby at every stage creating new enemies. As he increasingly trampled upon established constitutional procedure, he restricted the constitutional responses available to his enemies. He probably did not fully understand the implications of his actions until it was too late. Nor did the Roman oligarchs comprehend the magnitude of the woes they were destined to unleash by the murder of Tiberius Gracchus the apostate.

Appendix A: The Nature of the Evidence

This appendix has two purposes: first, to provide an explicit statement of where the author stands on the subject of the sources available for the life and career of Tiberius Gracchus; and second, to make available for easy reference a survey of the historiographical tradition that underlies any interpretation of the actions of the tribune and his contemporaries. I should note, in regard to the latter undertaking, that I do not seek here to amplify preceding "Quellenforschungen"; indeed, I have deliberately avoided doing so.

Plutarch and Appian

Plutarch and Appian are the major sources for the background to and the events of 133. Only they provide extended narrative accounts of that year. Plutarch, a Greek from Chaeronea, wrote his biographies around the end of the first century of the Christian era, while Appian of Alexandria must have written his histories near the middle of the second century. Both drew on the partisan accounts composed by authors contemporary with the Gracchi, but neither is himself consistently partisan.

Plutarch sought to chronicle his subjects' lives and to draw useful moral lessons by recording the virtues and failings of his characters. He therefore searched out works that were both sympathetic and critical. Appian has no special ax to grind. His works contain frequent inaccuracies and bias, but those faults are not his; they reflect the nature of the sources that he was faithfully—one is tempted to say slavishly—following. He is not dishonest but un-

critical, and his indulgence in light embellishments of the record
for reasons of style does not amount to falsification. If some of the
speeches found on his pages are fabrications, they are almost certainly the creations not of Appian but of the source he was using.[1]

With the exception of the two authors' renditions of the final assemblies that led to Tiberius' assassination, the accounts of Appian and Plutarch are now generally agreed to be compatible.[2]
Most of their differences consist of details supplied by Plutarch
but missing in Appian. Since Plutarch's version is considerably
longer than Appian's, its greater detail is not surprising, and a
lack of corroboration in Appian does not of itself invalidate any
of Plutarch's statements. If some are rejected it should be because
Appian, or some other source providing a more plausible account,
contradicts or compromises them, or because they are in themselves tendentious and improbable, arbitrary, or conflict with some
known fact about Roman history.

There has been considerable debate over whether Plutarch and
Appian used a common source and even more over which account
is superior. The task of providing answers to the two questions
will interest the historiographer more than the narrative historian,
for Plutarch and Appian can be used in reconstructing the events
of Tiberius' tribunate without those answers. I am inclined to believe that Plutarch and Appian shared a source, but our knowledge
of the historical tradition that connected them to the original historians of the Gracchan era is inadequate to determine which of
the latter might have been the ultimate sources. Even if we did
know this, we could settle only the most obvious issues because we
should still know too little about the earlier authors' biases and
viewpoints.

Reconstructing a narrative of Tiberius' tribunate and demon-

1. Two dissertations are especially worthy of note: Nagle, "A Historiographic Study of Plutarch's Tiberius Gracchus," and Luce, "Appian's Exposition of the Roman Republican Constitution."

2. Contra, Carcopino, *Autour des Gracques,* chap. 1. His arguments have
been amply refuted by Gelzer, "Review of Carcopino, *Autour des Gracques,"*
pp. 648–660; Fraccaro, "Due recenti libri sui Gracchi," pp. 291–320; Geer,
"Plutarch and Appian on Tiberius Gracchus," pp. 105–112. See also Astin,
SA, p. 323 with notes 3 and 4.

strating the superiority of one main source over the other would involve the same process. The details of both accounts would be analyzed and compared for their inherent plausibility and for how well they accorded with the other facts available. Once this process established superiority, knowledge of where it lay would not much help the narrative historian, for he would still have to take account of the possibility that in any given instance the poorer source provided the more reliable account. Resolving any specific factual conflict simply by preferring the version of the source judged generally superior would not only mean resorting to the crudest kind of indicator. It would also entail employing methodology that bordered on being circular: the superior author's superiority would have been established because an examination of details showed that a greater proportion of his were reliable. The choice of version when details conflicted would depend upon which came from the superior author.

The careful reader will no doubt have noticed that, as a working principle, I have tried to reconcile the accounts of Plutarch and Appian. I have declared them irreconcilable only when all the information they and other sources provide cannot be encompassed in a reasonable reconstruction. For example, the two seem at odds where Plutarch portrays the struggle for the land law's passage as a conflict between rich and poor, while Appian sees it as a controversy over the allies and their welfare. I consider the viewpoints divergent but not incompatible. The struggle over possession of the public lands was bound to be between the propertied and the propertyless, provided we understand that the latter would be spoken for by members of the propertied classes, as they must always be in an aristocratic society. Yet, since many of the occupants of the public lands would have been non-Romans, and since the land would be redistributed, at least in part, for military reasons, the struggle might easily develop into one between Romans and Italians as well. Appian may have chosen to emphasize this aspect because he believed the Social War to be a cause of the Civil War about which he was writing, as P. J. Cuff has suggested. Alternatively, it may have been because one of his sources, who was writing near the time of the Social War, was especially concerned with the Italian question. Or both reasons may have played a part.[3] The absence in Plutarch of any emphasis on the Italians' interests need not mean that Plutarch used a different source, or even that he would have objected to this aspect of Appian's version if he had read it. His concern was for character rather than for coherent, continuous narrative, so that he may simply have ignored an implication of the struggle of 133 that he saw as irrelevant to his main purpose. Even in their accounts of Tiberius' final assemblies, accounts generally thought to be hopelessly at odds, the differences finally seem more of emphasis than of substance, and I have drawn on the accounts of both authors. Of course, reconciliation cannot always be achieved; for example, a choice has to be made between the two versions of the fate Octavius suffered immediately after his deposition.

The skeptic might despair of achieving anything like an accurate account of the events of 133. The earliest surviving author to mention the Gracchi, Cicero, wrote nearly a century later, while two and a half centuries separate Plutarch and Appian from the period of which they write. The works that survive, moreover, are based on heavily propagandistic accounts, though if propaganda is to be effective, it must move within the limits set by plausibility. The closer it adheres to known truth, the more likely it is to convince. The versions of events preserved by Cicero, Plutarch, Appian, and the other extant sources trace their origins to contemporary authors writing to persuade a literate, upper-class public, many of whose members either witnessed, or knew witnesses of, the events. Their writings, and the works of the authors who may have been intermediaries between them and our extant sources, have been the subjects of innumerable scholarly studies.

Sources Contemporary with the Gracchi

We know of five authors who lived during the Gracchan period and who may have written about their own turbulent times. They

3. Cuff, "Prolegomena to a Critical Edition of Appian, B.C. I," pp. 177–188, esp. p. 180; Gabba, *Appiano e la storia delle guerre civili,* pp. 79–88, who believes the source is Asinius Pollio. Contra, see Badian, "Appian and Asinius Pollio," pp. 159–162.

are Cn. Gellius, Sempronius Asellio, C. Fannius, C. Gracchus, and
P. Rutilius Rufus. While none of their works survives, some of the
extant authors quote or refer to them. These passages, called fragments, were collected by Hermann Peter in his two-volume work,
Historicum Romanorum Reliquiae (Leipzig, 1906–1914). As far
as we can tell, the surviving sources ultimately depend on the
works of these five men. Unfortunately, the fragments are few and
not especially revealing, so that our knowledge of the authors, with
the exception of C. Gracchus, is thin.

Very little information exists about Cn. Gellius; indeed, the
uncertainty extends even to his identity. He may be either of two
Gellii from this period, one involved in a private lawsuit with the
elder Cato, the other, possibly his son, a "monetalis" in about 134.
He wrote a history of Rome in ninety-seven books that began before the city's founding and may have reached the Gracchan age.
The elder Pliny and Aulus Gellius read it, but the only other
historian who claims to have read him is C. Licinius Macer. His
effect on our surviving sources is therefore impossible to determine.[4]

Sempronius Asellio was serving as military tribune with Scipio
Aemilianus when Numantia fell. A member of Scipio's circle of
intellectual friends, he had read Polybius and wrote a history in
fourteen books that probably began in 146 where Polybius had
ended. He recounted the turbulent events of his own lifetime in
some detail and, although he was in Spain at the time, according to
Aulus Gellius he wrote that Tiberius Gracchus never ventured out,
during the last days of his life, without a bodyguard of less than
three or four thousand men. Plutarch, on the other hand, puts the
figure at never more than three thousand.[5] The evidence is hardly
overwhelming, but this discrepancy, and the little we know of
Asellio's Scipionic background, combine to suggest that his account of Tiberius' career would not have been sympathetic. It has
been hypothesized that Asellio was an indirect source for Plu-

4. Münzer, *RE,* s.v. "Gellius," no. 4. Cic. *Div.* i.55; Gell. xiv 2.21;
Sydenham, *Coinage of the Roman Republic,* p. 50. Badian, "The Early
Historians," pp. 11–13 with notes.

5. Gell. ii.13; Plut. *TG* 20.2.

tarch.[6] This is possible, of course, though Asellio may not have been read very widely. Aulus Gellius, who wrote in the middle of the second century of the Christian era, is the first author to mention him. We have no real way of knowing if any of the later historians used him, nor has enough of his work survived to permit assessment of its quality.[7]

Another member of the Scipionic circle, C. Fannius, wrote a history encompassing the Gracchan era. All the datable fragments refer to events during the author's lifetime. His identity, however, has been disputed. Plutarch mentions a C. Fannius who, along with Tiberius Gracchus, mounted the walls of Carthage in 146 and later wrote a history that mentioned the exploit.[8] Fraccaro has denied that this man was the consul of 122 who turned against C. Gracchus, but Münzer's arguments for the idea are more persuasive.[9] The first extant fragment of Fannius, which comes at the very beginning of his work, explains that with age and experience men grow wiser; this idea may have formed part of his defense of his public switch in political affiliation. His break with C. Gracchus and his obvious veneration for Scipio, whom he compares with Socrates (frag. 7), make it rather unlikely that he viewed Tiberius' activities with favor. This impression receives some support from the inclusion in his work of Metellus Macedonicus' attack on Tiberius (frag. 5), part of which appears in Plutarch.[10] Several authorities have argued that Fannius was Plutarch's principal source, though the view has not won universal acceptance.[11] He is also a candidate for one of Diodorus Siculus' ultimate sources.

6. Soltau, "Plutarchs Quellen zu den Biographien der Gracchen," pp. 357–368, esp. p. 364.

7. Badian, "Early Historians," pp. 17–18 with notes.   8. Plut. *TG* 4.5.

9. Fraccaro, "Sui Fannii dell'età Graccana," pp. 656–674; Fraccaro, "Ancora sulla questione dei Fannii," pp. 153–160; Münzer, "Die Fanniusfrage," pp. 427–442. See also Broughton, *MRR,* I, 519.

10. Plut. *TG* 14.3.

11. Peter, *Die Quellen Plutarchs in den Biographieen der Römer,* pp. 95–100; cf. Peter, *HRR,* 2d ed., p. cxcvii; Kornemann, *Zur Geschichte der Gracchenzeit,* pp. 20–37. Contra, Cauer, "Review of Kornemann, *Zur Geschichte der Gracchenzeit,*" cols. 599–607; Meyer, "Untersuchungen zur Geschichte der Gracchen," p. 399, n. 2.

On the period of the Gracchi, Diodorus is usually taken to be following Posidonius, who was a pupil of Fannius' close friend, Panaetius. Cicero knew Fannius' work, Brutus made an epitome of it, and Sallust, hardly a sympathizer with the established aristocracy, claimed that truthfulness was Fannius' most conspicuous quality.[12]

Cicero mentions a work of C. Gracchus (*scriptum ad M. Pomponium*) that is sometimes thought to have been a political biography of his brother. Plutarch mentions what may have been the same document, and says that in it Gaius asserted that his brother was inspired to confront the issue of land reform after seeing the conditions of the peasantry on his journey through Tuscany to Numantia.[13] If the work was available to Plutarch, Appian may also have been affected, directly or indirectly, by its partisan contents, which could offset the less flattering pictures of Tiberius emanating from Scipionic circles.

One of the latter may have been P. Rutilius Rufus' histories, for he also served with Scipio at Numantia. He was one of Metellus' legates in the war against Jugurtha and reached the consulship in 105. Thereafter he served with Q. Mucius Scaevola (C. Laelius' son-in-law) in Asia, where he fell foul of the province's nonsenatorial publicans. In Rome, his dubious conviction by the Gracchan jurors on the extortion court resulted in exile and minor martyrdom. In Smyrna, where he lived out his days among the people against whom he was convicted of having practiced extortion, he wrote history, and two works are attributed to him, the *Historiae* and *De Vita Sua*. Rutilius had a reputation for being a loyal friend and an unforgiving enemy; Plutarch, who clearly thought well of his work, nonetheless cautions that he may not be entirely trust-

12. Badian, "Early Historians," pp. 13–15 with notes. Peter, *HRR,* 2d ed., frag. 9.

13. Peter, *HRR,* 2d ed., frag. 1 = Cic. *Div.* i.36, cf. ii.62; Plut. *TG* 8.7. Schwartz, "Review of Meyer, *Untersuchungen zur Geschichte der Gracchen,*" p. 793, first suggested that the *scriptum ad M. Pomponium* was a political pamphlet written by Gaius. He has been followed by Cardinali, *Studi Graccani,* pp. 6–7, n. 1, and Taeger, *Tiberius Gracchus,* pp. 9–12, among others.

worthy when writing of an opponent.[14] If he was an ally of Scipio and Metellus, his work may not have treated Tiberius well, but the strength of his attachment to Scipio is not known, and Rutilius sounds like an independent man. He was also friendly with Lucilius, Panaetius, and Posidonius. If Posidonius used his histories, written in Greek, Rutilius' account may have influenced those of both Diodorus and Plutarch, yet so little is known of the works' contents that this sort of theorizing does not take us very far.[15]

Our sources may also have been influenced by the satires of Lucilius, yet another witness to the fall of Numantia and a member of the Scipionic circle. Despite his lifelong friendship with Scipio and his open enmity with several of Tiberius' political affiliates, he seems to have criticized strongly the Senate's treatment of the tribune. This fact indicates the need for caution when we infer political hostility in the historical accounts of Scipio's intellectual friends.[16]

Copies of senatorial decrees (*senatus consulta*) were also available, although Cicero complains that the state's clerks filed them arbitrarily. He knew of a book that contained all the *senatus consulta* for 146, and presumably other years had similar collections which any senatorial history writer could consult.[17]

Finally, sometime during his pontificate between 130 and about 115, P. Mucius Scaevola arranged the publication in eighty books of the *Annales Maximi* from Rome's origins to the present. These set out, year by year, the official events of state. Previously any senator who wished would have had the right to consult them, and their publication opened them to the general public.

Three other historians also wrote about this time, and although some evidence suggests that the events of the Gracchan tribunates

14. Plut. *Mar.* 28; Plut. *Pomp.* 37.

15. On Rutilius generally see Badian, "Early Historians," pp. 23–25 with notes, who takes the evidence as far as it will go. See also Soltau, "Plutarchs Quellen zu den Biographien der Gracchen," p. 363, for the view that his account influenced Plutarch's and Diodorus'. Cicero, in *Brut.* 114 and *Off.* iii.10, connects him with Panaetius and Posidonius.

16. Luc. *Sat.* xxvii, frags. 772–773, 790. See Cichorius, *Untersuchungen zu Lucilius,* pp. 145–149.

17. Cic. *Leg.* iii.46; Cic. *ad Att.* xiii.33.3; cited by Astin, *SA,* p. 1, n. 2.

The identity of Aelius Tubero, Livy's closest predecessor, is
puted, and little is known of the scale or nature of his writ-
s.[27] The same applies to a certain Vennonius to whom Cicero
d Dionysius refer, but about whom no other information exists.[28]

tant Writers on the Gracchi

The earliest extant source for the activities of Tiberius Gracchus
Cicero (106–43). He nowhere provides a continuous narrative
the early career and tribunate of Tiberius, but his writings con-
n numerous references to the events and personalities of the
iod. Though Cicero was born after both Gracchi died, he had
d the histories of Cn. Gellius, L. Calpurnius Piso Frugi, C. Fan-
s, and Sempronius Asellio, as well as some of the later his-
ians such as C. Licinius Macer and possibly even Q. Claudius
adrigarius. He knew the *Annales Maximi* and had consulted
er public documents as well.[29] He had also read widely among
ious selections of speeches from the Gracchan period. He
ised the orations of both Gracchi and was familiar with the
eches of several of Tiberius' opponents: Scipio Aemilianus,
Laelius, T. Annius Luscus, Q. Pompeius, and Q. Caecilius
tellus. He knew of the speeches of Scipio Nasica through a
nd and had read those of C. Papirius Carbo and M. Fulvius
ccus, two of the staunchest allies of the Gracchi.[30]
Cicero's letters provide very little information about the Grac-
n era. The speeches, on the other hand, refer often to the

7. Badian, "Early Historians," pp. 22–23; Ogilvie, *COL*, pp. 16–17.
8. Cic. *ad Att.* xii.3.1; Cic. *Leg.* i.6; Dion. Hal. iv.15.
9. See Cicero's writings, for Cn. Gellius, *Div.* i.55; for Piso, *Brut.* 106;
. i.6; *ad Fam.* ix.22.2; for Fannius, *Brut.* 81, 101, 299; *De Orat.* ii.270;
d. pr. ii.15; *Tusc. Disp.* iv.40; *Leg.* i.6; for Asellio, *Leg.* i.6; for Licinius
cer, *Leg.* i.7; for Claudius Quadrigarius, if he is to be identified with
odius," *Leg.* i.7; for the *Annales Maximi, De Orat.* ii.52. All cited by
n, *SA*, pp. 7–11 with notes.
0. See Cicero's writings, for Tiberius, *Brut.* 104; for Gaius, *Brut.* 125;
Scipio Aemilianus, *Brut.* 82, 295; for Laelius, *Brut.* 82, 94, 295; for
ius Luscus, *Brut.* 79; for Pompeius, *Brut.* 96/97; for Metellus, *Brut.* 81;
Nasica, *Brut.* 107; for Carbo, *Brut.* 104; for Flaccus, *Brut.* 108. All cited
Astin, *SA*, pp. 7–11 with notes.

had affected their views, they do not seem to have actually written
about those events.

L. Calpurnius Piso Frugi served as consul in 133 with P. Mucius
Scaevola and as censor in 120. He drew up the famous *lex Calpurnia* of 149, which established Rome's first standing court, designed to try charges of extortion in the provinces. While he was
no friend of C. Gracchus, his relations with Tiberius are less clear-
cut, and prosopographical analyses have not settled that issue.[18]
By the time he came to write his history, however, his attitude to
such tribunician activity seems to have been openly hostile, as is
evident from his account of Sp. Maelius (frag. 24). His treatment
of Maelius may have inspired the comparison between him and
the Gracchi that so pleased Cicero, who liked to picture himself as
both a new Servilius Ahala and a Scipio Nasica.[19] Piso's writings
were once thought to be the oldest source for the events of the
Gracchan period and to have been behind Diodorus' account.[20]
We do not know, however, that his histories reached Gracchan
times, for the last datable fragment in his work concerns events
that occurred in 146.

Another history-writing contemporary of the Gracchi was
L. Coelius Antipater, one of Livy's major sources. Cicero claims
Antipater knew C. Gracchus and had heard from the younger
brother about his dream that he was fated to suffer the same death
as Tiberius (frag. 50). Antipater's stock portrayal of C. Flaminius
is sometimes taken as evidence for hostility toward the Gracchi
(frag. 19). Whatever the case, his attitude does not much matter
for his history dealt with the Hannibalic War. No evidence exists
that he wrote of the Gracchan period.

18. For his hostility to Gaius, see Peter, *HRR*, 2d ed., frags. 39–43. Earl,
"Calpurnii Pisones in the Second Century B.C.," pp. 283–298 (see also, Earl,
Tiberius Gracchus, p. 14) argues that Piso was probably "benevolently
neutral," a view rejected by Astin, *SA*, pp. 316–318.
19. Cic. *Cat.* i.3; Cic. *Dom.* 86; Cic. *Mil.* 8; Cic. *Sest.* 143; Cic. *Phil.*
ii.26f.; Cic. *De Orat.* 153; Cic. *Rep.* i.6, ii.49, all cited by Nagle, "A
Historiographic Study of Plutarch's Tiberius Gracchus," p. 28, n. 8, and
Murray, "Cicero and the Gracchi," pp. 291–298, esp. p. 296.
20. Busolt, "Quellenkritik beiträge zur geschichte der römischen
Revolutionszeit," p. 321.

Finally, C. Sempronius Tuditanus, the consul for 129 directed
by the Senate to supervise the activities of the Gracchan land commission, also wrote history, but did not deal with the Gracchan
period.[21]

Intermediate Sources

The works of six other historians survive only in fragmentary
form. They were not quite contemporary with the Gracchi, yet
they may have written of the tribunes' activities. They are the possible intermediaries between the authors just discussed and the
extant sources. Accounts of the events surrounding Mancinus'
treaty with the Numantines survive in fragments by two of the
leading annalists before Livy, Q. Claudius Quadrigarius (frags.
73–75) and Valerius Antias (frags. 57, 58). It is normally assumed that their works contained the usual anti-Gracchan version
of the Mancinus affair and of the tribunates.[22] Claudius was a
wholly derivative historian whose remaining fragments reveal no
factional bias, not even the one his name might lead us to expect.
He occasionally added a rhetorical flourish to entertain his audience, but such creations do not seem to have compromised his
faithfulness to the record he slavishly followed. Valerius Antias is
probably the later of the two for he is not mentioned in Cicero's
list in the *de Legibus* (i.6), which was published in 52. Livy, who
was forced on occasion to use him, calls him a credulous and im-
pudent liar.[23] He has often been charged with fabricating archival
material to support his inventions. His accounts were often more
prolix than the comparable treatments by Livy.

Posidonius of Apamea and Rhodes (ca. 135 to ca. 50) was, as
we have seen, a pupil of Panaetius and the leading Stoic philosopher of his day. In addition to philosophy he wrote fifty-two books
of history which began in 146 where Polybius ended and continued until the dictatorship of Sulla. He wrote in Greek and is

21. Peter, *HRR,* 2d ed., p. cciii.
22. See, for example, Taeger, *Tiberius Gracchus,* p. 36; Meyer, "Untersuchungen zur Geschichte der Gracchen," p. 372.
23. Livy, xxvi.49.4, xxxix.43.1; cited by Badian, "Early Historians,"
p. 35, n. 104; more generally, see pp. 18–22.

Nature of the Evidence

often thought to be the source behind the acc
Greek authors, Diodorus, Plutarch, and App
histories are usually assumed to have favored
bility and therefore to have taken a negative a
activities. In fact, Posidonius' own contribution
clearly enough disentangled from the surviving
such conclusions. Even Diodorus, usually take
Posidonius in the part of his history that treats
presents an inconsistent picture. In one passag
as a fearless hero who will risk any personal
effect land redistribution, an aim the author ap
Diodorus sees such schemes as examples of dei
berius as a man who is aspiring to absolute po
contradiction makes it hard to avoid concludir
excerptor has allowed another author to pollute
fortunately, we are not in a position to know
mately derived from the Stoic philosopher.

C. Licinius Macer, an aristocrat whom Bac
last minute Sullan," quickly repented of his co
new establishment and found himself siding w
In his history he portrayed the Struggle of the C
temporary and a *popularis* viewpoint. He includ
own ancestor, C. Licinius Stolo, and insisted up
of the Licinian-Sextian rogations of 367 in prom
of the orders and of settled government. He r
expected to have provided a sympathetic acc
activities, especially if the *lex Sempronia agrar*
vertised as re-establishing the ordinances of 367
cupation of public lands. But Licinius only wr
his work began in the regal period, and the lat
fragments is to Pyrrhus, so that his writings may
the second century.[26]

24. See, for example, Cardinali, *Studi Graccani,* p.
Tiberius Gracchus, pp. 105–111; Gelzer, "Review of Ca
25. Cf. Diod. xxxiv/xxxv.6 and 33.
26. I have followed the account of Badian, "Early
See also Ogilvie, *COL,* pp. 7–12.

Gracchi and to their supporters and opponents, but the statements must be treated judiciously. While Cicero probably knew his history well, it is unlikely that, given his polemical purposes, he always researched his points scrupulously. For the most part he must be telling us what was believed, or what was at least believable, in the first century about the second. This does not mean, of course, that what he says is untrue, for truth might, on occasion, serve his purposes as well as invention, and it is much safer. His self-serving allusions rightly arouse suspicion, but each requires evaluation on its own merits.

Cicero's philosophical writings present different problems. They, too, contain numerous references relevant to a study of Tiberius Gracchus, as do the dialogues. In the *de Republica,* the *de Senectute,* and the *de Amicitia,* Scipio and Laelius have the role of interlocutors. In all these works the reader must decide whether the ideas that emerge from the speakers' mouths originated with them or with Cicero and whether the men portrayed as friends were in fact friends. There is probably no definite answer to the first question. All we may reasonably assume is that the canons of plausibility should have inhibited Cicero from crediting to anyone an opinion with which he was known to disagree. Again, the demand for dramatic plausibility should have prevented Cicero from presenting known enemies as friends, though the friendships that Cicero portrays do not necessarily imply close political affiliation.[31] His own opinion of Tiberius seems impossible to draw from his writings. He uses the image of Tiberius as a rhetorical device, to discredit an opponent before the Senate by comparing him to the seditious tribune, or to embarrass him before the assembly by showing how far short he falls of the caliber of the People's martyred hero. After his exile, Cicero displays a greater propensity to sympathize with the Gracchi who, like himself, had been condemned without due process. Before 57, he sided more readily with Scipio Nasica or Opimius, both of whom delivered summary justice when the state was in danger.[32] Thus, in the writings as in

31. See Zetzel, "Cicero and the Scipionic Circle," pp. 173–179. Throughout, my treatment of Cicero as a source has followed Astin, *SA,* pp. 7–10.
32. Nagle, "Historiographic Study," pp. 21–22.

the age of Cicero, Tiberius Gracchus had become an ambiguous figure. If the consul of 63 had a consistent, personal opinion of him, his public pronouncements do not reveal what it was.[33]

Ten of the lost books of Livy, forty-eight through fifty-eight, treated the events leading up to and including Tiberius' tribunate. Moving at the rate of slightly under two years per book, Livy must have provided his reader with an impressively detailed account. It is generally agreed, however, that he drew, not on the historians who were the Gracchi's contemporaries, but on the intermediaries from the next generation.[34] All that remains of the books are two brief and highly selective epitomes, the so-called *Periochae* and the *Oxyrhynchus Epitome*. The latter survived as a mutilated papyrus effectively covering only the years between 149 and 138. It at least tells us the year in which Livy placed each of its events. In addition to these abridgements there are various other works usually thought to have relied exclusively, or at least mainly, on Livy: Florus, the *de Viris Illustribus,* Julius Obsequens, Eutropius, and Orosius.

Florus probably wrote his *Epitome Bellorum* during Hadrian's principate. It does not follow Livy exclusively, for on a few occasions Florus disagrees with him, seeming to have consulted Sallust and Caesar, among others. The work is a confused and inaccurate compilation and presents a noncommital portrait of Tiberius. The *de Viris Illustribus,* usually incorrectly attributed to the fourth-century author, Aurelius Victor, consists of a series of very brief biographies of Republican figures from Romulus to Augustus.[35] A half-page piece on Tiberius is not obviously partisan. Julius Obsequens, who probably wrote sometime in the fourth century, compiled a table of prodigies from 249 to 12 B.C., based ultimately on the Livian tradition. Only those from 190 to 12 survive. Eutropius, who took part in the Persian campaign (A.D. 363) of the Emperor Julian, was commissioned by the Emperor Valens to produce a survey of Roman history. The work, in ten books, was extremely

33. Béranger, "Les Jugements de Cicéron sur les Gracques," pp. 732–763.
34. Walsh, *Livy: His Historical Aims and Methods,* chaps. 5 and 7.
35. Momigliano, *The Conflict between Paganism and Christianity in the Fourth Century,* p. 96.

compressed, beginning with Romulus and reaching Sulla's dictatorship by the fifth book. The author clearly culled the subject
matter for the Republic from the epitome of Livy, but the work
concentrates so exclusively on external affairs that it never even
mentions the Gracchi. Finally, in the fifth century, Orosius, a pupil
of St. Augustine, at the instigation of his teacher wrote a Christian
chronicle, the *Historiae adversum Paganos,* in seven books, extending from the creation of the world to A.D. 417. This chronicle
drew on pagan sources, including an epitome of Livy that seems
to have been more detailed than those extant. Orosius' work presents a consistently hostile picture of Tiberius Gracchus.

Finally, five other extant sources warrant brief mention: Di-
odorous Siculus, Velleius Paterculus, Valerius Maximus, Aulus
Gellius, and Dio Cassius. Diodorus wrote during the lifetimes of
Caesar and Augustus. Up to 146 he used Polybius as his source.
Thereafter he is generally thought to have followed Posidonius,
though, as we have seen, the pictures of both Tiberius and his
land-reforming activities are inconsistent. Velleius Paterculus wrote
his *Historiae Romanae* during the principate of Tiberius, and in
the second book, covering the period from 146 B.C. to A.D. 30, he
includes a brief and disinterested reference to Tiberius Gracchus.[36]
He makes the interesting and almost universally rejected claim
that Tiberius promised full citizenship to all Italians. His contemporary, Valerius Maximus, composed a collection of memorable
deeds and sayings (*Factorum ac Dictorum Memorabilium*) in nine
books as examples for rhetoricians to cite in their speeches. It follows a topical rather than a chronological pattern, and the material is gathered under such headings as Gratitude, Cruelty, and
Moderation. The chief sources for the Roman examples seem to
have been Livy and Cicero, though Valerius may have consulted
Varro, Coelius Antipater, and Pompeius Trogus as well. While
generally uncritical, the work gives a consistently hostile picture of
the Gracchi. It depicts them as the heirs to a great family tradition
who have fallen far below the standards set by their ancestors.
They wished to destroy the state but were fortunately prevented by

36. Vell. ii.2.1–4.7.

Nasica and Opimius.[37] The twenty books of the *Attic Nights* (*Noctes Atticae*) of Aulus Gellius date from the middle of the second century. This haphazard collection of short chapters deals with an enormous variety of topics. It contains a great deal of miscellaneous information about the middle Republic, preserving a large number of fragments from earlier writers. Our last author, Dio Cassius, entered the Senate during Commodus' reign and wrote a history of Rome from its origins to A.D. 229. Books xxii through xxv dealt with the Gracchan period, but they survive only as brief excerpts contained in various Byzantine collections. Both Gelzer and Taeger believed Posidonius was Dio's source of information.[38] Only he and Plutarch mention the proposals Tiberius put forward in order to gain re-election to the tribunate. He alone furnishes the following details: he claims Tiberius hoped for a triumph on his return from Numantia; he makes Octavius as villainous as Tiberius; he says Gaius intended to stand for the tribunate and Appius Claudius for the consulship for 132.[39] Whoever he was following, he seems to have lost his way.

37. Val. Max. ii.8.7, iii.2.17, iv.7.1 and 2, v.3.2e, vi.2.3.
38. Taeger, *Tiberius Gracchus,* pp. 105–111; Gelzer, "Review of Taeger, *Tiberius Gracchus,*" p. 74.
39. Dio xxiv, frag. 83.

Appendix B: The Dating of the Aelian and Fufian Legislation

Cicero is the only source for the date of the *lex Aelia* and the *lex Fufia*. Though it is now generally agreed that the two laws are distinct, there is little agreement about their dates. Cicero says only, "deinde sanctissimas leges, Aeliam et Fufiam dico, quae in Gracchorum ferocitate et in audacia Saturnini et in colluvione Drusi et in contentione Sulpici et in cruore Cinnano, etiam inter Sullana arma vixerunt," and "Centum prope annos legem Aeliam et Fufiam tenueramus." [1] Suggestions for dating the laws have ranged from 167 for the *lex Aelia* to 132 for both the *lex Aelia* and the *lex Fufia*.[2] Scholars have tried either to link them with an event they considered to have inspired the laws or to join them to some other piece of legislation that seems to come from the same general mold. Such attempts have verged on circularity, for the provisions of the laws are obscure and so the temptation is to slip from seeking an appropriate event to connect with the law into interpreting the law in light of an appropriate event. So, for example, Lange has dated the legislation to 153 because that year witnessed another, similar, political reform, namely the change whereby the consuls entered office on the first of January instead of the fifteenth of March.[3] While such a date is, of course, possible, there is no

---

1. Cic. *in Vat.* 23; Cic. *in Pis.* 10, delivered in 55 before the Senate.
2. See Astin, *"Leges Aelia et Fufia,"* p. 432, and Sumner, *"Lex Aelia, Lex Fufia,"* p. 347.
3. Lange, *De Legibus Aelia et Fufia commentatio,* reprinted in *Kleine Schriften,* I, pp. 274–341, and followed by MacDonald, "Clodius and the Lex Aelia Fufia," p. 164.

strong reason for connecting this reform with what we know of the provisions of the *lex Aelia* and the *lex Fufia*. Some scholars date the two laws to about 150, when the difficulties over the Spanish campaign had become acute, and see them as a reaction to a tribune who had attempted to override the wishes of the Senate.[4] This again is a possibility, though not more. We know that in 151 there had been trouble with the levy and that the consuls had been imprisoned by the tribunes. Also, Cicero informs us that at least one of the aims of this legislation was to muzzle "tribunicii furores."[5] If this is so, it is a bit surprising that a law passed just after 151, before which "there [was] only one dubious record of tribunician activity in the scattered sources," should have merited Cicero's praise, yet should have been so ineffectual that "in contrast, in the next eighteen years before the tribunate of Tiberius Gracchus, years of equally scattered sources for the events in Rome, there are no less than twenty-three recorded episodes of the tribunate."[6] G. V. Sumner has attempted to link this legislative activity with the tribunate of Tiberius Gracchus and so places both laws in 132.[7] He argues that the *leges Aelia et Fufia* reasserted the tribune's right of veto (*intercessio*) and believes that Tiberius' justification (as presented by Plutarch *TG* 15) of his deposition of Octavius for exercising his veto would be very much weakened by the fact that a law confirming the right of *intercessio* had been passed in the preceding generation. This argument is not very convincing, and Sumner's conclusion rests upon the assumption that the Aelian and Fufian laws specifically mentioned the tribune's right of veto, an inference based upon the fact that the laws established (or reasserted) a magistrate's right of *obnuntiatio*. Further, dating the legislation to 132 rather unhappily trims Cicero's *centum prope annos* to only seventy-four years. This is perhaps not an impossible approximation, but its improbability combines with the consequent necessity of making *in Gracchorum ferocitate* refer to

    4. Taylor, "Forerunners of the Gracchi," p. 24, following Frank, "Italy," p. 367. See also Weinstock, "Clodius" p. 216.
    5. Cic. *in Vat.* 18; Cic. *Post red. in sen.* 11.
    6. Taylor, "Forerunners of the Gracchi," p. 22.
    7. Sumner, *"Lex Aelia, Lex Fufia, pp. 344ff.*, esp. p. 348.

the *ferocitas* of only one Gracchus to weaken Sumner's case seriously. Finally, Sumner believes that the clause forbidding the passing (or, as he prefers, the proposing, though the Latin does not necessarily support this) of legislation during the *trinundinum* belongs to the *lex Fufia*. He sees the provision as a reaction to Tiberius' attempt to propose legislation designed to win him votes for a second tribunate. Yet there is no evidence that Tiberius proposed that legislation during the *trinundinum*. Indeed, the absence of the country voters suggests the opposite.

A. E. Astin would make the Aelian and Fufian legislation follow Scipio's election in 148 to the consulship for 147 and so would put the *lex Aelia* in 147 and the *lex Fufia* a little later. This thesis has the virtue of making the occasion of the legislation not a single event but an action that can be seen as the culmination of a growing trend. He believes that the clause in the *lex Aelia* that forbade the passing of legislation during the *trinundinum* was designed to prevent such last-minute law passing as, first, may have enabled M. Claudius Marcellus to hold his third consulship in 152, only three years after he had held his second (instead of the statutory ten), and, second, must have enabled Scipio Aemilianus, who was several years below the minimum age and had not yet held the praetorship, to be elected consul for 147. This line of reasoning, however, fails to consider the possibility that a law granting a candidate the sort of exemption envisaged might be drafted and passed before the *trinundinum*.

Attempts to date these laws precisely have to rely largely on guesses. The sources for the period are too fragmentary to allow much confidence in linking any particular occurrence with the shadowy provisions of the laws. Undoubtedly many of the important events and much of the legislation in these decades came and went without leaving a trace for posterity. The Aelian and Fufian laws themselves receive no contemporary mention and might not be known to us at all had the sixties and fifties of the first century B.C. developed differently. Unrecorded events and laws, even proposals that were never passed, might suggest a wholly different time that would have been appropriate for the passing of the laws of Aelius and Fufius.

Bibliography

Africa, Thomas. "Aristonicus, Blossius, and the City of the Sun," *International Review of Social History*, 6 (1961), 110–124.

Afzelius, Adam. *Die römische Eroberung Italiens (340–264 v. chr.)*. Copenhagen, 1942.

———. *Die römische Kriegsmacht während der Auseinandersetzung mit den hellenistischen Grossmächten*. Copenhagen, 1944.

Astin, Alan E. "Scipio Aemilianus and Cato Censorinus," *Latomus*, 15 (1956), 159–180.

———. *The Lex Annalis before Sulla*. Brussels, 1959.

———. "*Professio* in the Abortive Election of 184 B.C.," *Historia*, 11 (1962), 252–255.

———. "*Leges Aelia et Fufia*," *Latomus*, 23 (1964), 421–445.

———. *Scipio Aemilianus*. Oxford, 1967.

Aymard, André. "Deux anecdotes sur Scipion Émilien," in *Mélanges de la société toulousaine d'études classiques*. Toulouse, 1946. II, 101–120.

———. "Les Capitalistes romains et la viticulture italienne," *Annales Economies-Sociétés-Civilisations*, 2 (1947), 257–265.

Badian, Ernst. "Quintus Mucius Scaevola and the Province of Asia," *Athenaeum*, 34 (1956), 104–123.

———. *Foreign Clientelae, 264–70 B.C.* Oxford, 1958.

———. "Appian and Asinius Pollio," *Classical Review*, 72 (1958), 159–162.

———. "From the Gracchi to Sulla (1940–1959)," *Historia*, 11 (1962), 197–245.

———. "Review of Taylor, *Voting Districts*," *Journal of Roman Studies*, 52 (1962), 200–210.

———. *Studies in Greek and Roman History*. New York, 1964.

———. "The Early Historians," in *Latin Historians*, ed. by Thomas Allen Dorey. London, 1966. Pp. 1–38.

———. "Review of Weische, *Studien zur politischen*," *Journal of Roman Studies*, 57 (1967), 246.

———. *Roman Imperialism in the Late Republic*. Pretoria, 1967.

———. "Roman Politics and the Italians (133–91 B.C.)," *Dialoghi di Archeologia*, Anno IV–V, nn. 2–3 (1970–1971), 373–421.

———. "Three Fragments," in *Pro Munere Grates—Studies Presented to Henry Louis Gonin*, ed. by D. M. Kriel. Pretoria, 1971. Pp. 1–6.

———. *Publicans and Sinners*. Ithaca, 1972.

———. "Tiberius Gracchus and the Beginning of the Roman Revolution," in *Aufstieg und Niedergang der Römischen Welt*, ed. by Hildegard Temporini. Vol. I i. New York, 1972. Pp. 668–731.

Balsdon, John Percy Vyvian Dacre. "Some Questions About Historical Writing in the Second Century B.C.," *Classical Quarterly*, 3 (1953), 158–164.

Bandelli, Gino. "I processi degli Scipioni," *Index: Quaderni Camerti di Studi Romanistici*, 3 (1972), 304–342.

Barrow, Reginald Haynes. *Plutarch and His Times*. London, 1967.

Bauman, Richard Alexander. *The Crimen Maiestatis in the Roman Republic and the Augustan Principate*. Johannesburg, 1967.

Beauchet, Ludovic. "Patria Potestas," *Dictionnaire des Antiquités Grecques et Romaines*, ed. by Charles Victor Dahremberg and Edmond Saglio. Vol. IV i, 342–347.

Becker, James B. "The Influence of Roman Stoicism upon the Gracchi's Economic Land Reforms," *La Parola del Passato*, 19 (1964), 125–134.

Beloch, Karl Julius. *Der italische Bund unter Roms Hegemonie*. Leipzig, 1880.

———. *Campanien*. Breslau, 1890.

———. "Römische Geschichte bis zum Ende der Republik," in *Einleitung in die Altertumwissenschaft*, ed. by Alfred Gercke and Eduard Norden. Vol. III. Leipzig-Berlin, 1914.

Béranger, Jean. "Les Jugements de Cicéron sur les Gracques," in *Aufstieg und Niedergang der Römischen Welt*, ed. by Hildegard Temporini. Vol. I i. New York, 1972. Pp. 732–763.

Berger, Adolf. "A Note on Gellius," *American Journal of Philology*, 67 (1946), 320–328.

Bernstein, Alvin H. "Prosopography and the Career of Publius Mucius Scaevola," *Classical Philology*, 67 (1972), 42–46.

Bicknell, Peter J. *Studies in Athenian Politics and Genealogy*. Wiesbaden, 1972.

Bilinski, Bronisław. "De Capitolii loco, quo Tiberius Gracchus occisus est, observationes topographicae," *Meander*, 15 (1960), 417–430.

Bilz, Konrad. *Die Politik des Cornelius Scipio Aemilianus*. Stuttgart, 1935.

Bleicken, Jochen. *Das Volkstribunat der klassischen Republik*. Munich, 1955.

Bloch, Gustave, and Carcopino, Jérôme. *La République Romaine de 133 à 44 avant J.-C.* Paris, 1935.

——. *Histoire Romaine.* Vol. II. Paris, 1940.

Blum, E. "L'Origine des *Leges Repetundarum,*" *Revue Genérale du Droit de la Législation et de la Jurisprudence,* 46 (1922), 119–135, 197–206.

Bolkestein, Hendrick. *De Colonatu Romano ejusque origine.* Amsterdam, 1906.

Boren, Henry Charles. "Numismatic Light on the Gracchan Crisis," *American Journal of Philology,* 79 (1958), 140–155.

——."The Urban Side of the Gracchan Economic Crisis," *American Historical Review,* 63 (1958), 890–902.

——. "Tiberius Gracchus: The Opposition View," *American Journal of Philology,* 82 (1961), 358–369.

——. *The Gracchi.* New York, 1968.

Bourne, Frank C. "The Gracchan Land Law and the Census," *Classical World,* 45 (1952), 180–182.

——. "The Roman Republican Census and Census Statistics," *Classical Weekly,* 45 (1952), 129–135.

Bracco, Vittorio. "L'Elogium di Polla," *Rendiconti dell' Accademia Archeologica di Napoli,* 29 (1954), 5–38.

——. "Ancora sull' *elogium* di Polla," *Rendiconti dell' Accademia Archeologica di Napoli,* 35 (1960), 149–163.

Brink, Charles Oscar, and Walbank, Frank William. "The Construction of the Sixth Book of Polybius," *Classical Quarterly,* 4 (1954), 97–122.

Briscoe, John. *A Commentary on Livy Books XXXI–XXXIII.* Oxford, 1973.

——. "Supporters and Opponents of Tiberius Gracchus," *Journal of Roman Studies,* 64 (1974), 125–135.

Broughton, Thomas Robert Shannon. *The Magistrates of the Roman Republic.* 2 vols. New York, 1951–1952.

——. *Supplement to the Magistrates of the Roman Republic.* New York, 1960.

——. "Senate and Senators of the Roman Republic: The Prosopographical Approach," in *Aufstieg und Niedergang der Römischen Welt,* ed. by Hildegard Temporini. New York, 1972. Pp. 250–265.

Brown, Ruth Martin. *A Study of the Scipionic Circle* (Iowa Studies in Classical Philology I). Scottdale, Pa., 1934.

Brown, Truesdell S. "Greek Influences on Tiberius Gracchus," *Classical Journal,* 42 (1947), 471–474.

Bruns, Carl Georg, ed. *Fontes Iuris Romani Antiqui.* 7th ed. Tübingen, 1909.

Brunt, Peter Astbury. "Review of Westermann, *Slave Systems*," *Journal of Roman Studies*, 48 (1958), 164–170.

———. "The Army and the Land in the Roman Revolution," *Journal of Roman Studies*, 52 (1962), 69–86.

———. "*Amicitia* in the Late Roman Republic," *Proceedings of the Cambridge Philological Society*, n.s. 11 (1965), 1–20.

———. "The *Equites* in the Late Republic," in *Second International Conference of Economic History, 1962*. Paris, 1965. I, 117–137.

———. "Review of Earl, *Tiberius Gracchus*," *Gnomon*, 37 (1965), 189–192.

———. *Italian Manpower 225 B.C.–A.D. 14*. Oxford, 1971.

———. "Review of White, *Roman Farming*," *Journal of Roman Studies*, 62 (1972), 153–158.

Bruwaene, Martin van den. "L'Opposition à Scipion Emilien après la mort de Tiberius Gracchus," *Phoibos*, 5 (1950–1951), 229–238.

Burdese, Alberto. *Studi sull' Ager Publicus*. Turin, 1952.

Busolt, Georg. "Quellenkritik beiträge zur geschichte der römischen Revolutionszeit," *Neue Jahrbücher für Philologie und Pädagogik*, 161 (1890), 321–349.

Carcopino, Jérôme. *Autour des Gracques*. Paris, 1928.

———. "Les Lois agraires des Gracques et la Guerre Sociale," *Bulletin de l'Association Guillaume Budé*, 22 (1929), 3–23.

Cardinali, Giuseppe. *Studi Graccani*. Genoa, 1912.

Carney, Thomas Francis. "Rome in the Gracchan Age," *Theoria*, 15 (1960), 38–42.

———. "Prosopography: Payoffs and Pitfalls," *Phoenix*, 27 (1973), 156–179.

Caspari, Max Otto Bismark. "On Some Problems in Roman Agrarian History," *Klio*, 13 (1913), 184–198.

Cauer, Friedrich. "Review of Kornemann, *Zur Geschichte der Gracchenzeit*," *Berliner philologische Wochenschrift*, 25 (1905), cols. 599–607.

Cichorius, Conrad. *Untersuchungen zu Lucilius*. Berlin, 1908.

———. *Römische Studien*. Leipzig-Berlin, 1922.

Clarke, Martin Lowther. *Rhetoric at Rome*. New York, 1963.

Clausing, Roth. *The Roman Colonate: The Theories of Its Origins*. New York, 1925.

Coarelli, Filippo. *Monuments of Civilization: Rome*. New York, 1972.

Cook, S. A., F. E. Adcock, and M. P. Charlesworth, eds., *Cambridge Ancient History*. Vols. VIII–IX. Cambridge, 1930 and 1932.

Corbett, Percy Ellwood. *The Roman Law of Marriage*. Oxford, 1930.

Corpus Inscriptionum Latinarum. Berlin, 1863———.

Coulanges, Fustel de. *Recherches sur quelques problèmes d'histoire*. Paris, 1894.

Cousteau, Jacques-Yves. "Fish Men Discover a 2,200-year-old Greek Ship," *National Geographic Magazine,* 105 (1954), 1–36.

Crawford, Michael H. *"Foedus* and *Sponsio," Papers of the British School at Rome,* 61 (n.s. 28) (1973), 1–7.

———. *Roman Republican Coinage.* Vols. I–II. Cambridge, 1974.

Cuff, P. J. "Prolegomena to a Critical Edition of Appian, B.C. I," *Historia,* 16 (1967), 177–188.

D'Arms, John H. *Romans on the Bay of Naples.* Cambridge, Mass., 1970.

Degrassi, Attilio. "Un nuovo miliario calabro della *Via Popillia* e la *Via Annia* del Veneto," *Philologus,* 99 (1955), 259–265.

———. *Inscriptiones Latinae Liberae Rei Publicae.* Florence, 1965.

De Sanctis, Gaetano. *Storia dei Romani.* Vols. I–IV. Turin and Florence, 1907–1964.

———. *Problemi di Storia Antica.* Bari, 1932.

———. "Review of Haywood, *Studies on Scipio Africanus," Rivista di filologia,* 64 (n.s. 14) (1936), 189–203.

Dessau, Hermann. *Inscriptiones Latinae Selectae.* 3 vols. Berlin, 1892.

Dilke, Oswald Ashton Wentworth. *The Roman Land Surveyors, An Introduction to the Agrimensores.* New York, 1971.

Dohr, Heinz. "Die italischen Gutshöfe nach den Schriften Catos und Varros." Ph.D. dissertation, University of Cologne, 1965.

Drexler, Hans. "Zur Frage der 'Schuld' des Tiberius Gracchus," *Emerita,* 11 (1951), 51–103.

Drumann, Wilhelm Karl August. *Geschichte Roms,* ed. by P. Groebe. 2d ed. Vols. I–VI. Berlin, 1899–1929.

Dudley, Donald Reynolds. "Blossius of Cumae," *Journal of Roman Studies,* 31 (1941), 94–99.

Duff, Arnold Mackay. *Freedmen in the Early Roman Empire.* Oxford, 1928.

Earl, Donald C. "Calpurnii Pisones in the Second Century B.C.," *Athenaeum,* 38 (1960), 283–298.

———. "M. Octavius, trib. pleb. 133 B.C., and His Successor," *Latomus,* 19 (1960), 657–669.

———. "Terence and Roman Politics," *Historia,* 11 (1962), 469–485.

———. *Tiberius Gracchus: A Study in Politics.* Brussels, 1963.

———. "Tiberius Gracchus' Last Assembly," *Athenaeum,* 43 (1965), 95–105.

Errington, Robert Malcolm. *Philopoemen.* Oxford, 1969.

Ferguson, John. *Utopias of the Classical World.* Ithaca, 1975.

Ferrero, Guglielmo. *Grandezza e decandenza di Roma.* Vol. II. Milan, 1904.

Finley, Moses I. "The Alienability of Land in Ancient Greece: A Point of View," *Eirene,* 7 (1968), 25–32.

Flach, Dieter. "Die Ackergesetzgebung im Zeitalter der Römischen Revolution," *Historische Zeitschrift,* 217 (1973), 265–295.

Fraccaro, Plinio. "Sui Fannii dell'età Graccana," *Rendiconti della R. Accademia dei Lincei,* 19 (1910), 656–674.

——. "I processi degli Scipioni," *Studi storici per l'antichità classica,* 4 (1911), 217–414

——. "Studi nell'età Graccana," *Studi storici per l'antichità classica,* 5 (1912), 317–448; *Studi storici per l'antichità classica,* 6 (1913), 42–136.

——. *Studi sull'età dei Gracchi.* Vol. I. Città di Castello, 1914.

——. "Ancora sulla questione dei Fannii," *Athenaeum,* 4 (1926), 153–160.

——. "Due recenti libri sui Gracchi" (reviews of Taeger, *Tiberius Gracchus,* and Carcopino, *Autour des Gracques*), *Athenaeum,* 9 (1931), 291–320.

——. "Ancora sui processi degli Scipioni," *Athenaeum,* 17 (1939), 3–26.

——. *Opuscula.* 3 vols. Pavia, 1956–1957.

Frank, Tenney. "Italy," *CAH,* 8, 326–356. Cambridge, 1930.

——. *An Economic Survey of Ancient Rome.* Vol. I. Baltimore, 1933.

Frederiksen, Martin W. "Republican Capua: A Social and Economic Study," *Papers of the British School at Rome,* 27 (1959), 80–130.

——. "The Contribution of Archaeology to the Agrarian Problem in the Gracchan Period," *Dialoghi di Archaeologia,* Anno IV–V, nn. 2–3 (1970–1971), 330–367.

Friedländer, Ludwig. *Roman Life and Manners under the Early Empire.* Vols. I and IV. New York, 1910.

Fritz, Kurt von. *The Theory of the Mixed Constitution in Antiquity.* New York, 1954.

Fuks, Alexander. "Patterns and Types of Social-Economic Revolution in Greece from the Fourth to the Second Century B.C.," *Ancient Society,* 5 (1974), 51–81.

Gabba, Emilio. "Le origini dell'esercito professionale in Roma," *Athenaeum,* 27 (1949), 173-209.

——. "Ricerche sull'esercito professionale romano da Mario ad Augusto," *Athenaeum,* 29 (1951), 171–272.

——. "Note Appianee," *Athenaeum,* 33 (1955), 218–230.

——. *Appiano e la storia delle guerre civili.* Florence, 1956.

——. *Appiani, Bellorum Civilium Liber Primus.* Florence, 1958.

——. "Studi su Dionigi D'Alicarnasso," *Athenaeum,* 42 (1964), 29–41.

——. "Motivazioni economiche nell'opposizione alla legge agraria di Tib. Sempronio Gracco," in *Polis and Imperium: Studies in Honor of Edward Togo Salmon.* Toronto, 1974. Pp. 129–138.

Garnsey, P. "Review of Bauman, *Crimen Maiestatis*," *Journal of Roman Studies*, 59 (1969), 282–284.

Geer, Russell Mortimer. "Plutarch and Appian on Tiberius Gracchus," in *Classical and Mediaeval Studies in Honor of Edward Kennard Rand*, ed. by Leslie Webber Jones. New York, 1938. Pp. 105–112.

——. "The Scipios and the Father of the Gracchi," *Transactions and Proceedings of the American Philological Association*, 69 (1938), 381–388.

——. "Notes on the Land Law of Tiberius Gracchus," *Transactions and Proceedings of the American Philological Association*, 70 (1939), 30–36.

Gelzer, M. *Die Nobilität der römischen Republik*. Leipzig-Berlin, 1912 (reprinted in *Kleine Schriften*, I, 17–135) = *The Roman Nobility* (trans. by Robin Seager), Oxford, 1969.

——. "Review of Taeger, *Tiberius Gracchus*," *Gnomon*, 5 (1929), 296–303 (reprinted in *Kleine Schriften*, II, 73–80).

——. "Review of Carcopino, *Autour des Gracques*," *Gnomon*, 5 (1929), 648–660.

——. "Römische Politik bei Fabius Pictor," *Hermes*, 68 (1933), 129–166 (reprinted in *Kleine Schriften*, III, 51–92).

——. *Kleine Schriften*, eds. Hermann Strasburger and Christian Meier. Vols. I–III. Wiesbaden, 1962.

Göhler, Josef. *Rom und Italien*. Breslau, 1939.

Greenidge, Abel Hendy Jones. *A History of Rome, 133–104 B.C.* Vol. I. London, 1904.

——, and Clay, Agnes Muriel. *Sources for Roman History, 133–70 B.C.*, rev. by Eric William Gray. Oxford, 1960.

Gruen, Erich S. "The Political Allegiance of P. Mucius Scaevola," *Athenaeum*, 63 (1965), 321–332.

——. *Roman Politics and the Criminal Courts, 149–78 B.C.* Cambridge, Mass., 1968.

——. *The Last Generation of the Roman Republic*. Berkeley and Los Angeles, 1974.

Gummerus, Hermann Gregorius. *Der römische Gutsbetrieb, Klio*, Beiheft 5. Leipzig, 1906.

Gwynn, Aubrey. *Roman Education from Cicero to Quintilian*. Oxford, 1926.

Hall, Ursula. "Voting Procedure in Roman Assemblies," *Historia*, 13 (1964), 267–306.

Hanell, Krister. "Bermerkungen zu der politischen Terminologie des Sallustius," *Eranos*, 63 (1945), 263–276.

Hardy, Ernest George. *Six Roman Laws*. Oxford, 1911.

Harmand, Jacques. *L'Armée et le soldat à Rome de 107 à 50 avant notre ère*. Paris, 1967.

Harris, William Vernon. *Rome in Etruria and Umbria.* Oxford, 1971.
Haywood, Richard Mansfield. *Studies on Scipio Africanus.* Baltimore, 1933.
Heitland, William Merton. *The Roman Republic.* Vol. II. Cambridge, 1909.
——. *Agricola.* Cambridge, 1921.
Hellegouarc'h, Joseph. *Le vocabulaire latin des relations et des partis politiques sous la république.* Paris, 1963.
Henderson, M. Isobel. "Review of Scullard, *Roman Politics,*" *Journal of Roman Studies,* 42 (1952), 114–116.
——. "The Establishment of the 'equester ordo,' " *Journal of Roman Studies,* 53 (1963), 61–72.
Hill, Herbert. *The Roman Middle Class.* Oxford, 1952.
Hinrichs, Focke Tannen. "Der römische Strassenbau zur Zeit der Gracchen," *Historia,* 16 (1967), 162–176.
——. "Das legale Landversprechen in Bellum Civile," *Historia,* 18 (1969), 521–544.
——. "Nochmals zur Inschrift von Polla," *Historia,* 18 (1969), 251–255.
Holmes, Thomas Rice. *The Roman Republic.* Vol. I. Oxford, 1935.
Hopkins, M. Keith. "The Age of Roman Girls at Marriage," *Population Studies,* 18 (1965), 309–327.
Instinsky, Hans Ulrich. "Zur Echtheitsfrage der Brieffragmente der Cornelia, Mutter der Gracchen," *Chiron,* 1 (1971), 177–189.
Jacoby, Felix. *Die Fragmente der griechischen Historiker.* Berlin, 1923–1930; Leiden, 1940——.
Jhering, Rudolf von. *Der Besitzwille.* Jena, 1889.
Johannsen, Kristen. *Die lex agraria des Jahres 111 v. Chr.; Text und Kommentar.* Söcking-Sturnberg, 1971.
Jones, Arnold Hugh Martin. "De Tribunis Plebis Reficiendis," *Proceedings of the Cambridge Philological Society,* n.s. 6 (1960), 35–38.
——. *The Criminal Courts of the Roman Republic and Principate,* ed. by John A. Crook. Oxford, 1972.
Jones, Christopher Prestige. *Plutarch and Rome.* Oxford, 1971.
Kaiser, Max. "Der Inhalt der Patria Potestas," *Zeitschrift der Savigny —Stiftung für Rechtsgeschichte, Rom. Abt.,* 58 (1938), 62–87.
Katz, Solomon. "The Gracchi: An Essay in Interpretation," *Classical Journal,* 38 (1942), 65–82.
Kelly, John Maurice. *Roman Litigation.* Oxford, 1966.
Kontchalovsky, Dimitri. "Recherches sur l'histoire du mouvement agraire des Gracques," *Revue Historique,* 153 (1926), 161–186.
Kornemann, Ernst. *Die neue Livius-Epitome aus Oxyrhynchus. Klio,* Beiheft II. Leipzig, 1904.

Kromayer, Johannes. "Die Wirtschaftliche Entwicklung Italiens im II and I Jahrhundert vor Chr.," *Neue Jahrbücher für Pädagogik,* 17 (1914), 145–169.

Lange, Ludwig. *De Legibus Aelia et Fufia commentatio.* Giessen, 1861, reprinted in *Kleine Schriften,* Göttingen, 1887, I, 274–341.

——. *Römische Alterthümer.* Vol. III. Berlin, 1876.

Larsen, Jakob A. O. "*Sortito* and *Sorti* in CIL, I, 200," *Classical Philology,* 25 (1930), 279.

——. "The Judgement of Antiquity on Democracy," *Classical Philology,* 49 (1954), 1–14.

Last, Hugh. "Tiberius Gracchus," *CAH,* IX, 1–39. Cambridge, 1932.

Levi, Mario Attilio. "Intorno alla Legge Agraria del 111 a.C.," *Rivista di filologia e di istruzione classica,* 57 (1929), 231–240.

Lincke, Ernst Martin. *P. Cornelius Scipio Aemilianus.* Dresden, 1898.

Lintott, Andrew William. "Trinundinum," *Classical Quarterly,* 15 (1965), 281–285.

——. *Violence in Republican Rome.* Oxford, 1968.

Luce, T. James, Jr. "Appian's Exposition of the Roman Republican Constitution." Ph.D. dissertation, Princeton University, 1958.

McDonald, Alexander Hugh. "The History of Rome and Italy in the Second Century B.C.," *Cambridge Historical Journal,* 6 (1939), 124–146.

——. "Rome and the Italian Confederacy, 200 to 186 B.C.," *Journal of Roman Studies,* 34 (1944), 11–33.

MacDonald, William Francis. "Clodius and the Lex Aelia Fufia," *Journal of Roman Studies,* 19 (1929), 164–179.

MacInnes, John. "The Use of 'Italus' and 'Romanus' in Latin Literature, with Special Reference to Virgil," *Classical Review,* 26 (1912), 5–8.

MacMullen, Ramsay. *Enemies of the Roman Order.* Cambridge, Mass., 1967.

Malcovati, Henrica. *Oratorum Romanorum Fragmenta Liberae Rei Publicae,* 3d ed. Turin, 1966.

Marrou, Henri I. *Histoire de l'éducation dans l'antiquité.* Paris, 1965.

Marsh, Frank Burr. *A History of the Roman World, 146–30 B.C.,* 3d ed., rev. by Howard Hayes Scullard. London, 1963.

Meier, Christian. "Review of Badian, *Foreign Clientelae,*" *Bonner Jahrbücher,* 161 (1961), 503–514.

——. *Res Publica Amissa.* Wiesbaden, 1966.

Meyer, Eduard. *Caesars Monarchie und das Principat des Pompeius.* Stuttgart, 1922.

——. "Untersuchungen zur Geschichte der Gracchen," *Kleine Schriften,* I, 2d ed. Halle, 1924. Pp. 363–421.

Michels, Agnes Kirsopp. *The Calendar of the Roman Republic.* Princeton, 1967.

Molthagen, Joachim. "Die Durchführung der gracchischen Agrarreform," *Historia,* 22 (1973), 423–458.

Momigliano, Arnaldo, ed. *The Conflict between Paganism and Christianity in the Fourth Century, Essays.* Oxford, 1963.

Mommsen, Theodor. *Geschichte des römischen Münzwesens.* Berlin, 1860.

——. *Römische Forschungen.* 2 vols. Berlin, 1864–1879.

——. "Decret des Commodus für den Saltus Burunitanus," *Hermes,* 15 (1880), 385–411.

——. *Römisches Staatsrecht,* Vols. I, II (3d ed., 1887), Vol. III (1888).

——. *Römisches Strafrecht.* Leipzig, 1899.

——. *Römische Geschichte.* 3 vols. Berlin, 1903–1904.

——. *Gesammelte Schriften.* 8 vols. Berlin, 1904–1913.

Mørkholm, Otto. *Antiochus IV of Syria.* Copenhagen, 1966.

Münzer, Friedrich. "Die Fanniusfrage," *Hermes,* 55 (1920), 427–442.

——. *Römische Adelsparteien und Adelsfamilien.* Stuttgart, 1920.

——. "Norbanus," *Hermes,* 67 (1932), 220–236.

Murray, Robert J. "Cicero and the Gracchi," *Transactions and Proceedings of the American Philological Association,* 97 (1966), 291–298.

Nagle, D. Brendan. "A Historiographic Study of Plutarch's Tiberius Gracchus." Ph.D. dissertation, University of Southern California, 1968.

——. "The Failure of the Roman Political Process in 133 B.C.," *Athenaeum,* 48 (1970), 372–394; 49 (1971), 111–128.

Niccolini, Giovanni. *I Fasti dei Tribuni della Plebe.* Milan, 1934.

Nicolet, Claude. "L'Inspiration de Tibérius Gracchus," *Revue des Etudes Anciennes,* 67 (1965), 142–159.

——. *L'Ordre équestre a l'époque républicaine, 312–43 av. J.C.* Paris, 1966.

——. *Les Gracques.* Paris, 1967.

Niese, Benedictus. "Das Sogenannte Licinisch-Sextische Ackergesetz," *Hermes,* 23 (1888), 410–423.

Nitzsch, Karl Wilhelm. *Die Gracchen und ihre nächsten Vorgänger.* Berlin, 1847.

Ogilvie, Robert Maxwell. *A Commentary on Livy. Books 1–5.* Oxford, 1965.

Pais, Ettore. *Dalle guerre puniche a Cesare Augusto.* Vols. I–II. Rome, 1918.

Pareti, Luigi. *Storia di Roma.* Vol. II. Turin, 1952.

Paribeni, Roberto. *La Famiglia Romana.* Rome, 1947.

Pascal, Carlo. *Studi Romani.* Fasc. 4: "Il partito dei Gracchi e Scipione Emiliano." Turin, 1896.

Pauly, August Friedrich von, Georg Wissowa, et al. *Real-Encyclopädie der Classischen Altertumswissenschaft.* Stuttgart, 1894——.

Peter, Hermann. *Die Quellen Plutarchs in den Biographieen der Römer.* Halle, 1865.

——. *Historicorum Romanorum Reliquiae.* Vols. I–II. Leipzig, 1906–1914.

Plaumann, Gerhard. "Das sogenannte Senatus consultum ultimum, die Quasidiktatur der späteren römischen Republik," *Klio,* 13 (1913), 321–386.

Pürkel, Jürgen von. *Untersuchungen zum spätrepublikanischen Notstandrecht: Senatusconsultum und hostis-Erklärung.* Munich, 1970.

Rambaud, Michel. *Ciceron et l'histoire romaine.* Paris, 1953.

Rawson, Elizabeth. "Scipio, Laelius, Furius and the Ancestral Religion," *Journal of Roman Studies,* 63 (1973), 161–174.

——. "Religion and Politics in the Late Century B.C. at Rome," *Phoenix,* 28 (1974), 193–212.

Reid, James Smith. "On Some Questions of Roman Public Law," *Journal of Roman Studies,* 1 (1911), 68–99.

Riccobono, Salvatore. *Fontes Iuris Romani Anteiustiniani.* Florence, 1941.

Richard, Jean-Claude. "Qualis Pater, Talis Filius," *Revue de Philologie,* 46 (1972), 43–55.

Riddle, John M., ed. *Tiberius Gracchus.* Lexington, Mass., 1970.

Rimscha, Hans von. *Die Gracchen. Charakterbild einer Revolution und ihrer Gestalten.* Munich, 1947.

Rödl, Bernd. *Das Senatus Consultum Ultimum und der Tod der Gracchen.* Bonn, 1969.

Salmon, Edward Togo. "Roman Colonisation from the Second Punic War to the Gracchi," *Journal of Roman Studies,* 26 (1936), 47–67.

——. *Roman Colonisation under the Republic.* London, 1969.

Scalais, Robert. "Les Revenus que les Romains attendaient de l'agriculture," *Musée Belge,* 31 (1927), 93–100.

——. "La Politique agraire de Rome depuis les guerres puniques jusqu' aux Gracques," *Musée Belge,* 34 (1930), 195–241.

Schwartz, Edward. "Review of Meyer, *Untersuchungen zur Geschichte der Gracchen,*" *Göttingischer gelehrte Anzeiger,* 158 (1896), 792–811.

Scullard, Howard Hayes. "Scipio Aemilianus and Roman Politics," *Journal of Roman Studies,* 50 (1960), 59–74.

——. *From the Gracchi to Nero.* 3d ed. London, 1970.

———. *Roman Politics 220–150 B.C.*, 2d ed. Oxford, 1973.

Seager, Robin, ed. *The Crisis of the Roman Republic.* Cambridge, 1967.

———. *"Lex Varia de Maiestate," Historia,* 16 (1967), 37–43.

———. *"Factio:* Some Observations," *Journal of Roman Studies,* 62 (1972), 53–58.

Shatzman, Israel. "The Roman General's Authority over Booty," *Historia,* 21 (1972), 177–205.

Sherwin-White, Adrian Nicholas. "Violence in Roman Politics," *Journal of Roman Studies,* 46 (1956), 1–9.

———. *The Roman Citizenship.* 2d ed. Oxford, 1973.

Shochat, Yanir. "The Lex Agraria of 133 B.C. and the Italian Allies," *Athenaeum,* 48 (1970), 25–45.

Smith, Hanne. *"Factio, Factiones,* and *Nobilitas* in Sallust," *Classica et Mediaevalia,* 29 (1968), 187–196.

Smith, Richard. *The Failure of the Roman Republic.* Cambridge, 1955.

———. *Service in the Post-Marian Roman Army.* Manchester, 1958.

———. "The Anatomy of Force in Late Republican Politics," in *Ancient Society and Institutions: Studies Presented to Victor Ehrenberg.* Oxford, 1966. Pp. 257–273.

Smuts, Francois. "Stoïsyne Invloed op Tiberius Gracchus," *Acta Classica,* 1 (1958), 106–116.

Soltau, Wilhelm. "Plutarchs Quellen zu den Biographien der Gracchen," *Jahrbücher für Classische Philologie,* 153 (1896), 357–368.

Stadter, Philip A. *Plutarch's Historical Methods.* Cambridge, Mass., 1965.

Staveley, E. Stuart. *Greek and Roman Voting and Elections.* London, 1972.

Stern, E. von. "Zur Beurteilung der politischen Wirksamkeit des Tiberius und Gaius Gracchus," *Hermes,* 56 (1921), 229–301.

Stone, Lawrence. "Prosopography," *Daedalus,* 100 (1971), 46–79.

Strachan-Davidson, James Leigh. *Problems of the Roman Criminal Law.* Vols. I–II. Oxford, 1912.

Sumner, G. V. *"Lex Aelia, Lex Fufia," American Journal of Philology,* 84 (1963), 337–358.

Sydenham, Edward Allen. *Coinage of the Roman Republic.* London, 1952.

Szemler, George J. *The Priests of the Roman Republic.* Brussels, 1972.

Taeger, Fritz. *Tiberius Gracchus.* Stuttgart, 1928.

Taylor, Lily Ross. *Party Politics in the Age of Caesar.* Berkeley and Los Angeles, 1949.

———. *The Voting Districts of the Roman Republic.* Rome, 1960.

———. "Forerunners of the Gracchi," *Journal of Roman Studies,* 52 (1962), 19–27.

——. "Was Tiberius Gracchus' Last Assembly Electoral or Legislative?" *Athenaeum,* 41 (1963), 51–69.

——. "Appian and Plutarch on Tiberius Gracchus' Last Assembly," *Athenaeum,* 44 (1966), 238–250.

——. *Roman Voting Assemblies from the Hannibalic War to the Dictatorship of Caesar.* Ann Arbor, 1966.

Thomsen, Rudi. "Erliess Tiberius Gracchus ein Iustitium?" *Classica et Mediaevalia,* 6 (1944), 60–71.

Tibiletti, Gianfranco. "Il possesso dell' *ager publicus* e le norme *de modo agrorum* sino ai Gracchi," *Athenaeum,* 26 (1948), 173–326; *Athenaeum,* 27 (1949), 3–42.

——. "Ricerche di storia agraria romana," *Athenaeum,* 28 (1950), 183–266.

——. "Lo sviluppo del latifondo in Italia dall' epoca graccana al principio dell' Impero," in *Relazioni del X Congresso Internazionale di Scienze Storiche,* II (Rome, 1955), 235–292.

Toynbee, Arnold Joseph. *Hannibal's Legacy: The Hannibalic War's Effects on Roman Life.* Vols. I–II. London, 1965.

Toynbee, Jocelyn Mary Catharine. *Death and Burial in the Roman World.* London, 1971.

Trapenard, Camille. *L'Ager Scriptuarius.* Paris, 1908.

Treggiari, Susan Mary. *Roman Freedmen during the Late Republic.* Oxford, 1969.

Tyrell, Robert Yelverton, and Purser, Louis Claude. *The Correspondence of M. Tullius Cicero.* 6 vols. Dublin, 1904–1933.

Valgiglio, Ernesto. *Plutarco. Vita dei Gracchi.* Rome, 1957.

Verbrugghe, Gerald. "The *Elogium* from Polla and the First Slave War," *Classical Philology,* 68 (1973), 25–35.

Vretska, Karl. *C. Sallustius Crispus, Invektiven und Episteln.* Heidelberg, 1961.

Walbank, Frank William. *A Historical Commentary on Polybius.* 2 vols. Oxford, 1957–1967.

——. *Polybius.* Berkeley and Los Angeles, 1972.

Walsh, Patrick Gerard. *Livy: His Historical Aims and Methods.* Cambridge, 1961.

Wardman, Alan. *Plutarch's Lives.* Berkeley and Los Angeles, 1974.

Warmington, Eric Herbert. *The Commerce between the Roman Empire and India.* Cambridge, 1928.

Weber, Max. "Agrarverhältnisse im Altertum," in *Gesammelte Aufsätze zur Sozial- und Wirtschaftsgeschichte.* Tubingen, 1924.

Weinstock, Stefan. "Clodius and the Lex Aelia Fufia," *Journal of Roman Studies,* 27 (1937), 215–222.

Westermann, William Linn. "On Inland Transportation and Communication in Antiquity," *Political Science Quarterly,* 43 (1928), 364–387.

——. "Industrial Slavery in Roman Italy," *Journal of Economic History,* 2 (1942), 149–163.

——. *The Slave Systems of Greek and Roman Antiquity.* Philadelphia, 1955.

White Kenneth Douglas. "Latifundia," *Bulletin of the Institute of Classical Studies, London,* 14 (1967), 62–79.

——. *Roman Farming.* Ithaca, 1970.

Wilson, Alan John Nisbet. *Emigration from Italy in the Republican Age of Rome.* Manchester, 1966.

Wirszubski, Chaim. *Libertas as a Political Idea at Rome during the Late Republic and Early Principate.* Cambridge, 1950.

Wiseman, Timothy Peter. 'Viae Anniae," *Papers of the British School at Rome,* 32 (1964), 21–37.

——. "Viae Anniae Again," *Papers of the British School at Rome,* 37 (1969), 82–91.

——. "Note on Mucius Scaevola," *Athenaeum,* 48 (1970), 152–153.

——. *New Men in the Roman Senate 139 B.C.–A.D. 14.* Oxford, 1971.

Yeo, Cedric A. "The Overgrazing of Ranch-Lands in Ancient Italy," *Transactions and Proceedings of the American Philological Association,* 79 (1948), 275–309.

——. "The Development of the Roman Plantation and Marketing of Farm Products," *Finanzarchiv,* 13 (1951–1952), 321–342.

——. "The Economics of Roman and American Slavery," *Finanzarchiv,* 13 (1951–1952), 445–485.

Zancan, Leandro. *Ager Publicus.* Padua, 1935.

Zetzel, James Eric Guttman. "Cicero and the Scipionic Circle," *Harvard Studies in Classical Philology,* 76 (1972), 173–179.

Zumpt, August Wilhelm. *Das Criminalrecht der römischen Republik.* Berlin, I.ii, 1865; II.i, 1868; II.ii, 1869.

——. *Der Criminalprocess der römischen Republik.* Leipzig, 1871.

Index of Persons

Aelius Tubero, as historical source, 242

Aelius Tubero, Q., nephew of Scipio Aemilianus, 112n, 203n

Aemilia, wife of Scipio Africanus: death and bequest to Scipio Aemilianus, 53; and dowry of the Corneliae, 30, 54; family of, 42

Aemilius Lepidus, M. (cos. 187), 36

Aemilius Lepidus Porcina, M. (cos. 137): and *lex Cassia,* 115n; and Numantines, 63n, 71

Aemilius Paullus, L. (cos. 182): on education of sons, 21; family of, 42, 53, 112-113; on Spanish war, 65

Annius Luscus, T. (cos. 153): Cicero familiar with speeches of, 242; on deposition of Octavius, 196n, 210-213; and *elogium* at Polla, 136n

Annius Rufus, T. (cos. 128), 136

Antiochus III, ruler of Seleucid Empire, 27, 39n, 81

Antipater of Tarsus, 47

Antius Briso (tr. pl. 137), 115, 121, 185

Appian of Alexandria:
on agrarian commission, 199
on assassination, 219
dating and composition of histories, 231
on deposition of Octavius, 183-184
on Gracchan violence, 178n
on Ti. Gracchus' (cos. 177) land distribution, 34, 48
on Ti. Gracchus (tr. pl. 133): bid for re-election, 215-216; *intercessio,* 171n
as historical source, 231-234
on imprisonment of consuls in 151, 193-194
integrity of, 138
on *lex Sempronia agraria,* 94n, 132n, 138-152, 156, 159, 166, 168-169, 173-176, 178n

on Q. Mucius, 161n
on Numantine treaty, 63nn
sources for, 138n, 234n, 237, 241

Aristonicus, rebel king of Pergamum, 46-47

Asinius Pollio, Cn. (cos. 40), as historical source, 138n, 234n

Atilius, M. (pr. Farther Spain, 152), 58-59

Attalus Philometer, king of Pergamum, 39, 207-210

Augustine of Hippo, 245

Augustus, the emperor, 107

Aurelius Victor, as historical source, 244

Blossius of Cumae, 45-47, 221

Caecilius Metellus Macedonicus, Q. (cos. 143): attitude toward Ti. Gracchus (tr. pl. 133), 117, 210-211, 236; Cicero familiar with speeches of, 242; in Nearer Spain, 60; and Q. Pompeius, 210; and Scipio Aemilianus, 117, 210; speech to Senate on procreation, 133n, 170n

Caecilius Metellus Numidicus, Q. (cos. 109), 237-238

Caesarus, the Lusitanian, 58

Calpurnius Piso, Q. (cos. 135), 71

Calpurnius Piso Caesoninus, L. (cos. 112), 155

Calpurnius Piso Frugi, L. (cos. 133): consulship, 153; and Ti. Gracchus (tr. pl. 133), 111n, 239; as historian, 239, 242; and *lex Calpurnia,* 239; in Sicily, 72-73

Cassius Dio:
on Cornelia's betrothal, 29n
on Ti. Gracchus (cos. 177), 29n
on Ti. Gracchus (tr. pl. 133): bid for re-election, 216-217; in Numantine war, 69n

Servilius Caepio, Q. (*continued*)
Asellus' veto, 185; in Farther Spain, 61
Servilius Rullus, P. (tr. pl. 63), 122, 151, 200, 204n
Socrates, 236
Strabo, on Diophanes, 45
Sulpicius, C. (pr. 169), 37
Sulpicius Galba, Ser. (cos. 144), 59, 62

Tacitus, Cornelius, on Cornelia, 43
Tarquinius Superbur, 187, 226
Terence (P. Terentius Afer), on tenant farming, 92
Terentius Massiliota, L., tr. mil. of Q. Fulvius Flaccus, 32
Tremellius, Cn. (tr. pl. 168), 39
Tullius Cicero, M. (cos. 63):
on Cato's *De Agri Cultura,* 78n
on Blossius, 47
on Ti. Gracchus (cos. 177), 38, 40-41
on Ti. Gracchus (tr. pl. 133): and defections from cause, 111n, 203n; and deposition of Octavius, 185; and Mancinus affair, 69-70; and C. Porcius Cato's support of, 111; and speeches, 52
as historical source, 234, 242-245
on land commissions, 204n

on *leges Aelia et Fufia,* 247-248
on *lex Licinia* and *lex Aebutia,* 200
on *lex Sempronia agraria,* 110, 151-153, 156
on Mancinus, 66
on the military, 75n
as *pater patriae,* 107
on C. Quinctius Flaminius, 177-178
recalled from exile, 88n
on Scipio Aemilianus, 20, 242-243
sources for, 237-242
on tenant farming, 93-94
on urban plebs, 96n
on wealth in Italy, 77n

Valens, the emperor, 244
Valerius Antias, as historical source, 240
Valerius Laevinus, M., 79n
Valerius Maximus: on Ti. Gracchus (cos. 177), 29n; as historical source, 245-246
Varro (M. Terentius Varro): on exporting, 95n; as historical source, 245
Velleius Paterculus, as historical source, 245
Vennonius, as historical source, 242
Viriathus, the Lusitanian, 59-61

General Index

Achaean League, 27
Africa, 74
Ager Campanus, 133-134, 151, 158
Ager censorius, 129
Ager compascuus, 77-78
Ager publicus: equestrians receive as *trientabulum,* 79-80; exploitation of, 124, 132; and grazing, 78n, 135-136; and *lex agraria* of 111, 129-131; and *lex Licinia-Sextia,* 120, 124-125; and *lex Sempronia agraria,* 123, 137-159; origins of, 123-124

Annales Maximi: Cicero familiar with, 242; publication of, 238
Annuality, transgression of, 213, 219, 228
Arevaci, *see* Celtiberians
Arpinum, 94n
Asia: legation of Ti. Gracchus (cos.) to, 41; in Macedonian war, 74, 80; rebellion in, 46
Atella, 94n

Belli, *see* Celtiberians

087431